In the Fire of

Living in Dubai &
Doing Business in the
Middle East

REBECCA MEIJLINK

In the Fire of Capital

ISBN: 978-1-7395640-1-8 (Paperback)
ISBN 978-1-7395640-2-5 (E-book)
ISBN 978-1-7395640-3-2 (Hardback)
First edition 1.0 (23 September 2023), Updated 14 October 2023
Publisher: AlphaBet Select Ltd, London, United Kingdom

All inquiries should be addressed to the publisher, AlphaBet Select Ltd, London, United Kingdom. The publisher would appreciate being notified of any corrections that should be incorporated in future reprints or subsequent editions of the book. For our contact details, visit our website at www.alphabetselect.com.

Contents

PROLOGUE

Introduction to Cultural Differences
Embarking on an Adventure

PART I LIVING IN DUBAI

Chapter 1. Dazzling New Year's Fireworks
Chapter 2. Dubai: Gateway to the Middle East
Chapter 3. Arriving in Dubai and Settling in
Chapter 4. Finding a Place to Call Home
Chapter 5. Dress Code and Perfumes Decoded
Chapter 6. Social Norms and Etiquette
Chapter 7. Love and Relationships
Chapter 8. Marriage and Divorce
Chapter 9. Living on the Edge
Chapter 10. Understanding Taxation
Chapter 11. Transportation and Infrastructure
Chapter 12. Dubai's Culture Defined
Chapter 13. A Lifestyle for Every Budget
Chapter 14. Dubai's Low Rate of Petty Crime
Chapter 15. Heat, Health, and Happiness
Chapter 16. Glitz and Glamour
Chapter 17. Local Experiences
Chapter 18. Camels and Horses: Local Celebrities
Chapter 19. Learn how to Haggle!
Chapter 20. Religion and Law
Chapter 21. Empowerment and Equality
Chapter 22. The Future and Security of Dubai

PART II DOING BUSINESS IN THE MIDDLE EAST

Chapter 23. My Business in the Middle East
Chapter 24. Dress for Success
Chapter 25. Setting up for Business
Chapter 26. Banking Hurdles
Chapter 27. Culture of Business in the Middle East
Chapter 28. Formalities are Necessary
Chapter 29. Establishing new Connections
Chapter 30. GCC Cultural and Business Insights
Chapter 31. Insights beyond the GCC
Chapter 32. Who to contact in The Middle East?
Chapter 33. Regulatory Realities
Chapter 34. Pitching to get a Meeting
Chapter 35. Setting up Meetings
Chapter 36. Ensuring Successful Dialogue
Chapter 37. Long Selling Cycle
Chapter 38. Decision-making Process
Chapter 39. Negotiation Skills and Debt Collection
Chapter 40. Do your Due Diligence
Chapter 41. Exploring Investment Interest
Chapter 42. ESG and Islamic Finance
Chapter 43. Reverse Culture Shock

EPILOGUE

In the Fire of Capital
Author Biography

The Fire Keeps Burning

Fire is a symbol of passion,
Of the desire to succeed,
It can burn bright and fierce.

Fire is full of strength,
Giving the power to overcome,
It can help us face our challenges.

Fire is a source of light,
In the darkness, it can shine,
It can provide guidance and wisdom.

Fire is a symbol of the inner light,
Of knowledge and understanding,
It can help us to see the truth.

In the Fire of Capital

I wish to express my sincere appreciation to the countless individuals who have contributed, both directly and indirectly, to the creation of this book.

PROLOGUE

In the Fire of Capital

Introduction to Cultural Differences

I have dual nationality. My father is Dutch, while my mother proudly claims her British heritage. My father was born in Indonesia, and my mother was born in the UK to a Czech father and a British mother. From an early age, I was exposed to cultural clashes.

I vividly remember the cultural clashes in the family around a simple topic, such as gifting. My mother had spent hours thoughtfully selecting a gift and nicely wrapping it, which she presented to my Dutch grandmother on her birthday. However, my grandmother, unfortunately, did not like the present. She asked my mother for the receipt so she could exchange the gift for something more to her liking. My mother was horrified. It is considered incredibly rude by the British to ask for the receipt.

Growing up, I often witnessed such a typically British approach to gifting. My mother would go through an elaborate theatrical performance, receiving a gift, beaming with delight, and then discreetly tucking it away at the back of a drawer. Then, when the gift-giver visited us again, she would put the item back on display as if it had been there all along. Occasionally, she recycled a gift while keeping a meticulous mental record of who gave what. The underlying principle? To avoid offending or embarrassing anyone.

My grandmother's perspective was rooted in pragmatism. To her, it was simple. Why hang onto it if my mother had given her a gift she did not like nor want? It would be such a waste of money. In her eyes, requesting the receipt and exchanging the gift was the right thing to do. She was being honest by not lying and telling my mother the truth. But in my mother's eyes, she was impolite and plain rude.

I recall another incident where cultures clashed, again around presents. We ventured into what was then known as Czechoslovakia before the Wall came down in the seventies. You could only cross the border into communist territory if you had family ties. The contrasts in East and West regimes were stark. Things would get tense at the border. Border control stripped cars, including ours, down to their bare bones. The police officers, wielding blinding white lights and commanding German Shepherds, left an indelible mark in my memory. We crossed into new territory. Our journey led us to Prague, where we stayed with family. My brother and I did not speak any Czech but were resourceful, communicating with local children with the help of a Czech-Dutch dictionary. We made it work and had a good time.

Christmas came around. Prague in communist time was like a fairy tale city waiting to be dusted off. The city's medieval architecture was intact, and the city looked magical in the snow but covered in a layer of grime and neglect. The Czech family gifted my brother and me wooden toys for Christmas. I thanked them for their kind gesture, but my brother was not on the same page. He burst into tears as he unwrapped his present. The wooden toys were not the flashy ones he was accustomed to in the West.

At around seven years old, a couple of years older than my brother, I grasped the nuances of the communist East versus the indulgent West. I realised the significance of the gesture far outweighed the actual present. I struck a deal with my brother and promised to swap all my teddy bears for one of his if he would stop crying. As a little girl, I felt mortified by my little brother's emotional outburst.

He was perhaps too young to understand the cultural differences, or some may say he was being Dutch, like my grandmother, while I took the British approach.

These examples highlight when we are young, we are taught it is not a good idea to speak up. It starts at home and continues in school and at work. In some cultures, expressing our true thoughts and feelings is wrong and rude.

There is a balance between remaining silent, speaking up, and expressing our true thoughts and feelings while still being mindful of others. By only listening and remaining silent when faced with injustice, we are neither fair to others nor loyal to ourselves and our values.[1]

In the Fire of Capital

Embarking on an Adventure

Many women find themselves up against barriers hindering their progress and curbing their growth. This challenge is particularly evident in male-dominated industries, with the financial sector being a prime example. Doing business in finance in the Middle East as a woman can be even more challenging, mainly when operating as an individual rather than a well-established brand.

I had a career working for American investment banks, selling equities to institutional investors. In 2003, I took the leap and established my investment advisory business. After completing my studies in international law at Leiden University in the Netherlands, I spent 3 years working in Brussels, 12 years in London, 5 years in Monaco, and 10 years in the Middle East before returning to London.

When I moved from Monaco to Dubai, my knowledge of the Middle East was limited, pretty much non-existent. I understand the people with not-so-informed opinions about the Middle East because I used to be one of them. I did not speak Arabic or have any roots in the region. I was starting from scratch. The journey was a captivating ride. I was learning on the job. Over time, I got a better understanding, driven by curiosity, peeling back the layers one by one. I kept digging deeper and deeper, unravelling the complexities. I have made my fair share of blunders, but on the other side, I have had some great moments and wins.

I had the most culturally enriching experiences in the Middle East. Expats often leave Dubai without having had the opportunity to meet any Emirati. Through my business, I was fortunate to meet locals in many of the countries in the Middle

East. Understanding the culture shaped my perspective and taught me much about myself and our biases. For ten years, I immersed myself in daily life in the Middle East, making new connections, nurturing relationships, and navigating the maze. This journey could have been smoother sailing. I encountered challenges and made my fair share of mistakes.

Looking back, I wish I had had a book like this when I first landed in the Middle East. If you are thinking of taking the plunge, this will give you a peek into what you might encounter. I use stories and experiences with facts about the region, each example serving as a case study, supplementing the points and need-to-knows of the UAE and the broader Middle East.

The Middle East is a region that is constantly changing. Currently, there is an oil-fuelled boom taking place in certain countries in the Middle East. While walking the streets of London, I often overhear conversations about Dubai and receive continuous calls from CEOs of companies and fund managers attending conferences in the Middle East and wanting to learn from my experience. However, not all countries are booming. Countries such as Lebanon and Egypt are facing challenges, while Iran continues to feel the impact of sanctions.

It has been challenging to write this book, juggling various interests. Striking a balance between shedding light on realities without dwelling too much on the negatives or invertedly insulting someone is a fine line to tread. I strive to provide a balanced view, breaking down the barriers for those who have boxed the Middle East into a rigid stereotype or those simply fearful of the unknown. It is helpful to understand the history of Dubai and the progress it has made over the last decade to see the trends and appreciate the present.

I conducted interviews with people in Europe. During these interviews, I would ask people from all walks of life about my book's expectations. Additionally, I would inquire about their motivations for moving to the Middle East. I would also explore why they might choose not to relocate to the region. I aimed to improve my understanding of the perceptions of people in Europe to address them. Is what they think an accurate reflection, or have times moved on? This input gave me excellent insights. It also provided me with ideas to add to the book. I also picked up a couple of stories along the way.

I offer a glimpse into the journey while enlightening those considering moving to Dubai or doing business there. I hope this book serves as an accessible read, providing deeper insights into the modern Middle East, as a lot has changed in the last couple of years. It covers issues and subjects any newcomer to the UAE should know before their trip. The stories may inspire you to embark on your adventure into the unknown.

The book first runs you through all the practical and cultural matters you will encounter moving to Dubai, from buying a property to dating, and the second half discusses business practices in the Middle East.

The image of a campfire on the front cover symbolises the timeless tradition of storytelling, where people gather around its mesmerising glow to share their experiences, wisdom, and dreams. It is a powerful visual representation of human connection, as stories have always been a fundamental part of our shared history and culture. The warm glow of the fire, the crackling sound, and the flickering flames all create an inviting atmosphere. Whether it is the peaceful solitude of the desert or the comforting ambience of a European hearth, these settings have long been cherished for their ability to spark meaningful conversations.

The anecdotes and characters in the book are products of the imagination, loosely inspired by real stories and lessons I, friends, and business associates learned. The tales are illustrative examples intended to explain specific points. Any incidental resemblances to actual persons or events are entirely coincidental.

This book only scratches the surface. Some tales are too wild to put out there in the public domain for everyone to read. Those are shared, cosying up by a campfire or countryside fireplace with a select few. Other stories are locked up in the vault of my mind, never to see the light of day, too delicate and shocking to even put into words.

The information in this book is for entertainment purposes only and is not intended to give you legal or investment advice. The laws and regulations governing various topics change rapidly, and the information in this book may not be current. The government websites give you up-to-date information, in English, on any topic you would like to research in more detail. The footnotes provide you with links to the government websites. You should consult an attorney or qualified advisor before deciding on your situation. The publisher would appreciate being notified of any recommended corrections to incorporated in future reprints or subsequent editions of the book.

I am soaking up the sun in the South of France, cat-sitting for friends who have jetted off to Mauritius. They have put their apartment in the South of France up for sale. Unexpectedly, they called me and asked, "Would you like to keep an eye on our cat, keep him company with an occasional tummy rub, and oversee any viewings of our apartment while we are out of town?" And here I am. My work is flexible. I can work from anywhere. Having lived five years in Monaco, this opportunity to spend the summer in the South of France was wonderful. The views from the roof terrace are breathtaking, with a stunning sea view overlooking Monaco. In between my writing, I will explore the neighbouring villages, my favourite being Beausoleil-Sur-Mer.

The cat is not any ordinary cat. He is a stunning ragdoll. This fluff ball has won its fair share of beauty awards. I came here to have fun, see my old friends in the South of France and occasionally feed the cat. It is not quite like that. The cat dominates my day. He is a furry dictator (think Stalin but covered with hair and whiskers). My friends told me the cat has an attitude, and he certainly does. He indeed has a huge personality and meows all day long. Sometimes, I meow along with him. The cat is entertaining, and as we get to know each other, I am starting to enjoy his company more and more.

My friends have a garden at the back of their top-floor duplex penthouse apartment, and although this cat is supposed to be an indoor cat, he clearly was crossed with something wilder. He likes spending time outside in the back garden.

They told me he once jumped over the front balcony and broke his front paws. On another occasion, he went missing in action for five days. I have concluded that he is an explorer, and we have much in common. I suggested my friends put a cat tracker on the furry fellow. They advised me, "It might not be the best way to start your relationship with Banksy. I doubt he would appreciate a tracking device around his neck."

I found myself confined with the cat, creating an unexpectedly ideal setting for writing a book. I am grateful to my friends for locking me up with their cat.

In the Fire of Capital

PART I

LIVING IN DUBAI

In the Fire of Capital

Chapter 1.

Dazzling New Year's Fireworks

My plan was not to uproot my life in Monaco and move to Dubai. I went to buy a property. The city cast its spell on me. I got caught up in the "Dubai bug," a contagious energy capturing countless others like me. It is a tale of accidental moves, stories of people who never thought they would end up in Dubai yet suddenly drawn to its buzz. The vibes in the hotel lobbies were electric, humming with the sound of business transactions.

Europe in 2012 was not in good shape. A gloom seemed to hover over the continent. On the other hand, the atmosphere in Dubai reminded me of the buzz I had experienced on London's trading floor in the 1990s. I needed to be part of this. Fast forward, I made the leap and bought an apartment in Downtown Dubai, close to the Burj Khalifa.

My fiancé and I spent New Year's Eve in Dubai. As the apartment had no furniture, we decided to stay in the Address Marina Hotel, about 30 minutes by taxi from Downtown.

New Year's Eve in Dubai is like no other. The iconic Burj Khalifa took centre stage, showcasing a mesmerising symphony of fireworks. People from all corners of the world flock to Dubai. All are drawn by the promise of an epic New Year's Eve experience. The city came alive, with locals and tourists flocking together to Downtown Dubai.

Anticipation builds toward the midnight countdown. And then, the magic happens as the clock strikes twelve. Fireworks burst into a dazzling display with a spectacular light show using cutting-edge technology. We gazed in awe at the fireworks, with music playing to the beat of the bangs. Other landmarks like the Palm Jumeirah and the Burj Al Arab joined the firework display, creating a visual masterpiece across Dubai, etching itself into my memory.

New Year's Eve in Dubai is not just about fireworks. It is a city known for its lavish parties. Hotels and clubs pull out all stops, hosting unforgettable celebrations into the early hours. It is a night to remember, a story you tell your friends for years to come.

But let me rewind. New Year's Eve did not precisely unfold as planned. We were supposed to meet a friend at one of the Address Hotels in Downtown. Little did we know how crowded it would be. Downtown was sectioned into separate areas, and moving between them was impossible. Our plans crumbled, as we could not get to the hotel where we were supposed to meet our friend.

After the midnight fireworks, we could not find a taxi to return to our hotel in the Marina. There were no taxis. A pragmatic thought, why not spend a couple of hours in Dubai Mall and shop for furniture until the crowds had gone? The Mall was open 24/7. My fiancé was not thrilled with the idea. He preferred returning to the hotel.

We walked to a high-end hotel, the Ritz Carlton in DIFC (Dubai International Financial Centre). Luxury cars lined the streets in front of the Ritz, and after a bit of a wait, we finally secured a taxi and made it back to the Marina around four in the morning.

Waiting in the queue, I had an unexpected encounter with a glimpse of Dubai's nightlife. A young, good-looking, elegant blonde woman stood ahead of us, dressed in a glamorous, glittering gown reaching above the knee. A 4x4 car with a group of elderly Middle Eastern men slowed down. They exchanged glances with the hotel concierge. What unfolded next was like a scene out of a movie. The concierge chatted with the lady, who nodded at the men. She confidently walked over to their car and joined them in the front seat. As I watched her embark on her night's journey, I thought, *this girl is on an adventure.*

Meanwhile, our friend was facing his own New Year's hurdles. Stuck in Downtown, he watched the fireworks and then went to Business Bay. He was engulfed in a sea of people trying to get onto the metro. He noticed an older lady in distress. As he had military training, he swooped in to assist. Declaring an emergency, he cleared a path through the crowd and onto the metro. Dubai's chaos often spurs creativity, and everyone finds their unique way to navigate the tide.

The next day, we made amends for the New Year's calamity. We invited our friend to our hotel in the Marina for a delightful dinner and a good laugh about our disastrous New Year's Eve. It was a night to treasure.

I became better prepared for Dubai's New Year extravaganzas. Little did I know that Dubai would become the backdrop for many more New Year's celebrations.

In 2014, Dubai made history with an awe-inspiring display of pyrotechnics, an astounding 479,651 fireworks, illuminating the night sky in a mesmerising six-minute show. The event marked the end of a memorable year for the city. Dubai has been awarded World Expo 2020[2], and there are many reasons to celebrate. It was a record-breaking achievement, earning Dubai the title of "the largest fireworks display in the world." It is a testament to the city's boundless passion for grandeur and its ceaseless dedication to pushing the boundaries of what is possible.[3]

The following year, 2015, cast a shadow over the celebrations. As reported on CNN and other TV stations, a fire broke out at the 63-story Address Downtown Hotel on New

Year's Eve, a couple of hours before midnight, a sight sending shivers down the spines of those who witnessed it. Flames raged, presenting a formidable challenge. Dubai Government's response was remarkable, swift, and efficient.[4] Despite the incident, the show continued, albeit on a smaller scale. The organisers took measures to prevent any panic, ensuring people's safety. As fireworks painted the sky around the Burj Khalifa, the fire raged just meters away. The uncertainty hung heavy in the air, amplifying the anxiety.

The world watched, and in that moment, Dubai's resilience and capacity to manage adversity became a global talking point. Some say there is no such thing as bad publicity, and while Dubai's reputation continued to build meticulously in that moment, other countries' fireworks displays were relegated to the background.

Each year adds a new chapter to the tale, weaving a narrative of grandeur and resilience, creating unforgettable moments.

Chapter 2.

Dubai: Gateway to the Middle East

UAE Unveiled: Facts and Figures

Dubai is only one of the Emirates. The United Arab Emirates (UAE) is a federation of seven: Abu Dhabi, Dubai, Sharjah, Ajman, Umm Al Quwain, Ras Al Khaimah, and Fujairah. Each Emirate is under the leadership of a ruler known as a Sheikh. In 1971, the Emirates united. Citizens of the UAE are called Emiratis.[5]

The current President of the UAE is Mohammed bin Zayed Al Nahyan[6] (also known as MBZ). The President guides the Government of the UAE, complemented by a parliament made up of elected representatives.

The UAE has its flag, coat of arms, and national anthem. The flag comprises three equal horizontal lines with green at the top, white in the middle, and black at the base. There is also a wider vertical red ribbon.[7] The UAE's new coat of arms displays the UAE flag, surrounded by seven stars, representing the seven Emirates. The falcon is shown holding a parchment in its talons, which reads 'United Arab Emirates' in Arabic.[8]

The capital of the UAE is Abu Dhabi. Although Dubai tends to overshadow Abu Dhabi in terms of global recognition and brand awareness, Abu Dhabi is where the money is. The UAE's population in 2023 is an estimated 10 million with a land area of about 70,000 square kilometres, with ongoing land reclamation efforts altering this figure. The median age hovers around 33[9]. Islam is the official religion. Arabic is the official language, but many people speak English. Official documents are available in both Arabic and English. The currency is called dirhams (AED), pegged to the dollar.[1011]

In the pre-union days, travellers between Dubai and Abu Dhabi were required to carry a passport between the two cities for identification purposes. You can still glimpse history at the Abu Dhabi-Dubai border through a little building on the coast side of the motorway, now functioning as Saih Sheib Police Station.[12] During the COVID-19 pandemic, preventive health measures led to Abu Dhabi's domestic border with Dubai temporarily being reinstated.

Each Emirate still has its distinct character and its flag. Although united since 1971 under the UAE, you will realise when doing business in the UAE, you should treat them as separate. You may need to set up companies in each Emirate to enable seamless interaction across the UAE.

Abu Dhabi is the UAE's capital and the largest Emirate in terms of land area and population. It has abundant oil resources. It is home to the Louvre and the majestic Sheikh Zayed Grand Mosque, among the world's largest. Known to be more conservative than Dubai, Abu Dhabi oozes an air of tradition while embracing modernity.

Dubai is recognised as a global tourism destination, celebrated for its towering skyscrapers, such as the Burj Khalifa, opulent shopping malls, and groundbreaking initiatives. It represents the epitome of contemporary luxury and innovation.

Sharjah preserves the nation's rich heritage, upholding the UAE's conservative values. It is the custodian of cultural traditions and offers a glimpse into the past.

Ajman claims the title of the smallest Emirate. It shares similarities with its neighbouring Sharjah.

Ras Al Khaimah is a mix. It combines historical significance with contemporary advancements, showcasing an expanding industrial zone, a thriving real estate sector and luxurious high-end hotels.

Umm Al Quwain is a quiet and laid-back coastal retreat. Green and lush, it is favoured as a summer escape by numerous Abu Dhabi Royal families maintaining holiday homes in this Emirate. It is suitable for bird watching. It also has cheaper alcohol and more lenient alcohol regulations. Yet, they are conservative. They prefer the Bedouin lifestyle and like their camel farms.

Fujairah, nestled along the Gulf of Oman, captivates with its awe-inspiring mountains and pristine beaches. It is a strategically located port to bypass the Straits of Hormuz. There are various oil and gas companies in this Emirate, but Fujairah has no oil.

While the UAE contains seven Emirates, this book primarily focuses on Dubai. Dubai was the base camp from which I explored the region for a decade.

Visionary Leadership: Dubai's Ambitious Ruler

His Highness Sheikh Mohammed Bin Rashid Al Maktoum[13], born in 1949, often referred to simply as Sheikh Mohammed, holds the distinguished position of Ruler of Dubai and serves as the Vice President, Prime Minister, and Minister of Defence of the UAE.[14] The Al Maktoum family's reign as rulers of Dubai began in 1833[15]. His presence is hard to overlook, with his image projected onto buildings. You really cannot miss him. You might see him at conventions or other public gatherings.

Some describe His Highness Sheikh Mohammed Bin Rashid Al Maktoum as authoritative. His committed and visionary leadership has played an integral role in propelling Dubai's remarkable growth. I greatly respect how he oversees

Dubai's development, akin to a CEO guiding a corporation through rapid expansion. Like any company, Dubai has encountered its share of challenges, yet it continues to thrive under his guidance. His Highness Sheikh Mohammed Bin Rashid Al Maktoum is known for his unwavering determination and resilience, facing adversity head-on and emerging more robust than ever.

Dubai has undergone a phenomenal transformation, evolving from a modest fishing village and the Emirates' primary trading outpost into a global financial hub and a beacon for various industries. The city's motto is *Build, and they will come.* Dubai aims to captivate tourists and attract businesses. It also creates new eco-systems.[16]

His Highness Sheikh Mohammed Bin Rashid Al Maktoum's pursuit of excellence is unceasing. Many expats, like me, deeply admire his accomplishments and instrumental role in Dubai's metamorphosis. He has generated substantial wealth along his journey, benefiting many beyond himself.

Dubai demonstrated remarkable agility in diversifying its economy, driven by the necessity to do so due to its limited oil revenues compared to Abu Dhabi, which can rely on oil for its wealth. Dubai shifted its focus to the finance, tourism, real estate, logistics, and technology sectors. Currently, the oil-gas industry contributes roughly 1% to the economy of Dubai. According to an article on Bloomberg, it used to be almost half[17].

More recently, Dubai has seized the reins of the new economy, championing technological advancement. It has embraced digital transformation initiatives encompassing blockchain, artificial intelligence (AI), smart city solutions, and e-commerce. These technological strides bolster Dubai's competitive edge.

One noteworthy example of technological integration is using AI-driven technologies that improve operational efficiency, customer experiences, and social services in Dubai. Insights gleaned from AI have empowered Dubai to optimise infrastructure, refine customer service, and predict future trends. A quote from His Highness Sheikh Mohammed Bin Rashid Al Maktoum gives insight into his visionary thinking: "The future belongs to those who can imagine it, design it, and execute it."

In 2017, The Economist wrote: "The world's most valuable resource is no longer oil, but data."[18] The slogan *Data is the new oil* only holds if you effectively use data. Dubai is doing a remarkable job mining its data. AI applications, including facial recognition, predictive analytics, and sentiment analysis, have been harnessed to bolster security, healthcare, and financial services for residents, visitors, and businesses.[19] One intriguing question remains: How well does facial recognition handle sunglasses?

Dubai's transformation resembles Amsterdam's evolution from a quaint fishing village to a bustling global trading hub. Amsterdam, like Dubai, experienced decades of construction. Over centuries, the Netherlands evolved into an economic powerhouse, attracting traders worldwide. Strategic location and innovation catapulted the nation into a pivotal role in international commerce[20].

Today, the Dutch are still renowned for their logistics, shipping, finance, and technology expertise. Dubai's path of development and growth mirrors this trajectory, pointing towards a promising future. Dubai's 'Golden Age' is undoubtedly on the horizon.

Dubai has unveiled its ambitious 2040 Plan[21], a sustainable urban initiative centred around people. The plan includes improvements to public transportation and creating more green spaces. Shifting gears from mere construction,

Build, and they will come, Dubai is concentrating on cultivating an environment that fosters lasting residency. The people have arrived. The current question is how Dubai can get them to stay. The city already is a remarkable place. The aspiration is to transform Dubai into the world's best city to live in and retire.

The American Dream

Having experienced life in Monaco and Dubai, I found a striking contrast between the two countries. Monaco is deeply rooted in its historical heritage, while Dubai is about the future. Dubai ignites dreams, embodying the promise of the American Dream that may have dwindled elsewhere. Its export product is hope for a brighter and more promising tomorrow. The UAE is sending its first Arab mission to the moon in 2024.[22] A quote by His Highness Sheikh Mohammed Bin Rashid Al Maktoum echoes this promise of hope and aspiration: "They say the sky is the limit for ambition. We say the sky is only the beginning."[23]

In this city, the possibilities are limitless. Dubai has a Ministry of Possibilities[24]. It nurtures entrepreneurship, welcoming daring ventures with open arms, and understanding failure is integral to the journey. Dubai embodies the spirit of our generation, being constructed right before our eyes in a perpetual state of growth and transformation. One of the defining characteristics of Dubai is its resounding "can do" attitude. If a tourist points out a missing element, it miraculously becomes a reality within a year. The phrase "not possible" is a foreign concept in the vocabulary of His Highness Sheikh Mohammed Bin Rashid Al Maktoum. My departure from the South of France was partly due to the exasperatingly frequent utterances of *"Non, ce n'est pas possible"* or *"Ce n'est pas evident."* In Dubai, the prevailing attitude is embracing challenges head-on, willing to tackle any obstacle. His Highness

Sheikh Mohammed Bin Rashid Al Maktoum, encouraging everyone to dream big and make it happen, is known to have said, "'Impossible' is a word used by people who fear to dream big."[25]

What struck me on my first visits was how much everyone passionately loved being in Dubai. One of my friends thought the expats were overcompensating because of the perception of Dubai at the time. After moving to Dubai, I can confirm there is much to love about the city. While the initial impression of Dubai is often one of boundless possibilities, the reality is a little more complex.

Jennifer, who initially worked as a head-hunter, started importing perishable goods from Africa. She had no prior experience. The venture flourished until a shipment of spoiled fruits wiped out all her accumulated profits. What I loved about her experience is that it showed how individuals would dive into new ventures without fearing judgment from their peers. It is arguably easier for expats in Dubai, away from the prying eyes of friends and family. The city thrives on experimentation, and while many expats depart Dubai with a string of fantastic failures, they carry with them a treasury of experiences that would have been hard and much more expensive to come by in Europe. It often is part of the journey leading to bigger and better things.

It takes time to navigate and find your footing. Diya, an entrepreneur from India, said she thought Dubai was the land of opportunities and everything would be easy but found that, in practice, it was much more challenging than doing business in India. Nonetheless, the journey is an enriching one. You will need a lot of perseverance to succeed. A quote by Louisa May Alcott, an American 19th-century novelist, inspires us never to stop dreaming: "We all have our own life to pursue, our own kind of dream to be weaving, and we all have the power to make wishes come true, as long as we keep believing."[26]

Resilience: Turning Crisis into Opportunity

Dubai has a remarkable ability to transform every crisis into an opportunity. It has consistently positioned itself as a secure and stable haven for businesses and individuals, especially during regional turmoil. This resilience was evident during the Iraq War, the Arab Spring, and the recent COVID-19 pandemic.

The Russia-Ukraine war is the latest example of how Dubai can benefit from regional crises. Since the war began, it has seen an influx of Russian and Ukrainian businesses and individuals, as the war led to challenges for both countries, including economic instability, political uncertainty, and violence. Dubai is a haven for both, living peacefully alongside each other. As a result, there has been an increase in demand for property. Dubai will likely continue to see the benefits of the Russia-Ukraine war in the months and years ahead.

However, Dubai is not immune to the adverse effects of crises. For example, the Iraq War had a detrimental impact on the tourism industry. The Arab Spring also caused political instability. Moreover, the COVID-19 pandemic initially had a significant negative impact on Dubai's economy as occupancy rates of hotels plummeted and entertainment venues were empty.

As Yamin Mogahed, an American motivational speaker, eloquently said, "Resilience means you experience, you fail, you hurt. But you keep going."[27]

Chapter 3.

Arriving in Dubai and Settling in

Continuous Influx of Newcomers to Dubai

The COVID-19 pandemic altered Dubai's landscape. Before its onset, the city was a favoured destination for tourists and expats. Dubai's resolute policies in containing the virus yielded results, effectively curbing its spread. Yet, the policies protecting its residents affected the economy. The hospitality sector experienced a profound setback as tourists stayed away. Heavily reliant on tourism, the city bore the brunt of the downturn, triggering widespread job losses and prompting the departure of many. In addition to a decline in the number of tourists coming to Dubai, expats, facing the uncertainty of lockdown measures, left the city. Similarly, I boarded a repatriation flight to the UK and spent the following months in Europe.

Then, Dubai shifted gears and relaxed restrictions, increasing the number of new residents. Influencers on social media platforms flocked to the city, showcasing its safety and entertainment options. Their endorsements fuelled a global surge of interest in Dubai. With the reopening, I once again returned. The city became a hub for remote workers, as people could work from home during the pandemic.

I saw the emergence of the "Mayfair crowd." This group, affluent professionals from London's hedge funds and private equity funds, sought refuge in Dubai, drawn to the city's relaxed lifestyle. Many extended their stay, and some even went on to invest in real estate, praising the virtues of Dubai to their London peers.

Florence, COO of a hedge fund manager in London, attended an event targeting hedge fund managers. The event included a panel marketing the benefits of Dubai, focusing on the tax advantages for the funds and the individuals basing themselves in Dubai. She told me the room was packed, with over 200 attendees. A poll was done. More than 50 per cent of the people present were looking to move to Dubai or were already in the process of moving to Dubai.

Not only Dubai but Abu Dhabi also reap the rewards.[28] Buoyed by higher oil prices leading to greater liquidity in the Middle East and challenges in fundraising across Europe, coupled with the prospect of higher taxation in Europe, the UAE is a promising destination for fund managers to move to and raise capital in the region.

Historically, the business cards of global hedge funds would feature offices in London, New York, Singapore, and Hong Kong. The UAE is gaining traction and attracting attention from asset managers. It is considered mainstream to have the UAE as one of the regional offices of a hedge fund. Many hedge funds setting up in the UAE have been mentioned in the press, including Brevan Howard, which manages over $33 billion in assets. Arabian Gulf Business Insight reported that more than 200 hedge funds exist in the UAE.[29]

In addition to hedge fund managers, tech companies are looking to make the move. Dubai had been positioning itself as a tech hub before the pandemic. The pandemic accelerated the tech sector's growth as remote work became the norm. The UAE is the perfect market to assess innovative technologies. It is known as an ardent supporter of innovation. Its diverse population of over 200 nationalities makes it an ideal market to test new technologies that must adapt to different cultures and languages. Examples include self-driving cars, virtual reality, augmented reality, blockchain and artificial intelligence. Dubai continues to draw in startups from across the globe.

The influx of Russians and Ukrainians seeking refuge in the UAE, particularly Dubai, due to the conflict between Russia and Ukraine has brought about a complex set of economic and social dynamics.[30] Many Russians are clustered in the Marina in Dubai because of its Russian-language schools, churches, and clubs. The wealthy opt for a villa on the Palm. The arrival of Russians and Ukrainians has boosted the economy, increasing property prices.[31]

However, this has led to stereotyping Dubai as a destination for Russian money, raising concerns about potential money laundering or illicit financial activities. My European bank account was closed as my bank decided UAE residents were high-risk customers.

Dubai's authorities must balance providing refuge to those in need and ensuring proper financial and legal due diligence to maintain the city's reputation and stability. Dubai is collaborating with international partners to address potential concerns related to financial transactions and the influx of residents from specific countries. Emirati officials have said the UAE welcomes Russian investors and Ukrainian refugees while acknowledging the Western sanctions. Contrary to what those in the West say, it is hard these days for a Russian to open a bank account in the UAE.[32]

The transient nature of the expatriate community, while offering the opportunity to connect with people from around the world, can bring challenges when building and maintaining long-lasting friendships. I went through several best friends in my ten years in Dubai. As soon as I had bonded with someone new, they would leave Dubai. And then, eventually, it was me leaving Dubai. As your social circle changes frequently, you may occasionally experience periods of social isolation until you build new connections. Alan Watts, an influential figure in popularising Eastern philosophy in the West, whose work I much enjoyed, would say: "The only way to make sense out of change is to plunge into it, move with it, and enjoy the dance."[33]

Strike a balance between investing in your existing friends and embracing the opportunity to meet new people. Thanks to the transient nature of Dubai, you will end up with friends worldwide. It does not matter if you have not seen them for months or even years. The bond is still as strong as ever, with many good and bad memories to laugh about.

Speaking Arabic is Impressive but not a Necessity

Upon arrival, I enrolled in an Arabic beginner's course to fully immerse myself in the culture. Arabic did not come naturally to me. The unfamiliar sounds of the language posed a hurdle, and the script was entirely different. Arabic writing follows a right-to-left direction, starkly contrasting the left-to-right script of European languages. While I have retained only about 2% of the content from the intensive three-week morning-and-afternoon Arabic classes, phrases like *"Shukran"* (Thank you) and *"Inshallah"* (I hope so/God willing) still linger in my memory. I believe revisiting the course now would yield better results, as I have developed an ear for the sounds.

In class, most participants had prior exposure to Arabic. However, I found myself close to the bottom of the class, sympathising with those who had to do the exercises with me. The course I did was at the World Trade Centre. They do online courses, allowing you to learn at your own pace. An online course may have been better suited for me then and a better option for those starting from scratch. However, the in-person classes are a great way to make new connections.[34]

Over 400 million people worldwide speak Arabic, so it is worth learning. I admire expats who have mastered Arabic, a testament to their dedication.

Sarah, a digital transformation advisor equipped with a basic understanding of Arabic writing, used to begin meetings by noting down the date and time in Arabic at the top of the page of her notebook. The reactions on the other side of the table were often a mix of surprise and curiosity. It was an unexpected sight for a redheaded Irish lady to be writing Arabic. People's language skills should never be underestimated.

In Dubai, speaking Arabic is optional. Everyone speaks English. When calling your utility provider, you are presented with a greeting, "Press 1 for Arabic and press 2 for English."

Learning a few key phrases of Arabic will go a long way to showcase your efforts and respect for the local culture. I suggest you memorise the words: *"Marhaba,"* which means "Hello" and is a warm way to greet someone. *"Salam alaykum,"* translating as "Peace be upon you," is a standard and respectful greeting. *"Shukran"* is your go-to for saying "Thank you," a gesture of appreciation often used when served tea or coffee. To inquire about well-being, you can use *"Kayfa haluka?"* meaning "How are you?" For wishing someone a good morning, *"Sabah al-khair"* is appropriate. And if someone advises you to be patient or slow down, you might hear *"Shway, shway."*

Desert Escapades and Architectural Marvels

When you arrive in Dubai, step into the vastness of the desert and experience everything it has to offer. I remember how my footsteps left soft imprints on the golden sands of the sprawling desert. As I inhaled the dry air, I felt a sense of calmness wash over me. I had been waiting for a chance to immerse myself in the vastness of the desert and embrace its beauty. Every moment is a spectacle. The changing colours of the sky over the dunes are mesmerising. The desert is one of the world's best places to stargaze. To experience its mystique, spend a night under the open skies by camping in the dunes in traditional Bedouin-style camps. The warm glow of lanterns lights up the surrounding area, and you will be entertained by traditional music and dance performances while enjoying Emirati cuisine. This gives you a glimpse of Bedouin culture and way of life. Desert camps often offer cultural experiences such as henna painting, falconry displays, and learning about Bedouin culture and history.

Alternatively, more upmarket, you can opt for VIP camping or head to Dubai's lavish desert resorts to indulge in luxury. For a more relaxing and peaceful way to explore the desert, ride a camel through the dunes or take a leisurely ride around the camp. There are also many hiking trails. Seek solitude and hike to the top of the dunes, explore ancient ruins, or enjoy the peace and quiet and flora and fauna. You can also experience the desert by taking a hot air balloon over the dunes, providing breathtaking panoramic views. If you are looking for more action, go dune-bashing. Dune bashing is thrilling, driving a 4x4 vehicle over the dunes. It is a terrific way to experience the power and excitement of the desert. Or try sandboarding, gliding down the sand slopes.

Zara, a renewable energy specialist, is looking to return to Dubai. She told me that what she misses most about Dubai is not Dubai itself but what lies beyond. She appreciates how easy and safe it is in Dubai to ride into the desert on your own for an afternoon of dune bashing. In other countries, such as Egypt, where she lives, you would need military clearance and may have to pass through twenty military checkpoints – not to mention all the paperwork.

Returning from the desert to Dubai, I felt a sense of gratitude wash over me. The desert offered me moments of adventure, a profound connection to nature, and a peaceful escape from busy Dubai. Back there after a day in the desert, driving down the Sheikh Zayed Road, I marvelled at the city's architecture, a testament to its endless innovation and rapid development. From having one skyscraper in 1991, the city boasts an astonishing count of over 400 towering structures.

Among them stands the iconic Burj Khalifa[35], the world's tallest building. Stretching to a breathtaking height of 828 meters (2,716 feet), almost a kilometre tall, the Burj Khalifa is a true marvel of human engineering. Its sight is a never-ending delight, especially when it lights up the night sky with dazzling sparkle. Constructing the Burj Khalifa was a monumental achievement. Over 12,000 workers can proudly claim to have contributed to this towering achievement, adding it to their resume.

Upon entering the Burj Khalifa, you will notice a unique touch: its bespoke *fragrance*. You will discover many hotels and malls have their distinct fragrances.

The origins of the Burj Khalifa's name hold significant meaning. Officially named after Sheikh Khalifa bin Zayed Al Nahyan, the President of the UAE and the ruler of Abu Dhabi, the name symbolises his leadership, unity, and pride for the entire UAE. Curiously, the skyscraper was initially known as the Burj Dubai during its construction phase. Rumour has it that Abu Dhabi's financial bailout of Dubai following the 2009 crash came with the condition of changing the name to Burj Khalifa. Regardless of its origin, the Burj Khalifa is an awe-inspiring masterpiece.[36] With 163 floors, it is often referred to as a vertical city.

I was fortunate to experience a business meeting in the world's highest office in the Burj Khalifa. The experience of visiting their offices was fun. It felt like a private viewing and encapsulated "working at new heights." Gazing down from such heights creates a surreal sensation akin to peering out of an aeroplane. I find standing at the base of the Burj Khalifa, looking up, equally impressive.

The fountains on the lake in front of the building and next to Dubai Mall are a nice *intermezzo* from shopping in Dubai Mall. I always appreciate the sparkling Burj and fountain show. It is performed multiple times a day – and is free.

Dubai is also known for its artificial islands, notably the Palm Islands – Palm Jumeirah, Deira Island and Palm Jebel Ali.[37] Perhaps inspired by the Dutch, who mastered land reclamation to expand their territory, Dubai undertook similar endeavours to create these islands, using vast amounts of seabed sand and rocks at a cost of approximately USD 12 billion. The Palm Islands are amazing. It is worth watching documentaries about their construction and the challenges they had to overcome.

Another renowned reclaimed land project in Dubai is "The World," artificial islands that resemble a world map. I am proud to share that two Dutch companies, Van Oord and Boskalis, helped construct the island; the same companies also created the Palm Jumeirah.[38] The Dutch began to reclaim land in the late 16th century because of a growing population and the need for more farmland to feed them. René Descartes[39] once said, "God created the world, but the Dutch made The Netherlands"[40], referencing the clever methods the Dutch people used to reclaim land from the sea. Dubai created not only Dubai but also the World.

Since the completion of the Palm in Dubai, Monaco has picked up the idea of reclaiming land. As I sit here writing this book in Monaco, I have been able to visit the new reclamation projects. A colleague I used to work with told me over an enjoyable lunch in the Monaco Yacht Club of an apartment sold at €250,000 per meter. In the rest of Monaco, you will see average pricing at €50,000+ per meter. €250,000 is exceptionally high, but outrageously high prices are not unheard of. Monaco has a limited supply.

These prices quoted make Dubai look extremely cheap, even after the recent increase in prices for apartments, ranging from USD$3,000–9,000 per square meter, cheaper too than in the rest of the South of France. Dubai has plenty of land compared to Monaco, so it is less constrained on the supply side, which may explain the price differential.

The UAE proudly boasts an impressive list of world records. These achievements capture the nation's unwavering commitment to pushing the boundaries of innovation and excellence. A quote by His Highness Sheikh Mohammed Bin Rashid Al Maktoum, trying always to be the best in everything: "We are no less than Number One. Whoever convinces himself that he is not worthy of first position has adorned himself to failure from the beginning."[41]

Dubai holds over 425 Guinness World Records.[42] Some of these remarkable records worth mentioning are the world's largest hand-woven Persian carpet (in the Sheikh Zayed Grand Mosque in Abu Dhabi), the world's largest chandelier (Qasr Al Watanb presidential palace), the world's largest picture frame and the world's highest tennis court.[43] I recently attended a party in the Princess Tower[44] Penthouse in Dubai Marina on the 96th floor, the world's tallest residence until recently. The list keeps growing longer and longer!

Getting Settled In

My fiancé and I separated because of our differing life aspirations. While he dreamt of retiring in the serene South of France after a successful banking career in London, my aspirations were far from considering retirement. My spirit still craved adventure and continued excitement. Retiring was not an option. I thrive on contributing to society and seek enriching experiences. We parted ways amicably, recognising our diverging paths in life.

The apartment where I am currently cat-sitting belongs to him. I have spent two weeks here, gradually forming a bond with the ragdoll cat. We are defining our boundaries and navigating our "cultural differences." We agree feeding times are set at 7 a.m. and 7 p.m. in exchange for *not keeping me up at night*. Despite the cat's disregard for his name "Banksy," I have discovered he responds well to "Darling."

In a fascinating twist, life has brought me full circle, writing a book about the Middle East while situated in the South of France. Like the writers in movies who often craft their novels in the idyllic South of France, I find myself infused with similar inspiration. I aspire to fill the pages with practical advice for those embarking on similar journeys, and I trust you will also find the anecdotes entertaining.

Embarking on my Dubai journey demanded a mountain of paperwork. Simplicity was a rarity; red tape loomed large, accompanied by an array of small fees for document stamps, bank account openings, driving license changes, and the pursuit of a residency permit. The absence of taxes eased the burden of these seemingly inconsequential charges.

A valuable lesson emerged: always make inquiries and plan when dealing with government institutions. It is frustrating to embark on a journey only to discover you are missing a crucial document they forgot to mention on their website or had not gotten around to updating it. You will hear me often say: double- and triple-checking is key; trust but verify. The Dubai experience sharpens your ability to think independently. Rules change swiftly, and what is acceptable today might no longer be okay tomorrow. The initial setup is time-consuming. With the paperwork eventually completed, living in Dubai becomes remarkably simple!

Patience becomes a virtue you will need in ample supply in the Middle East. The art of providing answers people want to hear is another skill acquired swiftly. Striking a delicate balance between friendliness and effectiveness becomes crucial. People are open to making exceptions if you present a credible case, and personalising the conversation is the secret ingredient for success in the execution of your plans. Numerous services in Dubai come with a fee. Departments operate under their profit-and-loss structures. Fees are charged at every turn. These are not bribes but service fees.

For those seeking fast-track service, VIP options are available. For an additional fee, government employees may offer VIP treatment by arriving early, before official opening hours, to accommodate your special requests. The lesson here is to ask if there is a VIP service, locally referred to as *wasta* service, if you are having challenges getting something done and have a budget to pay for fast track. Money talks in the UAE. A couple hundred dirhams can fix most things. Throughout my journey, I had to navigate the processes independently. Joining a company or partnering with a local business alleviates the burden. I was on my own.

After buying a property and settling in, I embraced all Dubai had to offer, attending networking events and conferences and reconnecting with acquaintances and friends of friends. Meeting new individuals is a breeze, as there is a continuous influx of new people, but fostering genuine friendships is harder. The city is transient. People have come to Dubai to pursue leisure or business objectives. People come and go.

The Capital Club Dubai[45], a private business club in DIFC (Dubai International Financial Centre), emerged as an excellent networking venue. You will find countless other networking clubs in Dubai to match your interests. I also attended events organised by MBA networks, such as the London Business School. I joined several Business Councils, attending events of the Netherlands Business Council, The British Business Group, and others. They would often have great intellectual topics for discussion, followed by mingling over drinks.

Additionally, I dedicated time to studying the Middle East, immersing myself in serious documentaries and more entertaining films like *"Lawrence of Arabia"*[46]. There are excellent books on the history of the Middle East worth reading. This initial period, on arrival, is ideal for studying the region before your social and business diary becomes more demanding.

Monaco's residents rarely discussed their occupations. When you meet someone new, the first question is, "Do you live in Monaco?" "Which building do you live in?" "Where do you come from?" followed by "What are you invested in?"

The pretentiousness of Monaco's inhabitants offered delightful entertainment, and the distinct characters found there were captivating. To experience and indulge in the eccentricity of Monaco, I would go for a drink in the evening at the American Bar at the Hotel de Paris. Another wonderful place for people-watching is the premiere gala nights at the Monte Carlo Opera House, where the Princess Grace generation would turn up in their tiaras and fur coats. You could never ask anyone in Monaco what they did for a living.

When you meet someone new in Dubai, the initial question will be about which area you live in. However, the conversation will quickly veer towards business, what you do and the potential for collaboration. One of the key questions on everyone's mind is how long you intend to stay. Does the length of your planned stay in Dubai justify an investment in a long-term relationship?

Frequently, I was asked, "What brings you to Dubai?" My purpose was simple: to buy real estate, and my mission was completed. With my business, I could work from home or on the road. My location was flexible.

However, to end further inquiries, I decided to make the Middle East a new territory for doing business. I began travelling around the region, meeting with family groups to better understand their concerns and investment interests. Over time, I started advising potential clients (companies in Europe looking for money) and organising meetings with investors.

When I first started in the Middle East, I combined Euromoney's insightful conferences throughout the Middle East with one-on-one meetings and sightseeing. I had to learn the names of all the corporations, family groups and banks in the Middle East. Before I set foot in the Middle East, I had never heard of any prominent families' names. I arrived with a completely blank piece of paper. I would combine my travel in the region with a day of sightseeing in each country. I so enjoyed those trips.

After about a year, I knew the lay of the land, understood the visa process, checked out hotels, and had drivers in each country on my mobile. I was confident in the connections I had cultivated with regional investors, which laid the foundation for many successful roadshows.

Chapter 4.

Finding a Place to Call Home

Navigating Dubai's Property Market

While in Monaco, where I had been a resident for 5 years, following 12 years in London and 3 years in Brussels, Dubai caught my eye. In 2011, the financial sector was teetering on the brink of collapse. With some liquidity in the bank, I explored avenues for currency diversification and sought exposure to the US dollar through tangible assets.

Dubai emerged on my radar with its currency pegged to the US dollar. It piqued my curiosity and led me to delve into real estate opportunities within the UAE. Dubai had undergone a spectacular boom followed by a massive crash in 2009 due to the global financial crisis sweeping through in 2008, leaving its mark on Dubai's economy and property market.[47] During the boom, investors, enticed by easy credit, flocked to Dubai, hoping to profit from reselling properties. This speculative frenzy artificially inflated property prices, making it vulnerable in the downturn. The market, once soaring, suffered oversupply and entered a prolonged period of stagnation.[48]

My UAE expat friends were vocal in their caution against investing in Dubai. "It's highly volatile; you might lose everything!" They explained to me the limited property rights and the fact that Dubai's towering skyline was constructed upon a foundation of debt.

The aftermath of the property market crash was a landscape of forced sales, crystallising genuine losses for many. Property values plummeted by up to 60% in some areas, and investors, burdened by property-related loans, found themselves unable to meet their financial obligations. Defaults and foreclosures swept through Dubai. Development projects were abandoned. The ripples of the crisis extended beyond real estate. Sectors intertwined with construction and property felt the strain, too, leading to an economic downturn across industries.[49]

However, these risks were not new and were now better priced into the market, given the substantial 60% decline. The market's freefall in 2009 was a catalyst for much-needed reforms, resulting, for example, in credit limits for buyers being significantly tightened. While Dubai's property market went through soaring highs and a major crash, its narrative was of resilience and transformation. The crash laid bare the risks, prompting re-evaluation, reform, and a readiness to launch a new era in the city's real estate journey.

As I sat in Monaco, my thoughts often turned to Dubai's advantages over my residency in Monaco. It was like Monaco, with the same tax advantages and a sunny climate. What set Dubai apart was its potential for business and the mild winters. Monaco, while charming and idyllic, lacked any business dynamism. It was a lovely and safe place for residence and retirement. It was where you would live while conducting business outside of its borders.

I found myself exploring Dubai in the evenings through online searches. I discovered that not all areas in Dubai were open to expat property ownership. There were designated zones where foreigners could possess freehold properties, granting them complete ownership rights. Desirable villa areas along the coast could only be rented. Behind my desk, I immersed myself in virtual tours of DIFC, Dubai's financial district, and the Marina, growing familiar with the distinct neighbourhoods. My understanding of the market deepened, including insights into pricing. At conferences, I would quiz residents in the Middle East, probing them for insights into Dubai's property landscape.

The summer of 2012 marked a turning point. I noticed a slight market recovery, with property values climbing 10% within months. My experience with emerging markets taught me that when these markets move, they do so with intensity.

After a year of online research, I decided it was time for action. I booked a flight to Dubai and set my plans in motion. In retrospect, 2012 proved an excellent year to buy property in Dubai. It was close to the bottom.

The city has been in perpetual construction mode, its skyline framed by cranes, especially during the economic booms. Price fluctuations have mirrored those of other real estate markets, though heightened in magnitude. Dubai's government employs pragmatic measures, facilitating expat residency during downturns to stimulate interest in its real estate market. This influx of expats subsequently buying properties offsets the imbalance between supply and demand. Dubai's property market has seen fortunes made and lost, contingent on timing.

Options for investment are diverse: purchasing existing properties, acquiring units from flippers in development projects, or making down payments for off-plan properties. The latter allows for buying property at a rate lower than the potential market value upon completion and lures in expats.

I considered off-plan real estate developments outside the boundaries of my risk appetite. I had heard stories of development projects not being delivered many years later or specifications being changed by the developer. Besides, I was looking for an apartment I could immediately enjoy.

My Dubai quest began with viewings of apartments already on the market. It was not straightforward. Scrutiny was essential, ensuring the real estate agent was licensed. Amidst the chaos, professional agents stood out as dependable guides. I gained invaluable insights. Certain buildings appeared neglected, exhibiting a need for ongoing maintenance and care by the developer.

People used to complain about the quality of construction in Dubai. However, I found the apartments in Dubai looked marvellous. Interestingly, in Monaco, renowned for its super high-end standards, I discovered that many smaller apartments were worn. In the past, Monaco was not a place where people lived. An address for residency and tax purposes with a functional letterbox was all that was required.

I remember going for viewings in Monaco. The real estate agent would point out the location of the kitchen. Surprisingly, I only saw a simple wooden plank serving as the kitchen. A lot has changed, with significant investments being made by expats in Monaco. As a result, you can find nice small apartments in the area. However, when I looked in Dubai ten years ago, Monaco still had many run-down apartments.

Dubai's apartments were priced at 1/10th of what you would pay in Monaco. The flats all had a gym and swimming pool. The pricing was appealing. Additionally, all apartments in Dubai were equipped with proper kitchens, including fridges, washing machines and ovens. Quality is a relative concept. It depends on what you are comparing it to.

I would engage with residents in the lift to gain insights into the buildings' quality and ongoing maintenance. I would inquire about their personal experiences with the building and the developer behind it, seeking to understand the positive aspects and any drawbacks they may have encountered.

I liked Downtown Dubai. It ticked many of my boxes. It offered the convenience of Dubai Mall, the world's largest shopping centre, and proximity to DIFC, Dubai's financial district, and the airport. After five years in the South of France,

I had seen enough beaches, so the sea view was less critical. My focus was business and convenience. At the time, limited to a single developer, Downtown was meticulously maintained and manicured, an attribute I found missing in other areas. In other areas, such as the neighbouring Business Bay, strips of undeveloped sandy land would often emerge between buildings due to the many developers involved, with neither party assuming responsibility for these gaps.

I researched developers' reputations. It became evident that EMAAR was the prominent developer in Downtown Dubai, with a solid reputation. There were others with notorious reputations for consistently failing to meet project deadlines or failing to fulfil the promised visions they marketed when selling a development. In case of a market downturn, EMAAR might be more inclined to maintain the aesthetics of Downtown, considering the iconic Burj Khalifa served as Dubai's global symbol, featuring on tourists' photographs of the city.

I focused on a select few buildings within the area. I checked the distance to the nearest mosque. I called them "volcanoes," knowing they could erupt any moment. If you are someone like me, sensitive to noise, identify and locate the mosques in the neighbourhood. This way, you can ensure a good night's sleep. Conversely, the resale value may be better if you are close to a mosque.

I decided to purchase an apartment in a low-rise building and had a specific reason for doing so. I had heard from friends who used to live in a low-rise building in Singapore that a developer offered them a good deal if they agreed to move out. They exchanged their old apartment for a new one in a planned, glamorous, high-rise building to replace their low-rise apartment block. Therefore, as the buildings eventually reached the end of their life, you would have the option of a nicer apartment if the building were demolished for a higher-rise building.

I settled on an apartment on a mid-level floor. The prospect of living at extreme heights did not appeal to me. I discovered higher floors could be troubled by noise from rooftop machinery. Residing on lower floors came with the possibility of cooking smells from restaurants on the ground level.

As I became more comfortable with the market, I went up the risk curve. The term "flipper's trade" was coined for transactions like mine. The apartment was ready for occupancy, having been developed and reaching the stage where it was ready for handover, subject to the final 80% instalment by the buyer. I acquired the apartment from the flipper, who was compelled to sell it due to financial constraints before shouldering the remaining 80%. I bought out his 20% share and completed the transaction by fulfilling the remaining 80% payment to the developer.

I had engaged the services of a lawyer to guide me through the transaction. However, I ended up explaining *to the lawyer* the intricacies of the process instead of the other way around. While the partners may be seasoned, the subsequent layers are often filled with juniors who started work yesterday. This is a problem in a city with high turnover and a transient population.

Dubai operates on its own set of rules. A mobile phone number was imperative, the key to unlocking all processes. Setting up a bank account was similarly critical.

Upon returning to Europe, I was about to initiate a substantial wire transfer to the lawyer to purchase the apartment. However, a hurdle emerged when my bank in Dubai blocked the transfer. I was not informed that my first transfer could not be executed solely over the Internet. Instead, I was required to visit the bank in person for the initial transfer, and subsequently, online transfers would be permissible. Banking hurdles are a fact of life, I later learned.

Faced with this unexpected roadblock, I promptly hopped on an overnight flight back to Dubai. I needed to complete the transaction on the same day, in alignment with the contractual agreement with the seller. I had to quite literally 'go the extra mile.' Despite the inconvenience, I successfully resolved the situation and completed all the necessary tasks within a day. I had to get paperwork stamped at a government office to arrange a power of attorney for the lawyer.

Stepping into the building, a gentleman at the front desk said, "We are closed."

Baffled, I responded, "What do you mean you are closed? There is a sign here clearly indicating you are open!"

His gaze shifted again towards me as he uttered, "We are swamped!"

I quickly surveyed the waiting area, pondering that *it was not busy. I counted three people.* I thought something was odd, not understanding why I was not allowed in.

The desk attendant gauged I would not give up lightly, then inquired whether I was a resident or a visitor. I explained I was a visitor with aspirations of becoming a resident, hoping it would address the required single answer to the question. Yet, he repeated the question, expecting just one single answer. I confidently asserted, "Visiting," to which he finally relented. For access, wearing an *abaya* was a requirement, he said. He handed me an abaya. To my surprise, my elegant London attire, a short, light grey cashmere dress with a graceful roll neck, did not conform to the dress code.

As I hastily made my way to the airport in London during the winter months, I found myself in Dubai bundled up in my winter cashmere, realising that I had been in a rush and not given much consideration to my wardrobe for this trip. My dress was slightly above the knee, and although dresses and skirts were acceptable in the UAE, it became apparent that trousers were the preferred choice for government-building visits to ensure knee coverage. Government buildings maintained a dress code I unwittingly violated. Understanding and adapting to local customs proved essential. Note to self: *A review of my wardrobe would be necessary.*

In the process, it became evident that layers of bureaucracy, or "red tape," were commonplace. Information was not always readily accessible, necessitating a triple-check approach to received data.

On a positive note, officials were consistently open to hearing credible stories and making exceptions when warranted. Over the past decade, I have noticed a significant transformation, making purchasing property in Dubai smoother and more accessible.

Timing is everything in Dubai. I bought a property there in 2012. The property's value doubled in a couple of years, peaking in Q4 2014, coinciding with the announcement of the World Expo. I remember a veteran in Dubai urging me to sell. I should have listened.

New developments were announced weekly, all scheduled to be completed before Expo 2020. The subsequent oversupply of new properties led to a decline in prices, all the way back to levels I had bought in 2012. The VAT announcement in 2018 also did not help.

The lowest point for property prices was during the COVID-19 pandemic in 2020-2021, with a decline in property demand due to travel restrictions and economic uncertainty. You could find selling prices *lower than the construction cost.*

Then, in 2022, to resurrect the market, the Dubai government made it much easier for expats to get residency, which led to an influx of new expats. This soaked up some of the oversupply of properties, and prices started to rise again. In recent years, prices increased by more than 50% from the lows in 2020-2021. Some expect property prices in Dubai will continue to rise in the coming years as the population grows, soaking up the supply. Some say new development will not be able to keep up with the projected increase in population.

Suppose you plan to participate in the Dubai real estate market. In that case, I advise you to exercise caution when considering off-the-beaten-track land or development purchases unless an established developer is offering them with a proven track record. While everyone's risk tolerance varies, conducting thorough research and due diligence in any property venture is crucial to making informed decisions. I have heard terrible stories from friends who were conned. Of course, these are exceptional stories, but it is good to stay vigilant.

A fundamental rule to follow is to triple-check all information. Diligently verifying every detail and doing proper homework on counterparties can help you navigate the complexities of property transactions and make well-informed choices.

Allow for extras. The extras are all the fees you will pay to complete the paperwork. These are not bribes but official fees. There is no or barely any tax, so nothing is for free. Each department will have its fee for processing your paperwork. No one tells you about these fees. They are small but can add up. When buying a property, budget for the unexpected.

Tips for Renting and Tenancy

From a renter's perspective, engaging only with registered agents is crucial. To ensure their legitimacy, you can request to see the agent's RERA (Real Estate Regulatory

Agency) license card. This card will validate that the agent operates within legal parameters and not freelancing, which is prohibited in the UAE. Different coloured cards denote various authorisations.[50] When dealing with a real estate agent, you must pay a fee, typically a percentage of the annual rent. To initiate your search, Propertyfinder is a reliable website to consider starting your search from. It also includes contact details of real estate agents from all nationalities.

Conducting due diligence on your prospective landlord is recommended, as there can be unscrupulous ones. Rental prices can fluctuate dramatically from one year to another. The landlord is responsible for repairing the property, but landlords may refuse. This can be a problem for tenants living in a substandard property. Some landlords harass tenants or enter the property without permission.

Disputes about deposits are common. Take photos and do an inventory report before moving in to avoid a disagreement at the end of the tenancy. Landlords can often request a single upfront payment, primarily due to the challenge of conducting thorough reference checks on tenants who have recently arrived in the UAE. Just because someone agrees to pay you with one cheque does not mean background checks are unnecessary. I prefer tenants from large corporations, as they are easy to check out and have gone through a vetting process before being hired.

Rental contracts are standardised, streamlining the process for all parties involved. The government's website provides information, including links to useful resources.[51] Rental income is not taxed in Dubai. Gross yields for apartments stand at approximately 7%, while villas are around 5%.[52]

From a landlord's perspective, there are risks too. Evicting a tenant is difficult. For instance, a landlord can evict a tenant if there is a technical risk to the tenant's safety, if the landlord intends to sell the property (with a year's notice) or if the landlord wants to move in.[53] As a landlord, ensure you do not hand over any keys until the Tenancy Agreement is signed and the funds are in your account.

Barbara, a German lady in her thirties, works in the hospitality sector. After her parents died, she inherited some money. With it, she bought a couple of properties in Dubai. She planned to live off the rental income. Renting out the properties was not as straightforward as she had imagined. The tenant signed a tenancy agreement stating the rent would be paid on the first of every month. She now knows this was a mistake. She should have asked for postdated cheques. The first couple of months, he paid on time. However, in month three, he started missing payments. She tried to contact him, reminding him about the rent. He never responded. Barbara then sent him a notice to vacate, but he ignored it. In response, she went to the Dubai Land Department to file an eviction case. The case proceeded to court, where the judge ruled in Barbara's favour. The judge ordered him to vacate the apartment within 30 days. Unfortunately, he still has not left.

Barbara had another set of tenants, where she had the opposite problem. A young, happy Eastern European couple embarked on their first cohabitation. It did not work out between the couple. They had a falling out and then terminated the Tenancy Agreement as they each wanted to go their way. They had only been in the apartment for a couple of months. They provided the required notice and continued to pay the rent until Barbara found a new tenant. Tenants can give notice at any time, subject to the stipulated notice period. If the landlord fails to secure a new tenant, they may need to cover the void after the notice period.

A project manager named Jenny told me an entertaining story about her apartment. She had rented it out to a well-mannered married tenant who owned properties globally. She engaged with the tenant during a viewing, discussing his intended apartment use. He assured her he would barely be in the apartment, occasionally using it for business, and was well-equipped to handle repairs.

She inquired, "Do you know how to change a lightbulb?"

He confidently responded, "Yes, I am a trained engineer and quite handy with fixing things. Do you have a toolbox?"

Impressed by his skillset and replies, she decided to go with him. He also agreed to pay her in advance with one cheque for the year.

The tenant messaged her about a severely leaking boiler in the second week of the tenancy. He was travelling but arranged for his local business partner to oversee the situation.

Her usual plumber promptly assessed the situation, discovering something unusual: two stunning African women sitting on the sofa with a third person in the shower. The plumber then shared a video of one of the women testing the shower while dressed only in a white dressing gown. The woman claimed to be living in the apartment.

Jenny sent a message to the tenant, alerting him others may be using the apartment while he is travelling. She is still waiting to hear back from him.

I am eagerly awaiting the unfolding episodes of this intriguing saga.

Both tenants and landlords navigate themselves through the property market. Of course, tenants and landlords are fine most of the time.

Hotel Accommodation: Where to Stay in Dubai

If you want to stay in a hotel for a couple of months before renting or purchasing a property, then serviced apartments, often attached to hotels, may be the way to go. Dubai has many hotels, from high-end hotels to more affordable ones. Because many of the hotels have been built recently, they are in excellent condition, as are the three-star hotels. Before you book online, check when the hotel was constructed. Even a three-star hotel can feel luxurious if it is a new addition to the hotel landscape. Local brands can be better priced. It is standard practice for hotels to take a photocopy of your passport or Emirates ID.

I was unaware of the many Address and Rotana Hotels when I arrived in Dubai. In Downtown, you will come across hotels with the same brand name, The Address. Verifying the full name of the hotel you are meeting at is recommended.

Similarly, Jumeirah is a name that pops up everywhere, from luxurious hotels and resorts to beautiful residential areas. Before getting into a taxi, check exactly where you are going. Just saying Jumeirah will not be helpful. Aside from the many Jumeirah Hotels, there is also Jumeirah Beach, Palm Jumeirah, Jumeirah Village, Jumeirah Lakes Towers, Jumeirah Islands, and Jumeirah Golf Estates.

Dubai is home to the most incredible hotels in the world, from 5–7-star properties. The Burj Al Arab Jumeirah[54], built in the shape of a sail, holds the prestigious title of being the only 7-star hotel in the world. The Burj Al Arab's interior is decorated with around 1,790 square meters of 24-carat gold leaf. It stands on an artificial island.

In 2005, Roger Federer and Andre Agassi played a match on the helicopter pad of the Burj Al Arab to promote the ATP Dubai Duty-Free Tennis. They set a record by playing 211 meters above ground level. "It was an amazing experience," said Agassi. "When you first get over how high you are and start playing, it is an absolute joy, and it was a great time."

"It was amazing," Federer added. "We had this picture-perfect day, no sandstorms, a clear day, no winds."[55]

The world's tallest hotel is being constructed in Dubai. The Ceil Tower[56] in Dubai Marina will reach 365 metres high.

Make sure you can afford your hotel and pay your bills. The UK Government website warns that financial crimes, including fraud and the non-payment of bills (including hotel bills), can result in imprisonment and a fine. Bank accounts and other assets can also be frozen. Bail is generally not available to non-residents of the UAE who are arrested for financial crimes. Those convicted will not normally be released from jail until the debt is paid or waived, and they may even remain in jail after a debt has been paid if there is an outstanding sentence to be served.[57]

Obtaining Residency: Navigating the Process

Historically, to reside and work in the UAE, all expats were required to have sponsorship from a locally licensed and registered entity to obtain a work permit and residency visa. Such sponsorship was specific to the employer and location, entitling the employee to work solely for their sponsoring employer. The employment regime in the UAE was closely tied to the immigration regime, which was relatively static, with a few exceptions. As a result of this framework, any expatriate who wished to work in the UAE had to be sponsored and employed by a licensed UAE entity. After termination, the employee would have to leave the country.[58]

The new immigration laws represent a departure from these old rules, ushering in more relaxed procedures. Versatile visas and residency permits have been introduced. The UAE now offers a range of flexible and renewable entry visas spanning 60 to 90 days. This initiative benefits investors, skilled professionals, freelancers, and their families, serving as a magnet for talent and streamlining the bureaucratic hurdles accompanying relocation.[59]

Dubai effectively has opened its doors wide to individuals from all over the world. Whether you are interested in starting a business, pursuing a career, retiring in the sun, or simply enjoying the luxurious lifestyle the city has to offer, Dubai now provides a streamlined process for obtaining residency and a visa that is both efficient and hassle-free, making it exceptionally easy to pack your bags and move to Dubai.

You will find a visa tailored to your needs in the extensive list of options available.[60] The revised residency and visa policies are designed to stimulate population growth. More liberal regulations have already increased demand for residential real estate. Introducing the Golden Visa program has lured ultra-high-net-worth individuals and others to the UAE, offering long-term 5- and 10-year visas.[61]

Chapter 5.

Dress Code and Perfumes Decoded

Dubai's dress code and cultural norms are influenced by its blend of local customs, religious beliefs, and the diverse expatriate population. Understanding and respecting Dubai's dress code and cultural norms is essential to being a responsible visitor or resident. Some Westerners think they need to wear an abaya in Dubai. This is not the case. On the other end of the spectrum, women have asked me, "Can I wear shorts in Dubai?" and, "Can I wear a bikini on the beach?"

Modesty is key when dressing in public. Men and women should avoid revealing clothing, bare shoulders, short skirts, or shorts. Wearing loose clothing is most comfortable in the heat. Layering is a good idea. Dubai's temperature swings between cool air-conditioned indoors and hot outdoors. It is like stepping into an ice bath whenever you enter a building. However, outside, it can reach 40-50° Celsius or more, sweltering hot and resulting in a swing of 20+° when you step indoors. Always have a *pashmina*, jumper, or jacket at hand for dining indoors to ensure you do not catch the "air-conditioning cold" caused by the cold shock.

Avoid clothing with offensive graphics or slogans in Dubai's malls and other public areas. Be cautious with any other disrespectful clothing, such as overly revealing outfits. Mini skirts and tank tops are not a good idea. In Dubai Mall, I once saw a lady in hotpants, a bosom-revealing top, and super high heels. She was probably not arrested but might have been asked to leave the mall. She also might have seen people staring at her, including me, as such an outfit is considered inappropriate for Dubai and better suited to a strip club in Europe. Luckily, there are plenty of shops in Dubai Mall to buy another more suitable outfit for the occasion. Interestingly, Abu Dhabi used to have signs in front of the malls, alerting visitors to the dress code. The signs have now disappeared, and you only see them during *Ramadan*.

I had to get used to the casual wear during the day. I had come from Monaco, where everyone dresses up and goes out in high heels to get a loaf of bread around the corner. You could never overdress in Monaco. Dubai is much more casual in the daytime.

At night, people will dress up. On a night out in the Marina, you will see expats wearing skimpy outfits, oblivious to the dress code.

Even more conservative attire is required in some places, such as government buildings and religious sites. In the mosques, women should cover their heads and wear modest clothing, fully covering the arms and legs. Men should wear long trousers. Once you understand the sacredness of mosques, you will better understand all the rules. You will be required to take off your shoes before you enter. Moreover, do not speak loudly or laugh inside mosques. It is good to have a pashmina in the handbag, which you can buy cheaply on the markets or in the malls in Dubai, to cover your head when visiting a mosque or covering bare shoulders when entering a mall or government building.

There are no nudist beaches. Swimwear is acceptable on the beach and at pools, but topless sunbathing is prohibited. Always cover up when leaving the beach or pool area. So, it would be best to be slightly more conservative than in other countries. And remember your sunglasses and a wide-brimmed hat, as the desert sun can be fierce. For swimwear, locals may opt for the *burqini*, entire body covering beachwear made of lightweight swimsuit material.

Some women in the Middle East view European women as being too liberated and promiscuous. They may be concerned about the impact of Western culture on their own culture and family life and its influence on their children. I sometimes see girls walking around showing too much flesh, whether in London or Dubai, and I agree that this is not a good look. I feel embarrassed about their dress choice. It is a shame that some girls think they need to use their bodies in public to get attention, attract men, and be accepted and valued. This is a harmful stereotype, objectifying Western girls.

Respect the clothing choices of local Emiratis, who may adhere to their traditional attire. Contrary to the casual expatriate daytime wear, the local ladies take time putting on their make-up, grooming their hair and looking immaculate. The men equally look impeccable. An expat may feel anonymous, whereas an Emirati will bump into friends on the street or in the mall, just as in Monaco, where everyone felt compelled to dress up before leaving the house.

The *abaya* is a loose-fitting, long-sleeved, long dress covering the whole body worn by women in Arab countries. It is usually black, but they do also come in other colours. The abaya is a symbol of modesty and cultural identity for many women worldwide. Abayas can be expensive, with delicate embroidery. In Dubai, women wear expensive Western designer clothing under their abayas, designer handbags on their arms, and extravagant shoes embellished with crystals.

There are many ways women cover their heads. I will mention a couple, but this list is not exhaustive. They may cover their hair with a black scarf, called a *hijab*, which covers the head and neck but leaves the face clear. It is sometimes called a *shayla*, which is usually made from silk. The *niqab* headdress is black, with the veil covering the woman's head and face, leaving only the eyes uncovered. It has a rectangular opening for the eyes. The *burka* is the most concealing of all veils, covering the face and body. The eyes have only a mesh screen, making it hard to see someone's eyes. The burka is only worn by the most devoted women, for example, in Saudi. The *chador* is a full-body cloak worn by Iranian women in public.

The men wear the traditional long-sleeved, loose-fitting white robes to the ankle, referred to as the *kandura* or *dish dash*. They always look immaculate, perfectly ironed, and bright white without a single spot or stain. The dish dash is typically made of lightweight fabric, such as white cotton, and is designed to provide comfort in the hot desert climate. They often wear open sandals, the perfect footwear for the hot weather. The dish dash has evolved, with different countries having their variations in terms of style. Today, it is commonly worn for formal and casual occasions in the Arab world.

You can usually tell by the man's headgear and the slight differences in the dish dash what country they are from. The red and white chequered headdress, *kaffiyeh*, is usually associated with Saudi. In the UAE, it is primarily white with a black *agal*. After a bit of practice, you will soon recognise the differences in dress codes between the countries.

Oud perfume in the Middle East is extremely popular. It has a distinct smell. The scent can be overwhelming. When I first arrived, I used to think they had gone overboard and put on too much perfume. The smell was too strong for my liking, but I began to appreciate it over time. Its deep and complex fragrance sets it apart from any other perfume.

Oud perfumes, often expensive, were only worn by the wealthy and powerful. It created a sense of mystery and sensuality. While historically associated with men, Oud has also become popular among women. Oud is believed to have therapeutic properties, having a calming effect on the mind and body. It is commonly worn as a perfume but can be burned as incense or added to essential oils.

Oud is available in different forms, from pure wood chips to concentrated oils. In its pure oil form, it is applied by men and women as a cologne, while by burning woodchips, the perfume is infused into clothing and through the hair. You will also smell it in houses as they burn the wood chips. Oud comes from the resinous wood of agarwood trees[62], found predominantly in Southeast Asia.

Oud is one of the most expensive perfume ingredients in the world. Its price will depend on the quality, rarity, and place of origin of the wood.[63] A 12ml bottle of high-quality Oud can cost up to 3,000 US dollars. It is concentrated and may last for 8 hours or more. Because of its rarity and high price tag, Oud is often called "black gold." A kilo of Oud can be as expensive as a kilo of gold.

International perfume brands have started to use Oud as a base note to attract more clients from the Middle East. Examples are Giorgio Armani's Oud Royale and Tom Ford's Oud Wood.[64] As you navigate Dubai's aromatic landscape, you will encounter a wide range of scents and quickly recognise the smell of Oud.

Chapter 6.

Social Norms and Etiquette

How to Meet and Greet

Not all cultures have the same ideas about how men and women should interact. If you are talking to a Muslim man in the Middle East, respect his cultural norms. Muslim men have diverse attitudes and behaviours.

Some Muslim men believe they should maintain a certain level of distance in their interactions with women. This may include avoiding physical contact, such as shaking hands or hugging. It may also involve avoiding certain types of conversation, such as talking about personal matters. In some cultures, being alone together is not considered appropriate for men and women. Not all Muslim men keep their distance from women. Many have close relationships with women, including their wives, sisters, and mothers. Respectful behaviour, especially in terms of physical contact and conversation, is a common theme.

In the Middle East, you will encounter separate queues for men and women going through airport security and women-only public transportation areas. I appreciated the separate queues for men and women at the airport in Saudi. It felt like a VIP treatment to me. The line for women was always shorter, so I never had to wait for long.

As a result of the segregation between men and women in some countries in the Middle East, men have not had much opportunity to interact and have casual conversations with women. Muslim men may not know how to act around women and find it hard to distinguish between business and romantic interaction.

Cultural differences also extend to dating and relationships. Expectations around who pays for a date, transportation, and physical intimacy vary widely among European and Muslim women. All women, anywhere in the world, like to be treated with respect. They each have their interpretation of what constitutes respect, which may be confusing for men.

Muslim women expect respect, politeness, and courteous behaviour on a date. For them, physical intimacy may take time and should align with their religious values. Muslim women usually prefer to date someone who shares their faith and values, as this can provide a foundation for mutual understanding and compatibility. Transparency about intentions, past, and beliefs is essential in dating Muslim women. Building a connection with a Muslim woman may require time and patience. Developing trust and comfort is necessary before progressing to more intimate interactions.

In Europe, shaking hands is acceptable between a man and a woman. It means nothing. Kissing on the cheeks or a hug also means nothing. In the Middle East, any touch may be misinterpreted.

Also, I experienced a couple of times that men would find it hard to look me in the eye for long, and their body language would be closed, half turned away from me. To me, it comes across as them not being interested and rude. It can also come across as cold.

Within Europe, women may think differently about the relationship between men and women. Some are liberal and others conservative. These views can range from more traditional to more modern or egalitarian. Preferences vary regarding gestures like opening doors or physical contact, such as hugging or kisses on the cheek. Some women appreciate chivalry, like opening a door, while others may find them old-fashioned or too intimate. There is no one-size-fits-all approach, not in Europe and not in the Middle East.

There are basic rules. In the Middle East, it is considered courteous for a European man to stand up when a local woman enters a room. Refraining from physical affection is essential. When interacting with local women, following their lead regarding handshakes is best. If she extends her hand, reciprocate with a light-touch handshake. When interacting with Arab women in public, a man should limit conversations to business matters and only engage in conversation if formally introduced. Maintaining eye contact and respecting personal space are essential when interacting with women professionally. And no flirting. You may think it is harmless, but you can get the woman in trouble by overstepping the line.

I have always struggled with the light-touch handshake, as my handshake is firm. In Europe, a weak handshake may be associated with a weak personality. Instead of a weak handshake, which is not me, I prefer to do a light bow and a smile to local men while placing my hand on my heart. If a local man or woman extends their hand to me, I will shake hands with them.

I remember my first experience meeting with a Muslim lady from the US at a hedge fund conference in Monaco. I reached out my hand to her to introduce myself and received no reciprocity. I found it awkward and wondered if she was afraid of catching germs. When I later saw her washing her hands in the ladies' toilet, I was sure she had a germ phobia. At the time, I had no idea of the Middle Eastern practice of not shaking hands, as this was years before moving to the Middle East.

While there are restrictions on interactions between men and local women in public, it is acceptable for a man to stand close to another man. In many Middle Eastern cultures, including the UAE, men holding hands is a gesture of friendship and does not indicate a romantic relationship. You may see male Emiratis holding hands. It might initially seem odd, as you would never see this in Europe. However, in many Middle Eastern countries, including the UAE, it is common for men to hold hands as a sign of friendship. It does not indicate they are having a gay relationship. The traditional cute nose touch greeting in the Middle East, sometimes called the "Eskimo kiss," is a unique way for men to greet and show friendly affection to each other.

Beware of the Signals You Send Out

While waiting for a taxi outside Jumeirah Emirates Towers, a Saudi gentleman standing nearby started a conversation and, at the end, asked me where I was going. He offered me a lift, and strangely, I agreed. His Land Rover, a traditional car I love as it reminds me of my time in the English countryside, might have played a part in swaying my decision. Once in the car, our conversation swiftly turned to business matters. As I shared details about my capital-raising business, he suggested a meeting with his business partner. Our initial plan was to meet at Jumeirah Emirates Towers.

However, during a meeting, I received a text notifying me of a venue change. The new meeting spot would be in a villa on the Palm. The person I was meeting with advised me against accepting the invitation and called his female friend from Saudi to seek her perspective. After explaining my situation to her, she offered me invaluable advice: "It is not just about your comfort level; it is also about the perception. You are sending the wrong signals by accepting such an invitation."

Following her counsel, I phoned the host and proposed meeting him and his business partner at a public location near the villa. He responded with a light-hearted laugh. He understood my concerns, telling me it was not a private villa but a "public villa." I relayed his response to the Saudi lady, who insisted I should not go alone, regardless of his assurances. She advised me to move to Plan B and take a chaperone along. I called Bernard, a partner at a law firm. I asked him if he was available and asked: "Would you like to be my chaperone for a business meeting on the Palm?" With his penchant for spontaneous adventures, he eagerly agreed. I subsequently messaged my new Saudi business contact, asking if it was acceptable to bring a business associate, and he consented.

Bertrand was on my doorstep within an hour, and we drove to the Palm for the meeting. It was fitting that he joined me, as the business partner only spoke French. With the few French words I had picked up in Monaco, I managed to engage in a meaningful conversation, but Bertrand's presence made it so much easier as he was fluent in French. Interestingly, their business discussions took place in what indeed was a "public villa." Upon entering, I bumped into someone who was on the way out and whom I had met earlier that week, highlighting the interconnectedness of Dubai.

In general, going alone to someone's private residence is not advisable. It can inadvertently convey the wrong impression. In various Middle Eastern cultures, women are seen as upholders of their family's honour. A woman visiting a man's house alone might be perceived as not respecting her family's honour and, therefore, lacking modesty. Opting to meet in public or bringing a male chaperone along is much more sensible. Similar caution applies even in the UK. I would not go to a guy's house in the UK alone if I did not know him well already, as I would be concerned about giving him the wrong signals.

Respect, Humility and Humour

Humour in Dubai is a way of life. Amidst the tumultuous existence in this dynamic and perpetually evolving city, humour becomes a coping mechanism for dealing with daily challenges. Humour also fosters friendships among Dubai's diverse population. It is important to have humility and to show respect to the locals.

A friend, new to Dubai and keen to meet new people, decided to join a golf club. The golf community in Dubai is thriving, with over 10 world-class golf courses. Dubai's golf courses are often located within gated villa communities, offering residents exclusive access to the course and other amenities such as clubhouses, restaurants, and fitness centres. Some of the homes have stunning views of the golf course. Dubai is the perfect place to live and play if you love golf. Dubai is also home to the most prestigious golf tournaments in the world, including the Dubai World Championship and the DP World Tour Championship.

After attending a golf tournament, he gate-crashed a party organised by a prominent family for their inner circle. The young family member spotted the intruder and instructed one of his men to push him into the pool. He then photographed my friend in his wet suit, with water dripping down his face, next to two girls in their bikinis. The next day, he immediately told his boss at work what had happened, fearing the photograph of him next to two scantily clad women might get him into trouble. His boss was sympathetic. He got off lightly, he said. He did learn a lesson: to be careful whose party you gatecrash.

Humour can present pitfalls. What is considered funny in one culture may not be considered funny in another. In business, I always recommend that clients cut out the jokes as they sometimes do not translate. Always laugh at the host's jokes, even if you do not catch the punchline. Using humour can be sensitive around specific topics. Jokes about religion or politics should be avoided. Jokes involving women or sex also are not a good idea.

Ginni told me a story of a tourist in Egypt, walking down the street when he saw a group of men praying. He stopped to watch them and started making fun of them. The men were offended and shouted at him. The tourist was arrested and taken to the police station. He was fined and deported from Egypt. In many Muslim cultures, making fun of praying people is considered disrespectful. The tourist in this story was punished for his lack of respect.

Humour can be a powerful tool but can also be dangerous if used unwisely. What may seem like a harmless joke to one person can be deeply offensive to another. Be sensitive to the culture and beliefs of others when telling jokes.

Etiquette for Visiting an Arab Home

Arabs have a strong culture of greeting and welcoming guests. Show respect and gratitude when you are in their home. When entering, greet everyone individually. Islamic traditions and customs play an essential role in shaping dietary preferences. The staple of the Arab diet is pita bread. Alcohol is forbidden. Consumption of pork, certain carnivorous animals, and unscaled fish is restricted. Meat must be butchered in accordance with the Qur'anic ritual known as *halal*, which means "permitted." Lamb is the most common meat. As a guest, accepting what is offered to you is always polite. It is best to initially refuse an offering of tea or coffee rather than quickly accepting or asking for it but with the view of accepting. This gesture shows not only respect and politeness towards your Arab host but also a certain refinement. Accept any drink with your right hand only. Similarly, using the right hand when eating, offering, or passing items around is customary. Leaving food on your plate indicates you are full and is considered a compliment. If you finish your plate, they will keep giving you more. Avoid discussing sensitive topics such as politics, religion, alcohol, and male-female relations.

Silent Conversations: Gestures in Communication

Never use your left hand to shake hands. In many Middle Eastern cultures, this is considered rude because the left hand is deemed unclean, as it is used for personal hygiene tasks such as wiping after using the toilet. Using your left hand to shake hands is a sign of disrespect. In some cultures, such as Saudi, eating with your left hand is also considered rude.

Pointing the heel of your foot to your host is also considered bad-mannered because the foot is seen as another unclean part of the body. Pointing it at someone would be impolite, showing they are not worthy of your attention. It will be seen as an insult to their hospitality. In Europe, crossing one leg over the other is seen as a relaxed pose and would signal the person is at ease and enjoying the conversation.

It is best to avoid all hand gestures as there are hand gestures you should not make. Pointing with the index finger is rude. Instead, it would be better if you used your whole hand. The 'thumbs up' is also an impolite gesture. It is used in the West to indicate something is good or to show approval, but it can be interpreted as a vulgar gesture. The OK sign, with the thumb and index finger forming a circle, used in the West to indicate something is okay, can be interpreted as a gesture for female genitalia. The peace sign, with the index and middle fingers extended and the thumb and pinkie fingers tucked in can be interpreted as a gesture for the devil.

Chapter 7.

Love and Relationships

City of Hearts: Romance and Dating Dynamics

Dating in the Middle East can be a unique and challenging experience. Dubai is a fascinating city for dating, as it is home to a large expat population from all over the world. It is an environment where people constantly mingle, form connections, and potentially embark on new romantic adventures. Everyone will have something interesting to say, making it hard to decide on the right partner with so much choice. For those content with the single lifestyle, Dubai offers an array of possibilities, regardless of age. The city's cosmopolitan environment and diverse population create an atmosphere where people from various backgrounds and age groups mingle more freely. This can appeal to older individuals who may be divorced or seeking companionship, as they may feel less judged or scrutinised in Dubai than they would in their home countries. Those in their early twenties can also revel in the city's exciting social landscape and diverse encounters.

Because Dubai is a transient city, finding someone looking for a long-term relationship can be difficult. You are always wondering whether you will be staying or whether your new date will be staying or moving back to their home country. Most expats have come to work, make money, have fun, and then leave again. As a result, the single scene in Dubai is dynamic. Cultural expectations around dating can vary depending on the individual's background. Despite the challenges, dating in Dubai can be fun. There are many ways to meet people. You can go to bars and clubs or attend cultural events. And because the city is so diverse, you will meet people from all walks of life.

For individuals already in committed relationships or married, relocating to Abu Dhabi rather than Dubai may be worth exploring. Abu Dhabi offers a more settled and less frenetic atmosphere, making it an appealing choice for those seeking a calmer pace while still enjoying the benefits of the UAE's unique lifestyle. Abu Dhabi is more family-oriented. Recently, it has become more like Dubai, appealing to the singles, too. Whether single or attached, the UAE presents captivating experiences for individuals from all walks of life. It is a place where people can embrace their independence, foster enriching connections, and create memories to last a lifetime.

Although born in Saudi, one of my male friends spent most of his life in the US. As a Muslim, he decided to move to the Middle East, but like me, he had limited knowledge about the region, although he was fluent in Arabic. He had a job interview lined up in Kuwait. As he started researching the country, he encountered restrictions on alcohol and nightlife. This sparked a sense of panic as he pondered, *How will I connect with someone in Kuwait as a single man if I cannot socialise at a bar?*

His friends convinced him to consider Dubai instead, where he was assured that the social dynamics were more accommodating for single men. However, he found the experience of meeting people to be quite challenging. He explained, "Back in the US, I could easily strike up a conversation with someone, but in the Middle East, it would not be appropriate to make such romantic advances in public." Additionally, he faced the constraint of being unable to pursue a romantic interest within his workplace, which could result in termination. Many of his friends frequented certain bars and nightclubs, known for the significant presence of airline stewardesses who were seemingly "working on the side." He eventually returned to the US, where he met his Muslim wife and lived happily ever after.

Frequently, my girlfriends in London would inquire about the gender distribution in Dubai. While providing an exact figure is challenging, it is evident Dubai does exhibit a notable surplus of men compared to women. Various sources have suggested ratios such as seven men to three women, translating to at least two men for every woman. This intriguing statistic is quite ironic considering the common perception of the Middle East, where the gender dynamic often leans towards men having multiple wives. The gender ratio can fluctuate based on different age groups and industries.

I warn friends that Dubai attracts individuals who find it easy to move away from their home country, making them less rooted than the average person. Both males and females in Dubai tend to have strong 'alpha' personalities, the explorer types, which often make it harder for them to commit. Many have moved to Dubai for financial security, with emotional security less of a priority. The surplus of men in Dubai stems from the influx of male expats seeking employment opportunities, often leaving their families behind. You also see women who have left their husbands and families in their home country. This particularly holds true for those from the Philippines, working in beauty salons or serving as maids.

What people may not know, and to my surprise, is that there are many single Muslim women in the Middle East for reasons identical to European women delaying marriage.[65] The percentage of single women in the Middle East is like that of Europe. The average age of marriage is rising due to education, employment, and changing social norms. In addition to marrying later, more women delay having children, like in Europe.

PDA Pitfalls in Dubai

Initially, I did not understand the term PDA. Were my friends referring to Personal Digital Assistants? I learned PDA stands for Public Displays of Affection.

In Dubai, the legal framework restricts any public display of affection. Public displays of affection (PDAs) are frowned upon in many Middle Eastern countries. While expats may feel comfortable engaging in hand-holding or other forms of PDA, it is important to consider the broader cultural context. While PDAs might not necessarily lead to legal consequences, they can result in uncomfortable situations or disapproving looks from locals. Expressing affection is more acceptable in private settings, within homes, private gatherings, or designated areas where it is permitted. Public displays of affection between people of different sexes, especially unmarried couples, will attract more attention and may be met with disapproval.

In summary, while cultural norms and attitudes may vary, erring on the side of caution by refraining from public displays of affection in Dubai and other GCC (Gulf Cooperation Council) countries is the way to go.

The First Kiss Requires Planning

Where is the appropriate place for an inaugural kiss? In contrast to the European norm where the first kiss may happen at your doorstep, should you have been accompanied home by your date, this scenario does not seamlessly translate to Dubai. Inviting a gentleman into your apartment for the farewell kiss could lead to unintended and uncomfortable advancements, which might be best avoided. You risk an unplanned and unwelcome acceleration in the relationship.

My next-door neighbour, Nora, was dating a charming American businessman named George. Nora had always held a fondness for dashing, well-travelled American men. The paths of Nora and George crossed during their early morning jogs on Dubai's tranquil beachfront at the break of dawn, around 6 a.m. There was an immediate spark between them. George gallantly invited Nora for coffee dates, lunches, movies, and the opera and asked her to an elegant villa soirée in Jumeirah.

Over the next six months, their bond deepened. However, George had yet to show any physical interest. Her patience was being put to the test. She concluded she needed to be more direct.

One humid evening in Dubai, they met for a drink at one of the premier hotel bars. Nora was excited to see George. George ordered a bottle of exquisite champagne, signalling the beginning of an enchanting evening.

After a few drinks, she leaned close and whispered in his ear. "I have been thinking about you a lot lately," she said. "I would like to get to know you better."

George smiled. "I would like that too," he said. Suddenly, his hand found its place on Nora's knee in a bold move. They fell under a magic spell and felt like they were the only two people in the universe.

That wonderful moment, their first kiss, was abruptly shattered, and alarm bells started ringing in her head. An unsettling hush fell over the bar as gazes converged on Nora and George, casting a spotlight of unwanted attention upon their shared moment.

Swiftly and purposefully, the hotel's security team arrived at the scene. Before Nora could even attempt to articulate her plea for leniency or offer an explanation, the security personnel's stern intervention rendered any discourse futile. She did not get to explain whether an exception could be made. It had taken six months for their relationship to blossom, and there were no special areas to execute the first kiss. The swift verdict was delivered with a finality not allowing for any negotiation: "Leave the premises without delay."

The story of Nora and George shows the strict boundaries defining public displays of physical affection in Dubai. No exceptions are made. As their tale underscores, the Emirates' code of conduct is unwavering and unforgiving in its prohibition.

The story takes another unexpected turn as Nora, rising from her seat, is suddenly engulfed by a disorienting dizziness, causing her to lose her balance. She stumbles forward, finding herself in George's embrace. He was caught in the delicate act of steadying Nora while orchestrating their exit. The hotel lobby witnessed their hurried departure, a silent chorus of disapproving expressions and sidelong glances echoing their retreat.

He recounts safely taking her home by taxi. Yet Nora's recollection of the events remains obscured, and the sequence of events from the hotel lobby to her bed remains a tantalising enigma. Was Nora's memory blurred by the oppressive heat and humidity of the night, or could her drink have been tampered with? Two small glasses of champagne rarely, if ever, lead to such a state and memory loss. Drink spiking does occur.

We concluded that the most likely explanation for Nora's dizziness when getting up from the bar was dehydration caused by the sweltering weather. It serves as a reminder to be mindful of dehydration, especially when drinking alcohol. If you drink alcohol, also have plenty of water to stay hydrated. Avoid drinking on an empty stomach, which can also lead to dehydration. Always remember you can be arrested for being drunk in public.

The unforeseen episode left Nora and George reeling with anxiety. They could have been in prison. They were terrified that the CCTV footage of their kiss had been captured, and they would face legal repercussions or even be deported from the country. They tried to find out how long the footage would be kept and were relieved to learn it was held for only three months. They decided to avoid each other for three months to be safe. This deliberate avoidance created a distance between them, and the spark that had been ignited began to fade.

A year later, Nora was browsing in the aisles of Waitrose in the Dubai Mall. She wore her favourite outfit, flowing beige linen trousers and an elegantly draping silk shirt. As she went around the corner of an aisle, she bumped into William, Irish and divorced, whom she had met weeks earlier through the introduction of a mutual friend. Nora was delighted to see him again. They agreed to have coffee at Le Pain Quotidien, Nora's favourite coffee shop near the mall entrance.

They talked for hours, sharing intimate details about their lives. Nora felt a connection with William. When it was time to leave, William reached out to take Nora's hand. However, her past encounter with George and the stern intervention by hotel security were not forgotten; thus, with an unexpected swiftness, Nora retracted her hand, her voice gently yet firmly echoing the unspoken societal etiquette, *"Such displays are not suitable in public here."*

There was a flicker of surprise in William's expression, his understanding of the cultural intricacies not yet fully crystallised. A swift apology was extended to Nora, a verbal acknowledgement of the boundaries he had unwittingly crossed. Attuned to the cultural subtleties, he extended an invitation beyond the coffee shop's confines, a prospect for dining at his house. He invited Nora to come over to his villa in Emirates

Hills, one of the high-end gated villa communities, for dinner to meet his daughter. Nora agreed, and they made plans to meet the following weekend.

On the day of the dinner, she arrived at William's house, feeling nervous. She had never met his daughter before and did not know what to expect. But William's daughter was funny and intelligent. Nora and William's daughter hit it off immediately, and they spent the evening talking and laughing.

The daughter started encouraging Nora to consider William as an eligible prospect. Nora joked with me the daughter was going to end up in sales. The daughter insisted her father loved shopping and was happy to spend the whole afternoon in Dubai Mall buying lots of stuff, including clothes and jewellery. She added Nora should join her dad on a shopping trip to Emirates Mall the following weekend.

After dinner, the daughter went to bed. William and Nora sat on the couch and talked for a while longer. Nora told William about her experience with George. He listened attentively, and when Nora was finished, he apologised again for making her uncomfortable. She appreciated his apology and leaned over, kissing him on the cheek. William smiled and leaned in. It was their first kiss.

Lesson learned: if you decide to kiss someone for the first time, do so in a private setting where others will not see you.

Nora and William continued to see each other but encountered the societal norms surrounding unmarried couples residing together in Dubai. According to the rules, such arrangements were not allowed.

The reality often diverged from the letter of the law. A subtle understanding emerged between security guards and unmarried couples in most residential buildings. The guards would usually look the other way if the couples were discreet and did not cause trouble. A gratuity slipped into willing hands seemed to ensure the concierge and security guards benevolently averted their gaze. However, you did run the risk a neighbour might call the police.

Francesca, whom I met over tea through Nora, warned that living together unmarried carries serious risks, and Nora should understand the potential consequences properly. She gave an example of a housekeeper stealing from her unmarried friends. Her friend could not file a report of the theft with the police because if she did, the maid would disclose their unmarried status to the police, forcing them to act. In such circumstances, it is often the woman who is punished.

At the time, the law also rendered it illicit for unmarried couples to share the same hotel room in Dubai. However, crossing this boundary rarely led to repercussions. Most tourists were utterly ignorant of these rules. Today, cohabitation no longer carries the weight of criminality, liberating individuals from past constraints and dispelling the spectre of imprisonment and penalties.

Civil partnerships have found a place within the UAE's legal framework, though within specific parameters. Due to the prevalence of Sharia Law, same-sex partnerships and couples where the woman is Muslim but the man is not, are impossible.

Dating Apps in Dubai: Looks Can Deceive

Advancements in technology have changed the dating landscape. You no longer need to rely on friend-led introductions. Digital platforms open the doors to many possibilities, with popular dating applications operating in Dubai. Among the favoured platforms are Tinder, Bumble, and Hinge. These are ideal when you are single and moving to a new city.

A word of advice: stay vigilant when using dating apps. A couple of years ago, according to the local newspapers, Dubai police revealed they had received a reliable tip-off about African gangs who were luring men by posting and sharing photos of girls on social media platforms and via emails. When the victim arrived at the specified address, he would find a different girl than the one he had chatted with online.[66]

It was also reported that the gang would threaten victims and take their belongings, including mobile phones and credit cards, after taking pictures of the men in indecent positions. If the victims reported the matter to the authorities, they would be threatened with the posting and sharing of their videos online with their contacts. The victims would end up sharing their mobile phone passcodes and credit card security pins and paying large sums to avoid online defamation and protect their family members.[67] Be cautious about the perceived anonymity in Dubai.

Sexual Assault and Rape is Rare

Friends in Europe ask me whether it is common to be harassed. Personal attacks, including sexual assault and rape, are relatively rare but do happen. The UK Government website notes the UAE imposes life imprisonment for males who rape a female, and the death penalty can be applied in certain cases. However, UAE law places a high burden of proof on the victim to demonstrate that the sexual relations were not consensual, especially when the victim had consumed alcohol or where the alleged attacker was known to the victim. If the sexual relations are determined to have been consensual, either party may still face prosecution for the offence of sex outside marriage in certain circumstances.[68]

Forbidden Fruits

All homosexual sex is illegal, and same-sex marriages are not recognised. The Dubai government has announced it will no longer prosecute people for homosexuality. It is still illegal to have same-sex sexual relations in the UAE, and there is no law against discrimination based on sexual orientation. As a result, gay men in Dubai still face challenges.

An acquaintance who used to rent an apartment in a high-end hotel in Dubai told me that certain men dressed themselves in abayas. Cross-dressing is illegal. He would spot the men in the bar of his hotel in disguise. He found this bizarre, assumed they were gay, and whispered what he suspected was happening in my ear.

People previously asked me about prostitution and believe all prostitutes in Dubai are Russian. Prostitution is everywhere in the world where money flows, including Dubai. As a woman, I do not recognise the telltale signs of this trade. One of my male friends, who shall remain nameless, said, "I have been approached by women from all sorts of nationalities, not only in the high-end hotels, nightclubs and bars but also in the shopping malls and even at the metro station."

Prostitution is illegal in Dubai, and the police take a strict stance against it. High-profile cases have occurred in recent years of people being arrested and deported for prostitution. Josie, an investment analyst, told me a story of a guy getting fired from her company because his employer found out he had entertained his client with prostitutes, something part of any entertainment in the UK in the old days but not a good idea to do in Dubai.

Chapter 8.

Marriage and Divorce

From Courtship to Family: Marriage in Dubai

Samantha, a dentist, found herself in an unexpected situation with a charming gentleman from Switzerland. On the fourth date, waiting for the right moment, she asked if he had been married. His response caught her off guard. To her astonishment, he said, "I thought you were aware I am married." The arrival of the bill spared them the awkward moment. Eventually, as he grasped her conservative stance on dating married individuals, he became a dear and valued friend.

While in the Middle East, I noticed a trend among men not wearing wedding rings. Expats, upon arriving, learn about the local culture, which allows for multiple wives. However, Western men often misinterpret this, leading them to believe it is acceptable to maintain multiple girlfriends. This is not the case.

I recall a disheartening story of a man who faced the consequences of his actions. He was employed at a prestigious institutional asset management firm in the UAE. His highly-paid job was instantly terminated due to his extramarital affair with a local lady while being married with children. This tale serves as a reminder that cultural norms and societal expectations must be understood and respected in the context of relationships.

Arranged marriages are still common in the Middle East. Families often play a central role in arranging marriages. Arranged marriages are not always forced marriages. The couple may also have a say and can meet and get to know each other before they marry. In countries like Pakistan and India, arranged marriages are still the norm. They have become less common in countries like Turkey and Lebanon.

I discussed this with an Uber driver from India in Dubai, his arranged marriage. I told him marriage in Europe used to be a business arrangement, but now there is pressure on finding love. "Weeding through unsuitable candidates with great expectations of love has not worked for me," I said. I asked him what the arranged marriage had been like for him.

He said, "Initially, you think, how am I going to stay with this one person my parents have selected for me? But as the years pass, love grows." He told me he was still incredibly in love with his wife after more than 30 years of marriage. It was a sweet story.

While arranged marriages can work out, they do not guarantee happiness. Similarly, falling in love does not guarantee happy endings either, as evidenced by the high divorce rates in Europe.

I remember talking to one Iranian man who had returned from the US to Iran, summoned by his family. They felt he had taken enough time to fall in love and had failed at finding a wife. His time was up, and the family had lined up a nice Iranian girl for him whom he was encouraged to marry. His family, more flexible than many, gave him little choice. Time was up.

In rare cases, arranged marriages are between cousins. Some people believe it is wrong to force couples to marry their cousins. Cousin marriage is legal in many countries in the Middle East. Some people choose to marry their cousins because they believe it is a way to preserve family ties.[69] During her check-up, a pregnant friend heard at the hospital that IVF is commonplace in the Middle East.[70] If a couple is forced to marry their cousins, they may use IVF to have children to avoid the risk of genetic disorders. Couples in forced marriages may never have sex and instead use IVF to produce offspring. Notably, couples therapy is less common in the Middle East, where doctors might prescribe antidepressants to address relationship challenges.

In Western societies, forced marriages can take on different forms beyond the traditional understanding. When a woman becomes pregnant unexpectedly, the arrival of a child can serve as a catalyst for the decision to marry, influenced by a sense of responsibility towards the unborn child or societal pressures and expectations of friends and family. This can lead to marriages based on a mutual desire to create a stable and supportive environment for the child's upbringing.

In Western societies, there is a common assumption that Arab men will have multiple wives. While this is possible, it is not a universal rule and does not necessarily mean they can maintain one wife with multiple girlfriends. The practice of polygamy, which involves having numerous wives, is indeed permitted in certain Middle Eastern countries. However, it is not uniformly accepted. In jurisdictions where polygamy is legally sanctioned, such as Saudi, men are allowed to marry up to four wives, provided specific conditions are met. The laws of the UAE also recognise this practice. According to Islamic law, a Muslim man may marry up to four wives, with the crucial stipulation that he treats each spouse equally and justly. In cases of subsequent marriages, the man is required to seek permission from his first wife. Furthermore, he must demonstrate his ability to financially support both households before judicial authorisation for a second marriage is granted.

Not all men in the Middle East express an interest in polygamy, and such unions are becoming increasingly rare within the region. The assumption that all Arab men engage in polygamous relationships oversimplifies the complex realities and choices.

In Iran, a unique marital arrangement exists known as *sigheh*, or temporary marriage. This practice allows couples to engage in a marital contract valid for a specific and predetermined duration, ranging from mere hours to months or even years. Temporary marriage is not without its controversies and complexities. Some regard it as a form of prostitution, raising concerns about the potential exploitation of women.

A non-Muslim Western woman marrying a Muslim man would need to convert to Islam before entering the marriage. This conversion typically involves an understanding and acceptance of Islamic beliefs and practices. Both partners must thoroughly understand each other's cultural backgrounds when entering such a marriage. In the unfortunate event that the marriage faces difficulties or ends in divorce, especially if children are involved, there can be complex legal and cultural considerations. The issue of child custody and the ability to leave the country may become difficult due to differing legal frameworks and cultural norms. The children may be considered part of the father's family, affecting custody and visitation rights. Navigating these potential challenges requires careful planning, legal advice, and a deep understanding of Islamic and local legal systems.

Married non-Muslim expats also should carefully study the detailed rules. Bernadette agreed to join her boyfriend Ted in Dubai, as he had been offered a well-paid, high-level job with a private company. They had read that it was illegal to live together without being married. The day before they moved to Dubai, they married in the UK. Bernadette did not fully understand that her husband had complete control over her. Her husband had to write and sign letters on her behalf for her to obtain an alcohol license, a driving license, and a bank account.

Having had a high-level executive position, adjusting to this dependency took time. Even though it was her money in the bank account, she was a secondary signature.

Untangling the Knot: Divorce Dynamics

Divorce in the Middle East can vary, depending on the specific country and cultural practices. Islamic law, or Shariah, influences divorce laws, which govern many aspects of personal and family matters. Divorce is allowed but considered a last resort when all efforts to reconcile have been exhausted. The process and requirements for divorce may differ between Sunni and Shia sects of Islam and between different countries. Grounds for divorce include irreconcilable differences, infidelity, abuse, desertion, or failure to fulfil marital duties. In some countries, like Saudi and Iran, men have more rights and easier access to divorce than women. Ongoing efforts are made to reform laws and provide more protection for women in divorce proceedings. Women are often confronted with limited financial resources and lack the necessary means to sustain themselves.

Unfortunately, Bernadette's relationship turned sour. She filed for divorce. Her husband then changed the locks on the apartment, locking her out with no access to her belongings. When she went to the police, she was told, "This is a domestic issue. What have you done to upset your husband? Go home and resolve your issues with him."

Divorce rates are rising in the Middle East, like Europe, because of changing social norms, economic hardship, and domestic violence. This adds to the number of single Muslim women. However, single women in the Middle East often have fewer legal rights than those in Europe. For example, single women in the Middle East may not be able to own property or travel without the permission of a male guardian.

I recently met Leila, a successful fintech entrepreneur. She told me she was travelling in business class from Asia on Kuwait Airlines to London. She got chatting with a Kuwaiti lady sitting next to her. She said she was visiting her sister in London, who had a baby. She had gotten divorced. Her husband had proposed a second wife, but she would not accept the situation. She was upset. They had a country house in Kuwait. As she suspected he had been unfaithful, she followed him to the country house one day and caught him in bed with another woman. Leila asked her if it is easy to get divorced in Kuwait. She whispered she had threatened to tell the Imam he had anal sex with her. They quickly settled. Leila, being conservative, was shocked to hear her say this.

Chapter 9.

Living on the Edge

The cost of living can be high compared to other countries. This is evident in education. Public schools are available to all Emirati citizens, regardless of their socio-economic background or geographic location. The more conservative Emirati families prefer to send their children to public schools, as schooling is in Arabic. Some also opt for public schools, as they look to limit exposure to the Western curriculum at an early age. Other Emiratis may prefer private schools. Among the expats, cultural preferences come into play, with Indian families choosing private schools following the Indian curriculum and British families gravitating towards private institutions adhering to the UK curriculum. This choice ensures a seamless transition for their children when returning to their home countries.

Private schools in Dubai have become increasingly expensive while offering great facilities and quality education. This has led families to reconsider living in Dubai as the financial strain of private schooling becomes a pressing concern.

The cost of living in Dubai is also influenced by its heavy reliance on imported goods, resulting in higher prices than elsewhere for many products. While this phenomenon is not unique to Dubai and can be observed in various global cities, it impacts everyday expenses, including grocery shopping. Around 80-90% of the food consumed in the UAE is imported from other countries. You can find all your local brands in Dubai, like Marmite, hot cross buns, and Cadbury's chocolate. I love Dutch liquorice and find it easier in Dubai than in London!

Interestingly, the UAE takes proactive measures to ensure food security by maintaining a food bank. Expats joke that in the face of an unforeseen crisis, the welfare of camels ranks above that of expats. Behind the humour lies a valuable lesson. Dubai is committed to ensuring its self-sufficiency. It is good to know there is a backup plan, even if it means sharing snacks with our camel friends.

Dubai is actively working towards enhancing its self-sufficiency, particularly concerning food production. The establishment of Food Tech Valley[71] shows Dubai's determination to explore innovative agricultural solutions to ensure food security. This initiative leverages cutting-edge technologies, including hydroponics and vertical farming, to optimise crop production locally despite the desert's arid climate and limited water resources.

The evolution of entertainment and social norms in Dubai over the years reflects the city's efforts to modernise and cater to its diverse population and international visitors. It is interesting to observe how the entertainment scene has transformed and adapted to meet the preferences and expectations of residents and tourists. You can enjoy live music and a more relaxed approach to dancing in restaurants. These changes reflect Dubai's efforts to create a vibrant atmosphere, appealing to a wide range of people. This did not exist when I first moved to the Middle East, when dancing in public in restaurants was considered inappropriate and limited to nightclubs only.

While Dubai has become more lenient in its entertainment offerings, alcohol regulations remain strict. Business practices involving alcohol, such as after-work drinks at the pub, may need to be adjusted in Dubai. Networking and socialising can still occur, but be mindful of the preferences of Muslim colleagues.

You will not find alcohol on the shelves of the supermarkets, only alcohol-free beers and alcohol-free wines. Alcohol is only sold in specialist shops for personal use. Only non-Muslims, 21 years or older, are allowed to buy and consume alcohol. Not all bars and restaurants will serve alcohol; they need a permit. Restaurants attached to a hotel will have an alcohol license.

The UAE has a strict zero-tolerance policy for drunk driving, ensuring road safety. Penalties for drunk driving can be severe, including fines, license suspension, and even imprisonment. While there may be venues serving alcohol, it is advisable to avoid excessive or disruptive behaviour in public, like public drunkenness, as this could be seen as disrespectful and could land you in prison. And you should most definitely avoid harassing people when you have had one too many.

Good news arrived in January 2023. The government suspended the 30% tax on alcohol sales for a year to reduce the cost of living and bring prices more in line with other Emirates. You still need a license to buy alcohol in specialist shops. The fee for obtaining a licence was scrapped.[72]

Remember, you can only enjoy your bottle privately or in licenced public places. So, walking on the streets with a can of beer in your hand is not appropriate.

Besides alcohol, you should be aware of the rules around drugs. The UAE has strict anti-drug laws, and possession, use, or trafficking of illegal substances can lead to severe legal consequences, including lengthy prison sentences. The UK Government website warns of a zero-tolerance policy for drug-related offences. The penalties for trafficking, smuggling and the possession of drugs (including residual amounts) are severe. Sentences for drug trafficking can include the death penalty. Possession of even the smallest amount of illegal drugs can lead to a minimum three-month prison term or a fine between AED 20,000 and AED100,000. The Emirati authorities count the presence of drugs in the bloodstream as possession. Some herbal highs, like Spice, are illegal in the UAE. Possessing and concealing money from drug-related offences and performing transactions using money from drug-related offences are also crimes which could lead to imprisonment and a fine.[73]

Some skincare products and E-cigarette refills may contain ingredients that are illegal in the UAE, such as CBD oil. If found in possession of such products, they will be confiscated, and you may face criminal charges. A list of narcotic, psychotropic and controlled drugs where this rule applies, allowed quantities and documents to present can be found on the UAE Ministry of Health website.

Importing pork products and pornography into the UAE is illegal. Videos, books, and magazines may be subject to scrutiny and may be censored.[74] Although it is also officially forbidden to sell pork in supermarkets, you will often find it in a separate section in some outlets.

Chapter 10.

Understanding Taxation

Adjusting to living in a tax-free environment is a mental shift for expats arriving in the UAE. There is no personal income tax, social security tax, or payroll tax for expats. There are no tax-related filing obligations for individuals. While the landscape has evolved with the introduction of certain taxes, the overall burden remains remarkably low compared to Europe. Businesses are subject to the UAE Corporate Tax. Firms posting annual profits exceeding Dh375,000 will be taxed 9%.

Interestingly, Middle Eastern individuals grapple with the concept of high taxes in Europe. In the Middle East, a deep-rooted familiarity exists with the concept of *Zakat*, a form of religious tax aimed at providing for those in need. This duty is viewed as a personal obligation and a voluntary act of compassion. While there is no external compulsion to contribute, abstaining from Zakat is considered a serious transgression with consequences.

The UK Government website warns that if you're considering undertaking or promoting fundraising or other acts of charity in (or while passing through) the UAE, bear in mind that these activities, including those conducted online and via social media, are heavily regulated. You should be fully aware of the legal requirements and seek professional advice as necessary. Non-compliance can incur criminal penalties, including heavy fines and imprisonment.[75] I know someone who got in trouble for setting up an unregulated charity.

Taxes are enforced by governing authorities. Some advocate that devout Muslims ought to minimise their tax liabilities, and curbing one's tax obligations is seen as aligning with virtuous principles. However, an opposing viewpoint asserts that evading taxes constitutes a breach of legal statutes and religious duties. This dialogue shows the interplay between faith, law, and financial obligations.

Considering this debate, Alice, a senior accountant at a prestigious firm, speculated that introducing direct taxation in the UAE would be challenging, "The nationals have never been used to any form of income tax, which may be why the government opted to introduce indirect taxes on consumption instead."

The absence of personal income and low corporate taxes are attractive features for individuals and businesses entering the UAE. It results in higher take-home pay and business profits. When considering the future, the absence of citizenship, long-term security and access to social benefits are considerations for individuals and families. An expat will always remain an outsider.

There are exceptions. An Emirati passport is occasionally offered to exceptionally gifted expats. However, it still does not make you an Emirati, with all the same benefits as the locals. There is, therefore, always a sense of insecurity in Dubai. Losing one's job often also means losing the right to live in Dubai or simply being unable to afford to stay. Regardless of whether you have lived in Dubai for 5 years or 50, the concept of permanent residency does not exist in Dubai. Dubai lacks social benefits commonly found in other countries.

Only after returning to the UK after living in Dubai did the NHS suddenly seem like an incredible luxury to have access to. In the UAE, expats are responsible for their healthcare expenses. Ideally, the company you work for will provide you with this health insurance as part of your salary package, but not all will, and the coverage may not be sufficient. The absence of state-provided pensions means individuals must take active steps to plan for retirement and secure their financial future.

In conclusion, while Dubai's economic opportunities, tax benefits, and high quality of life are appealing, the lack of specific social benefits, long-term residency options, and pathways to citizenship can create challenges over time. The wealthy will not be so concerned by the lack of permanent residency and benefits. That is something the working classes worry about. Once you understand what you are getting into, you are not setting yourself up for disappointment. It is all about expectations.

Chapter 11.

Transportation and Infrastructure

Dubai is not a pedestrian-friendly city. You can walk around Downtown Dubai, but other areas may require a car. It is a sprawling city with no central hub. Driving conditions can be challenging, especially on busy multi-lane roads like Sheikh Zayed Road. There are different nationalities on the road, each with their own driving style. Not all drivers will use their indicators. Stay alert and drive defensively.

The Sheikh Zayed Road is Dubai's most famous road. It was named in honour of the then-ruler of Abu Dhabi. This road begins at Abu Dhabi's Corniche as Sheikh Rashid Bin Saeed Al Maktoum Street, more casually known in Abu Dhabi as Airport Road. The name changes from Sheikh Rashid Road to Sheikh Zayed Road when you cross the border from Abu Dhabi into Dubai. By naming their grandest streets after each other, the founders of the UAE made a symbolic gesture to strengthen the union during its early days.[76]

The roads in Dubai are excellent, with no potholes to worry about. Most journeys within the city will not take more than 30-50 minutes. However, the traffic can be heavy and congested.

The roads in Dubai can also be challenging to navigate, making it easy to miss a turning. Expats joke that if you miss a turn, the next one could be in Saudi! It is not as bad as that, but you get the point.

If you ever get into an accident, always remain calm and avoid being confrontational. Getting angry will only worsen the situation and could get you into trouble. And never use any swear words. If you are uncomfortable driving in these chaotic conditions, it is best to avoid it.

Be careful at night and stick to the middle lane. Locals are known for racing their sports cars at night. You do not want to get in their way.

You can opt for other modes of transportation, such as taxis or public transport. I looked at the seven-lane Sheikh Zayed Road and used taxis instead. I prefer to be driven and believe viewing the car as a symbol of freedom is overrated. How can being stuck in traffic jams be seen as freedom? Dubai has a modern metro system, but it only covers part of the city. There are also buses and water taxis. The car or a taxi is most practical.

Cars are cheap in Dubai. The expat population is dynamic, with many people seeking work opportunities. This has led to a busy second-hand car market, as expats often sell their cars before leaving the country. As a result, you can find a wide range of used cars at various price points.

Maria, a private banker, told me that during the global financial crisis of 2008-2009, expats facing financial challenges would abandon their cars at the airport and exit the country to avoid legal repercussions. This then led to an oversupply of second-hand vehicles, resulting in discounted prices, providing an opportunity for buyers to find good deals.

You will see a lot of white cars on the road. Dubai's relentless heat can turn a car into an oven, causing interiors to become unbearably hot. White cars can deflect significant sunlight and heat, helping keep the interior temperatures cooler than darker-coloured vehicles. The reflective properties of white paint also prevent the car's engine from overheating. They also stand out more prominently in the desert landscape. White is also often associated with luxury, elegance, and purity. Owning a white car is a status symbol. Interestingly, white cars tend to hold their resale value well. Their heat-deflecting properties and their association with luxury can make them more appealing to potential buyers in the used car market. It took time to get used to white cars.

When purchasing a car, consider the total cost of ownership, not only the initial cost but also the ongoing expenses. These include the cost of servicing and maintenance, insurance premiums, vehicle registration fees, parking, potential traffic fines, adherence to traffic rules, and obtaining a driving license.

Before making a car purchase, thorough research is essential. People have been duped. Consider the vehicle's history, condition, and mileage. Inspect the car thoroughly to avoid surprises, and take the car for a spin to check the comfort, performance, and handling. Get a trusted mechanic to inspect the vehicle thoroughly. Of course, it is an extra expense, but it is worth it in the long run. Ensure all necessary documentation, such as the car's ownership history, maintenance records, and legal paperwork, is in order. You need to be a resident of the UAE to register a vehicle.

Converting a foreign driving license to a Dubai license can be straightforward, but sometimes, they may ask you to retake the driving test. To determine if your driver's license is eligible for conversion to a Dubai license, you can use the Roads and Transport Authority (RTA) online portal.

A client told me an amusing story concerning his wife, who had to retake the driving test at the police compound in Abu Dhabi. The night before the test, she was nervous. He told her, "Let's go to the police compound and practice. That way, you will be familiar with the area and less nervous tomorrow."

They drove to the compound. It was 10:30 p.m. The compound was empty, and the gates were open. They switched seats, and his wife got behind the steering wheel.

As she was going around the block, a police officer abruptly stopped them. "What are you doing here?"

Suddenly realising this may not have been a clever idea, the husband explained, "My wife has her driving test here tomorrow, and she is nervous, so we came here to practice."

The police officer laughed out loud. "Please switch places," he said. "And good luck with your driving test tomorrow."

She passed the test and is an expert on all the rules.

Maintaining a safe and steady pace when driving on highways in the UAE is crucial. The speed limit in Dubai is 120 km/h (75 mph) on highways and 60 km/h (37 mph) in residential areas. If a fast vehicle approaches you from behind, make way even if you drive within the speed limit. Moving too slowly is considered a risk and can lead to hefty fines. It is essential to adhere to speed limits, not just the maximum but also the minimum speed limits. You will see blue signs indicating the minimum speed limits. Do not drink and drive. The legal blood alcohol limit in Dubai is 0.00%. Also, do not use your phone while driving.

Maria told me a scary story of a young British expat living in Dubai for two years. He was driving home from work one night when he got into a car accident. He was speeding, ran a red light, and t-boned another car. He had no injuries, but the other driver was severely injured. The expat was arrested and charged with reckless driving. He was also charged with a visa violation because he was driving without a valid UAE driver's license. He was found guilty of both charges and sentenced to two months in jail and a fine.

He was eventually released from jail after serving one month but faced deportation. He had to apply for a special visa to stay in Dubai. He was also banned from driving for six months. This experience was a wake-up call. He had taken his privileges for granted and vowed to be more careful. He also learned that laws in Dubai are strict, and expats who break the law can face grave consequences.

Maria warned me your car's air conditioning system must work properly. She occasionally opens a window to let in fresh air. In the extreme heat, chemical fumes can be released from the plastics inside the car. These fumes can cause headaches and nausea, which can sometimes be fatal. Maria experienced the effects firsthand while driving from Dubai to Abu Dhabi. The chemical fumes became so intense that she started getting dizzy and had to pull over.

Taxis are everywhere in Dubai. The arrival of platforms like Uber has transformed the way people get around. The advanced navigation systems ensure drivers have accurate and up-to-date directions, reducing the likelihood of getting lost and providing a smoother ride for passengers. This is well worth the premium if you can afford to spend a little more.

In the early days of my arrival in Dubai, directions were always given based on landmark buildings. I remember getting into a taxi once and asking the driver to take me to Downtown. He did not know Downtown. I then tried Burj Khalifa. He did not know where that was either. I thought there may be a language barrier, so I pointed to the Burj Khalifa. He still did not show any sign of enlightenment. I explained patiently that it was a landmark in Dubai. It turned out it was his first day on the job. Finding yourself in a taxi with a driver who spoke no English was common. I often used to print off maps before getting into a cab. There are also traditional taxis, often cheaper, with navigation systems.

I love to chat with taxi drivers. I have learned so much about Dubai from them over the years. Some have been driving taxis for decades and are knowledgeable about the city. Others are starting out. They are all passionate about Dubai and marvel at the new buildings being constructed.

Dubai has pink taxis at the airport, identified by their pink roofs, driven by women. These taxis cater specifically to women who may feel uncomfortable in a cab driven by a male driver. However, I felt awkward when I first got into a pink taxi. I expected a taxi driver to lift my heavy luggage into the trunk, but I thought it was inappropriate for her to lift such heavy objects.

This made me realise I was as guilty of stereotyping as anyone else. The existence of female taxi drivers allows women to work in traditionally male-dominated fields and exercise their choice of occupation. One should support and respect the choices individuals make, regardless of gender.

In recent years, Dubai has poured billions of dollars into developing new transportation networks. The city's metro system is one of the most modern in the world and is currently being expanded. To stay ahead of the population growth, Dubai has also continued to invest in a network of highways and roads and a light rail system. The efficient transportation networks and logistics facilities also make it easy to move goods around. The free zones create an environment conducive to international business, allowing Dubai to become a significant player in global trade and commerce.

Dubai has long been known for its world-class infrastructure, from its state-of-the-art airports to its massive seaports. Dubai International Airport (DBX) is known for its efficiency and capacity to handle significant numbers of international travellers. It is a gateway to the world and ranks among the busiest airports globally for international travel.

One of the most significant investments has been the development of Dubai World Central (DWC), a massive new airport complex. DWC will be the world's largest airport, with the capacity to manage over 160 million passengers annually.[77] A quote by His Highness Sheikh Mohammed Bin Rashid Al Maktoum underlines his ambitions: "We do not want an airport for Dubai; we want Dubai to be an airport for the world."[78]

Dubai has also made significant investments in its seaports. The UAE boasts 12 commercial trading ports other than oil ports.[79] The city's Jebel Ali Port is the world's largest artificial port and one of the busiest ports in the Middle East.[80]

Dubai is an excellent base for frequent travellers like me. Situated at the crossroads of the Middle East, its strategic location makes it an ideal central hub for globetrotters. Whether my journeys took me to the GCC or other continents, Dubai's connectivity simplified my travel plans and enhanced my overall experience.

The well-connected Dubai International Airport is clean, and all its processes are efficient. Emirates Airlines gets you everywhere, plus there are local low-cost airlines such as FlyDubai. Emirates Airlines has a modern fleet of aircraft, including the iconic Airbus A380 and Boeing 777. Flying FlyDubai is as mundane as taking a bus.

Chapter 12.

Dubai's Culture Defined

People often argue that Dubai does not have a soul and is a materialistic playground for adults. The concept of a place having a soul is often subjective and can vary based on individual experiences, expectations, and cultural backgrounds. Every person living in Dubai has their own unique story and journey. Behind the flashy cars and buildings are stories of individuals from diverse backgrounds who have come together to make Dubai their home.

People say they do not feel Dubai has a soul because it is all new and was built quickly. I have always said in response that it is a place where you need to bring your soul. It would be best to be clear about who you are before you move to a place like Dubai, or you may get swept up in the excess. Its luxury lifestyle can be addictive and leave you broke at the end of the journey. Dubai is for some, but not for everyone.

Others say there is no culture. Dubai has created its own culture of enthusiastic individuals. Everyone is looking to succeed and is open to meeting other people. It is entrepreneurial – which I found highly motivational. The *can-do* attitude prevalent in Dubai's culture encourages individuals to pursue their goals and dreams. This positive outlook can be seen in the many success stories of individuals and businesses thriving in the city.

His Highness Sheikh Mohammed Bin Rashid Al Maktoum leads by example. He is an entrepreneur surrounded by excellent advisors. He has not shied away from taking risks. His visionary approach and commitment to innovation have played a significant role in shaping Dubai's culture of growth and progress, inspiring many.

Because so much is newly built in Dubai, it can feel like it lacks authenticity, with some referring to the city as 'plastic-fantastic.' Plastic-fantastic is often used to describe places that appear artificial or lacking in authenticity due to their rapid development and modern aesthetics. It is a superficial opinion; there is much more to Dubai.

While the city's modern infrastructure and luxury lifestyle may dominate its image, efforts to preserve and promote cultural heritage are evidenced by initiatives such as Dubai's historic neighbourhoods, museums, and cultural events. The city's cultural scene is thriving, with various art galleries, museums, and theatres. The Opera House[81], a tribute to Dubai's maritime history, hosts performances throughout the year ranging from operas to concerts and ballets to musicals. Alserkal Avenue[82], a hub for contemporary art exhibitions, showcases local and international talent. You will also find many galleries in DIFC.

Visitors and residents can explore the Jumeirah Mosque or immerse themselves in the traditional *souks* (markets), such as the Gold Souk or Spice Souk, where they can experience the charm of old Dubai.

The citizens take pride in preserving their cultural traditions through various events and festivals throughout the year. From Ramadan celebrations to the lively festivities during Eid Al-Fitr or Diwali, something is always happening, bringing people together to celebrate their shared heritage. The Emirati culture is often invisible to outsiders because they are a tiny minority and tend to be quite private and reserved. Move away from the glitter and glamour and uncover the Old Dubai and Dubai Creek.

Chapter 13.

A Lifestyle for Every Budget

A Sanctuary of Safety

Dubai stands out as an ideal destination for women. The city offers a blend of safety, cleanliness, upmarket amenities, and affordable services, making it an appealing choice for women. Dubai's commitment to cleanliness and convenience is truly exceptional. The streets in Downtown are meticulously cleaned every day, very different from the littered streets I encountered upon returning to London. I used to wake up every morning not by the call to prayer from the mosques but by the sound of the cleaning machines.

The chance of experiencing harassment in Dubai is low compared to other places around the world. You can also walk on the street without receiving any unwanted comments from men or construction workers whistling at you.

Dubai's emphasis on convenience is equally remarkable. You can have your groceries delivered within 20 minutes. Not only groceries – anything is delivered.

Dubai is known as a shopping haven, with many upmarket shopping malls. For women with a penchant for luxury, the city's offerings extend to purchasing gold, diamonds, custom-made jewellery, and even fur coats. The city's shopping scene caters to various preferences, making it an exciting destination for retail therapy. Dubai is equally renowned for its services, providing opportunities for relaxation and self-care. From massages to manicures and pedicures, the city has many options for indulging in rejuvenating treatments.

Interestingly, cosmetic procedures and maintenance services attract both men and women. It is not necessarily much cheaper, but you have the privacy of healing, so you can go back home with no one noticing your nose job.

One distinctive aspect of Dubai is the affordability of domestic staff, making certain aspects of daily life more convenient. Engaging services such as house painting or hiring live-in chauffeurs, nannies, and cleaning staff can enhance the quality of life without straining the budget.

Public places are highly equipped to cater to children's needs, with features such as creches, play areas, and spotlessly clean changing rooms.

Married couples in Dubai can maintain a lifestyle akin to that of singles, enjoying the city's offerings to the fullest. This lifestyle, however, might make transitioning back to Europe financially challenging, as recreating a similar lifestyle in their home countries could prove to be cost-prohibitive.

Overall, Dubai is an enticing destination for women seeking a safe, upscale, and indulgent experience with a unique lifestyle combining luxury, convenience, and exploration.

Dubai has earned its reputation as a global shopping destination like no other. The city's name beckons visitors with an irresistible invitation: "Do buy." Dubai has more than 70 shopping malls, including Mall of the Emirates[83], which features an indoor ski slope, and Dubai Mall[84], the largest shopping mall in the world. Dubai Mall has over 1,200 shops, an indoor ice rink, an aquarium, and a virtual reality park. It took me weeks to find my way around.

The biggest shopping mall in the world is getting bigger and bigger. A Chinatown extension was recently added, catering to the Chinese expats. I recently talked to a friend in Shanghai who wanted to know more about doing business in the Middle East. She told me the Chinese domestic market was slowing down, and many Chinese companies were now heading to the Middle East to raise capital.

Diversity in Dubai's Living Experience

Dubai's reputation for luxury and opulence is undeniable, with the sight of high-end cars like Rolls Royce, Ferraris, and Aston Martins commonplace on its roads. Yet, amidst the shimmering supercars, the cityscape includes various everyday vehicles cruising along the highways. Dubai balances extravagance and practicality, showcasing a blend of lifestyles.

And while Dubai is often synonymous with luxurious high-end apartments for the ultra-wealthy, the reality is more diverse. The city's real estate caters to an array of budgets and preferences. Whether you are a first-time homebuyer or are seeking a reasonable rental option, Dubai ensures inclusivity. In recent years, the local real estate industry has shifted focus towards creating more affordable housing solutions, recognising the importance of accessibility for residents across all income levels.

For those with budget constraints, Dubai provides a range of affordable apartment and villa options in neighbourhoods like Dubai Land, International City, and Discovery Gardens. Furthermore, neighbouring Emirate Sharjah offers significantly lower rents, making it an attractive alternative for those seeking cost-effective living arrangements. Dubai is where people from all walks of life can find a home matching their aspirations and financial circumstances.

Chapter 14.

Dubai's Low Rate of Petty Crime

One of the remarkable aspects of Dubai is its reputation as a place where you can confidently adorn yourself with gold and diamonds without the apprehension often associated with such displays in other cities like London.[85] The city boasts a notably low crime rate, particularly petty crimes, often prevalent in urban environments. This safety results from stringent law enforcement and robust security measures helping to deter incidents such as pickpocketing and theft, making them uncommon occurrences. While Dubai might attract individuals with questionable business intentions, contributing to financial crime, the prevalence of petty crime is low. Of course, like any big city, it is always wise to monitor your belongings and stay aware of your surroundings.

Susan, who works in human resources at a government entity, left a wallet behind in a shop at Dubai Mall. She did not realise it was missing until hours later. As she hurried back to the shop to recover her wallet, she did not doubt it would be there with all its contents. She walked into the shop, and the staff were waving her purse. They returned her purse with everything in it. In too many other countries, the thought of recovering your wallet intact would seem unlikely. Stories of lost items, like phones left in taxis, being promptly returned to their owners are common in Dubai.

A light-hearted joke circulates among residents: "You can spot a tourist in the UAE by observing whether they take their phone and handbag to the restroom." This humorously highlights the contrast between the safe environment in Dubai and the typical vigilance travellers maintain in other places.

Security measures within residential complexes are also thorough, with surveillance cameras strategically placed throughout. Sometimes, the emphasis on security can be slightly excessive, leading to permits being required even for minor repairs in an apartment.

Leaving the door to your apartment open might sound like a surreal concept in many parts of the world, but not in Dubai. Residents in the apartment buildings may leave their doors unlocked, even when they go on extended holidays. In villa neighbourhoods, finding houses without locked doors or cars is common. Susan even used to give her credit card – with the PIN – to a petrol station attendant, another example of the trust residents have in the city's security systems.

Many women I spoke to in Europe who had never been to the Middle East told me they worried about walking alone on the streets in Dubai. Contrary to these misconceptions, walking alone, especially for women, is safe in Dubai. Compared to women's apprehensions about walking alone in European cities, Dubai's safety level is notably higher. Instances of harassment are rare, and locals and expats feel comfortable walking around the city, even at night.

Online crime is a more significant issue. Recently, the police warned about online scammers impersonating UAE government bodies and companies such as DHL, Emirates Post, and the Central Bank.[86] I have personally had scammer emails from all of them. I also received dodgy phone calls from people pretending to be officials from the Central Bank asking for personal or bank details. As they would say they were calling from the Central Bank of Dubai, I immediately knew it was fake. The Central Bank is based in Abu Dhabi.

As a result, I rarely pick up the phone from unknown numbers. Many people are like me, making reaching someone on their mobile for business difficult.

They target people by phone and email. I received the following email from someone cloning Emirates Airlines: "Dear Valued Client, we are delighted about your upcoming Emirates flight! To confirm your reservation, kindly provide your credit card details by Clicking here, ensuring your seat, and locking in the fare. This link will stay active for 48 hours. We are looking forward to welcoming you on board. The Emirates team." I almost fell for this as I had a flight scheduled on Emirates Airlines, but I decided it was odd. I then checked the sender, and it was an irregular email address.

Another example received the same day, coming from someone pretending to be the government, explicitly asking for money: "Dubai Government - Urgent Payment Notice. Dear Rebecca, we are writing to you with utmost urgency. As part of the Dubai government's commitment to providing the best services and facilities to all visitors and residents, we require your immediate attention to a critical matter. Failure to address this issue promptly could lead to severe consequences during your stay in Dubai. Your cooperation is crucial to avoid any disruptions or inconveniences. Please immediately click the link below to settle the outstanding administrative fees for your recent entry to Dubai. It is of the utmost importance that you do so without delay. Pay Now 67.18 AED." Because there are so many little fees to pay in Dubai, for a split second, you think it is real and maybe something is outstanding. Fake again.

The search and investigation teams at the Dubai Criminal Investigation Department (CID) are experienced in handling security issues. I have complete confidence in their ability to tackle any situation. Officers stay updated with the latest crime prevention methods, including using the artificial intelligence capabilities of the Criminal Data Analysis Centre of Dubai Police to track down criminals and prevent crime.[87]

Chapter 15.

Heat, Health, and Happiness

Two Seasons: Hot and Very Hot

Dubai's weather is a topic of both praise and caution. The city experiences two distinct seasons: the hot season and the very hot season. Aside from the scorching summer months, the climate is remarkable throughout the year. Most days, about 90% of the time, begin with the comforting warmth of the sun, a natural gift. Rainfall with occasional sandstorms or haziness is rare. The summer season spans from April to October, and the winter season stretches from November to March.

During the summer, the temperatures skyrocket, and humidity levels soar, often surpassing 40° Celsius and sometimes even reaching a sweltering 50°. Dry heat is great. You can hang your washing outside, which is bone dry within 30 minutes. The heat feels like a cosy duvet cover wrapped around the body, comforting and soothing. The humidity can sometimes be intense. I recall stepping out of my apartment and frequently experiencing the immediate fogging up of my sunglasses due to the humidity.

On the other hand, the winter months bring about a much more pleasant temperature, hovering around a comfortable 25° Celsius. December and January are considered the coldest months of the year, and ironically, they are also the peak months for tourism. It is a unique sight to see me bundled up in a winter coat as I find it a little chilly while my European friends stroll around in their swimsuits and trunks, enjoying the mild winter of Dubai.

While this climate offers certain advantages, such as the ability to enjoy outdoor activities during milder winter months, the scorching heat of the summer can be intense and even oppressive. The period from early May to late September is especially marked by sweltering temperatures reaching a blistering 50° Celsius. During this time, the city can feel deserted as most people seek refuge in air-conditioned spaces, akin to sitting next to a warm radiator in London's winter. Often, the men will stay in Dubai while their families go to Europe to enjoy a cooler summer. The ideal scenario for me would be experiencing the wonderful summer months with its social calendar in London and winter with its many conferences in Dubai, striking a balance between the two.

Like many residents seeking a break from the relentless heat, I decided to escape to Amsterdam, known as the "Venice of the North," one scorching August for some cooler weather. The opportunity to spend a month in this captivating city with its iconic canals was a welcome prospect. My apartment was nestled beside the picturesque canals, offering a privileged view stretching over the tranquil gardens of the esteemed Mayor of Amsterdam. Behind the historic facades of the canal houses, lush and green gardens lay hidden from the public gaze.

Touching down at Schiphol Airport in Holland, I had keenly anticipated a refreshing change and maybe rain. However, the temperature unexpectedly soared to 30° Celsius. A wave of intense heat enveloped me as I stood in line for a taxi. Nonetheless, I was determined that my holiday in Amsterdam would be a delightful interlude. And it was. I spent my time leisurely strolling along the serene canals and reconnecting with dear friends. The city's charm and cultural allure offered a soothing balm to my senses, providing a welcome break from Dubai.

Yet, even amidst the scenic splendour of Amsterdam, an unexpected adversary emerged: the relentless mosquitoes hovering around the canals. These tiny creatures left me covered with itchy red bumps. It served as a reminder that nature's inhabitants can pose challenges even in the most idyllic settings. The unexpectedly elevated temperatures in Amsterdam and the limited availability of air conditioning resulted in a constant battle against mosquitoes while attempting to stay cool. Despite the picturesque canals and charming surroundings, the lack of air conditioning compelled me to return to Dubai, a mosquito-free and air-conditioned sanctuary.

A wave of appreciation washed over me when I arrived in my familiar Dubai apartment. In seeking relief from the scorching summer months, I concluded that there is no place like Dubai with its climate-controlled comforts. Dubai has fewer insects than other parts of the world, thanks to the city's hot, dry climate. Insects need water to survive, and the dry climate in Dubai makes it difficult for them to find water sources. The city's urban planning also minimises stagnant water, another insect breeding ground.

Mosquitoes do come out when the weather is warm and humid. You may encounter mosquitoes if you are living in a villa, especially if you are on the water, but you will not find them in apartment buildings. Dubai has a comprehensive mosquito control program. It institutes the regular spraying of insecticides, draining of standing water, and inspection of mosquito breeding grounds. This program has helped to keep the mosquito population in Dubai under control. Other insects you may encounter in Dubai include cockroaches, ants, and spiders. I never saw a spider in any apartment blocks, but I have spotted big ones in the villa areas.

I am writing my book, enjoying the serene beauty of the South of France. Additionally, I am happily engaged in the delightful task of cat-sitting throughout July. Nestled in the comfort of my friend's apartment, modern air-conditioning is a blessing. It is around 30° Celsius, which feels like the scorching 40+° summers I grew accustomed to in Dubai. The hot weather in the South of France this summer has kept me engrossed in the pages of my book.

I have good news. The weather is changing in the UAE. The UAE is pushing the boundaries of science and technology to tackle challenges related to weather and climate. During a conference, I spoke to an official from 'The Weather Department' in Abu Dhabi. He told me the UAE has been investing in advanced technologies to modify weather patterns. It has invested in innovative solutions, like cloud seeding, to enhance rainfall and combat water scarcity. Extending the winter season would benefit agriculture, water resources, and the tourism industry.

Weather modification has its origins in military applications. For example, the US military has experimented with cloud seeding for years to induce rain or snow and to create artificial fog to obscure enemy targets. The UAE's focus is on harnessing this technology for civilian benefits. While weather modification can offer promising outcomes, it raises intriguing questions about potential cross-border effects. Instances like the reported extreme flooding in a neighbouring GCC country prompt consideration of international responsibility for weather-related events crossing territorial boundaries.

An Uber driver told me that as Dubai embarks on ambitious green initiatives, such as planting forests and increasing green spaces, it strives to mitigate the effects of the desert heat. He said Downtown Dubai is already cooler than elsewhere because of all the trees planted over the last few years. The creation of lush oases within the desert landscape, facilitated by extensive use of sprinklers, showcases Dubai's determination to provide a cooler and more sustainable environment for residents and visitors alike. Dubai's weather, while presenting challenges, serves as a catalyst for innovative solutions and forward-thinking.

A Healthy Lifestyle in Dubai

People commonly experience weight gain after moving to Dubai, often humorously called the "Dubai stone." This could be attributed to a combination of factors, including a potentially slower metabolism, unhealthy eating habits, and adjustments in exercise routines due to the new environment. I can relate to this challenge, as I also found myself striving to shed the additional kilograms I gained in Dubai. A witty piece of advice from an acquaintance who had liposuction done: "Always remember it is more expensive to shed the weight than it is to put it on."

Interestingly, intermittent fasting has gained popularity among expats in Dubai as an effective weight management approach. During Ramadan, Muslims observe a fast from sunrise to sunset. They refrain from eating, drinking, smoking, and engaging in sexual activity from dawn to dusk. The purpose of the fast is to cleanse both the body and mind, allowing Muslims to focus on their spiritual journey. Expats sometimes join in during Ramadan, fasting to lose a couple of pounds!

Obesity has emerged as a significant concern in the Middle East, and it is worth noting that, according to the Economist, a higher proportion of women are affected than men. This trend could be attributed to lower workforce participation among women who spend more time at home. Women have limited opportunities to engage in sports. While young girls and boys can be seen playing football together on the streets, societal norms discourage physical activities for girls once they reach puberty. This leads to a decline in their active lifestyle, as they become more sedentary and spend time indoors socialising with friends. According to some women, Arab men prefer women to be curvier. Women even take weight-gaining pills to be more attractive to men![88]

In 2013, the Dubai government offered gold as a weight loss initiative. Every calorie counted. Contestants had to lose at least 2 kilograms during the month. They would receive one gram of gold for each kilogram of weight lost.[89]

Most apartments have swimming pools and gyms, which should encourage residents to maintain an active lifestyle. I find the repetitiveness of a gym monotonous and have more fun engaging in activities like tennis or horse riding. Dubai is a car-centric city, and many people rely on their cars to get around. As a result, residents may not get enough exercise. This is why I decided to live in Downtown Dubai, as it is easy to get around on foot. Daily walks are a great way to keep the blood circulating and stay active and healthy. Walking helps me to clear my head and relax. You can alternatively walk along the beach or stroll through the park. For those who enjoy getting their heart rate up, Dubai offers diverse indoor and outdoor activities to suit all interests. The latest craze is paddle tennis.

Dubai may resemble London, but transitioning to this new environment requires your body to adapt. Having spent years in the region, although I am not a medical professional, the key ailments are sunburnt nose syndrome, the desert dehydration drama, hair loss and the air-conditioning cold.

The sun is much stronger in Dubai than in other parts of the world. Wear sunscreen and a hat whenever you are outdoors or seek shade during the peak sun hours. Interestingly, despite the abundance of sunlight in the Middle East, Amal, my local GP, told me many residents suffer from vitamin D deficiency due to spending prolonged periods indoors. To get enough vitamin D, aim to get sun exposure every day. So do not avoid the sun altogether.

I would start my day with a 10-minute coffee session on my terrace, soaking up the natural warmth; a good way to get vitamin D and start your day off right. The desert air in Dubai can sap moisture from your body. It is crucial to stay properly hydrated, a lesson Nora learned when she was going out drinking with George. Dehydration can sneak up on you, causing fatigue, muscle aches, nausea, and headaches. I also experienced these symptoms firsthand when I first moved to Dubai.

It is not uncommon for people to experience hair loss when they move to the Middle East. I panicked when I saw my hair on the tiles. Some attribute this to the desalinated water, which can make hair brittle and more prone to shedding. The exact cause of hair loss in the Middle East has yet to be fully understood. Another reason may be the desert air. The sand particles can irritate the scalp and damage hair. The stress of moving to a new country may also contribute to hair loss. The use of air conditioning in the Middle East can dry out the hair and scalp, leading to hair loss. Also, the intense sun can damage hair and make it more susceptible to breakage.

Anti-hair loss solutions are a booming business in Dubai. I tried several things to help with my hair loss, including washing my hair with Evian water. I would even carry my water to the hairdresser to rinse my hair. I put filters on all my taps. I suggest you get your water supply tested. Hair loss is not the only concern; people have also reported skin problems. I also have filters on every tap in my London home and drink distilled water most of the time. I wore a hat outdoors and stayed indoors whenever a sandstorm raged through the city.

Over time, I began to suspect hair loss might be linked to a deficiency in zinc. It may also be due to a lack of Vitamin D. Psychological factors might also be at play. For example, the light-coloured tiled floors in most apartments can make it seem like you are losing more hair than you are, compared to how European carpets conceal fallen hair. Or, it could be breakage, not actual hair loss. And if all this fails, there are plenty of cosmetic surgeons happy to assist you in bringing back a full head of hair.

The sudden changes in temperature between the hot outdoors and the cold indoors can cause a chill, which can lead to a cold. Be sure to dress in layers. Your body will need to adapt to the significant temperature swings. This can be a challenge, especially if you are not used to it. I often felt disoriented and dizzy in the first couple of months.

I vividly remember the first time I got an air-conditioning cold. I was visiting a friend in Abu Dhabi for the weekend. She booked a fabulous suite at the St Regis Hotel on Saadiyat Island. It was a great mini holiday. We spent the day at the beach and laughed, catching up and exchanging war stories. However, when we returned to the hotel, the air conditioning was so cold, although incredibly refreshing, it might have been too much of a shock to my system. I ended up falling ill a couple of days later.

It is possible that the air conditioning was set to an extra low temperature, as Bill Clinton was also staying in the hotel during our visit. Getting the staff's attention was hard as they were all attending to Bill. Over the years, I noticed a correlation between the level of luxury in hotels and the temperature they maintain. The more opulent and lavish a hotel is, the cooler and more refreshing its indoor temperature tends to be.

I have learned since then to be more careful about the temperature changes. I try to avoid going from hot to cold too quickly and dress in layers.

Be aware of the potential air quality challenges and take steps to protect your health. The air quality in Dubai is not as good as in other countries due to vehicle emissions, industrial pollution, and dust storms. This can cause a variety of health problems, including respiratory ailments. In my personal experience, upon my arrival in Dubai, I got an eye stye, which my eye specialist told me is a common occurrence among expats due to the prevalence of sand and construction dust. I always made sure to stay indoors during sandstorms, not only to help prevent eye styes but also to minimise the risk of respiratory problems.

Pursuit of Happiness and Well-Being

A quote by His Highness Sheikh Mohammed Bin Rashid Al Maktoum underlines the government's commitment to happiness: "The fastest way to happiness is by instilling happiness in the hearts of others. The job of governments is to create an environment where people can achieve their happiness."[90]

Dubai's commitment to fostering happiness and well-being has achieved remarkable progress. One example is the National Program for Happiness and Positivity in 2016.[91] Dubai has soared from its 68th ranking in the World Happiness Report in 2016 to an impressive 21st position in 2022.

At the heart of this initiative are the dedicated Happiness and Positivity Councils, made up of citizens and residents of Dubai. These councils serve as dynamic platforms for collaboration and dialogue, creating a bridge between the government and the community. By channelling the collective wisdom and insights of its diverse population, these councils play a crucial role in identifying areas for improvement and offering valuable feedback to help shape policies.

By nurturing a culture of positivity, inclusivity, and well-being, Dubai has improved its global ranking while enriching the daily lives of its residents. As the city continues as a role model of progress and positive change, its commitment to happiness sets an inspiring example for nations worldwide. Through collaboration, collective effort, and a deep-rooted commitment to the well-being of its people, Dubai is paving the way for a brighter, happier future!

Chapter 16.

Glitz and Glamour

A Day at the Races

Attend the Abu Dhabi Grand Prix for a glitzy, fast car experience. The arrival of Formula One in the capital was a turning point, positioning Abu Dhabi as a place for entertainment. They brought in big names like Paul McCartney, Beyoncé, and Lionel Richie, to name a few.[92] One year, I was invited by a client aboard a luxurious yacht to witness the race, and it was an unforgettable way to spend a day with a concert at night. The experience was fun and offered great networking opportunities, with many investors at the party.

The Abu Dhabi race track differs from the Monaco Grand Prix track. Monaco's track is narrow and winding, while Abu Dhabi's is wider and more open. I had previously observed the Monaco race from the first-floor balcony of the illustrious Hotel de Paris, providing a panoramic view of Casino Square in Monaco. Witnessing a Formula 1 driver navigating the challenging corners of Casino Square at breathtaking speeds was a mind-blowing spectacle. The intense focus and split-second decisions required to navigate such a treacherous course left me in awe, aware that a slight misjudgement could result in a collision into the unforgiving walls. My admiration for the skill and bravery of these drivers reached new heights.

Abu Dhabi is a faster track, but it also removes some challenges. However, both tracks are thrilling and will surely pump your adrenaline. While the track in Abu Dhabi may lack Monaco's sharp corners and tight spaces, it nevertheless captivates the hearts of true motor enthusiasts passionate about speed and competition.

One of my friends recalled visiting an Emirati mansion in Abu Dhabi. He owned more than twenty race cars. He would take them out on the Formula One racetrack and compete against his friends.

You may occasionally come across speeding cars at night on the highways. You may even get invited to a race if you own a fast car. If you drive a fast car, it is assumed you will want to race. The girl in question recalled being in her boyfriend's car in Abu Dhabi on the way to the airport when a young Emirati in a pickup truck next to them at the traffic lights said, "Do you want to race?"

Her friend agreed. He had a Porsche 911. The traffic lights changed to green, and they were off. Looks can deceive. The pickup truck disappeared from their sight within no time. The Porsche must have been doing 170 kilometres an hour. Who knows what speed the pickup truck was doing? They never got the chance to congratulate him on his victory. I am not recommending you accept these invitations to race. Although it is rude to decline an invitation, there are strict speeding limits in the UAE to consider.

If you want something for the kids to enjoy, fast car related, you can visit Ferrari World Abu Dhabi. This theme park is located on Yas Island and features a variety of rides and attractions, all themed around Ferrari.

More than Glitz and Glamour

Dubai caters to the desires of those drawn to fast cars, glamour, and glitz. It is what Dubai is best known for abroad. The city puts on events designed to captivate your senses and elevate your adrenaline. There is also a buzzing expat scene, with Friday brunches. There are cool bars and adrenaline-pumping activities, such as skydiving. There is always another new glamorous restaurant opening up. And, of course, there is no shortage of nightclubs in town.

Transitioning from dazzling Monaco to buzzing Dubai marked a shift from my glamorous 30s. In the past, my life consisted of hopping between Monaco, St. Tropez, St. Moritz, and St. Barts, attending opulent soirées aboard luxurious yachts and elegant balls across Europe, and networking at exclusive clubs in London. A collection of glamorous experiences had underscored my life in London and Monaco. Despite the abundant glitz and glamour in Dubai, my interests had evolved. I still relished the occasional evening when I dusted off my ball gown, but my preferences had shifted. I was looking for genuine connections and authentic experiences to enrich my life.

I was fascinated by the local culture and connecting with the Emiratis and other locals in the region. I loved attending unique events like the Emirates Airlines Festival of Literature, where poetry flowed like the desert winds, whispering profound tales in the tranquil dunes. The desert's serene expanse provided an ideal canvas for introspection, lending depth and significance to my reflections. Dubai, for me, became more than glitz and glamour; it was a place where the desert's secrets intertwined with the city's vibrancy, inviting me to explore the essence beneath the surface.

Chapter 17.

Local Experiences

Immersive Local Experiences

During her early days in Dubai, Eva, Dutch like me, had the pleasure of meeting a Saudi gentleman called Mohamed. What started as a simple introduction quickly blossomed into a genuine friendship. She vividly remembers their first coffee meeting at Emirates Towers, which a mutual friend had arranged. Apprehensive due to warnings about Saudi men, she maintained a cautious demeanour, as he was quite clearly a flirt.

However, as she observed and got to know him better, she was in awe of his skills. He was a top athlete. Beyond his sports prowess, Mohamed embodies the spirit of a global citizen. She told me that with his profound insights into the region's nuances and understanding of European perspectives, this Saudi national brings valuable expertise. This unique blend equips him to bridge the gap between the East and West, making him a remarkable diplomat who adeptly extricates people from challenging predicaments, including legal entanglements and time in prison. Their conversations were always engaging, primarily confined to coffee sessions.

One amusing exchange captured their evolving rapport when Mohamed asked, "How can we truly understand each other if we do not share a dinner?"

"I am thoroughly enjoying our coffees," she replied. "I believe we are truly getting to know each other. Don't you feel we have created a bond?"

His laughter marked a turning point, leading to a lively, banter-filled friendship.

When she embarked on her first journey to Saudi, he extended a daunting invitation: "I am going to introduce you to the former head of Border Control."

Her initial reaction was a mix of trepidation and intrigue. She conveyed her feelings and said, "This is my first trip to Saudi, and any mistake could have long-lasting consequences."

As she tried to comprehend the significance of this introduction, she realised his underlying motive was to protect her well-being and ensure she had someone to rely on. His genuine concern and protective nature were remarkable, providing a comforting embrace throughout my travels.

She often extended an invitation for him to accompany her during client meetings. She proudly proclaimed, "Allow me to introduce my esteemed friend from Saudi." His eloquent endorsements bolstered her credibility in her client's eyes. Equally, he enjoyed showing her off to his friends.

Celebrating Saudi National Day

Eva received an invitation to join the Saudi National Day celebration held in Dubai. Arriving early, Eva was amidst a crowd of distinguished individuals making their entrances. Mohamed, who had invited her, had not yet arrived. She was standing alone next to an Emirati gentleman who, it turned out, like her, had dual nationality, in his case, Emirati and Iranian. He was the General Manager of a prominent family enterprise in the UAE.

She decided to start a conversation with him. "I seem to have arrived a little early. My friend who invited me is not here yet. I am Eva."

"I am in the same situation," he replied. "I am here on my own and do not know anyone." She was surprised he did not know anyone as he came from a well-known family. She found it amusing that he felt as out of place as she was.

She had a similar revelation while chatting with an Omani delegate during a conference. He asked her about her experience in Saudi and told her he had never been there, so he was curious to hear about her trip there.

This was a moment of profound realisation for her, as it affirmed that while there are similarities between the countries in the Middle East, each country also has its unique personality. Her encounter with the Omani delegate helped her to appreciate the diversity. Not everyone knows each other.

Breaking Fast: The Ritual of Iftar

During Ramadan, which lasts 29 to 30 days, there are many options for *iftar*, the evening meal that breaks the fast, from lavish hotel buffets to intimate private gatherings and unassuming street-side stalls. Iftar is more than a meal. It is a time for profound reflection and gratitude. It provides an opportunity for locals and expats to pause and appreciate the blessings of life. Families and friends gather around beautifully decorated tables. An aura of unity emanates from this shared experience as Emiratis and expats from all walks of life joyfully participate, share laughter, and weave stories together.

One year, Eva had the honour of being invited to an iftar hosted by the Consul General of one of the GCC countries. She arrived at 7 p.m. and found herself seated among a distinguished group of diplomats, including the Consul General of Singapore, the Consul General of Lebanon, and the Consul General of the Netherlands. They had engaging conversations throughout the evening. However, as the night progressed, the crowd started to disperse.

Feeling the evening was just beginning, she decided to stay longer. While her Saudi friend Mohamed was busy with hosting duties, she took the opportunity to approach a group of local individuals who had gathered in a semicircular formation. They all wore elegant white dish dashes and enjoyed each other's company. Spotting an unoccupied seat, she approached them and politely asked, "May I take this seat?" She was welcomed into their midst with warm smiles. Eva sat down and joined in the conversation.

To her left sat a notable figure, the head of Police, which surprised her. Then she introduced herself to the person on her right, who turned out to be the head of airport security. Engaging in conversation, the chief of the police shared intriguing insights, notably expressing a sentiment of underappreciation by expats for Dubai's safety and security. The city undoubtedly is an incredibly safe place. Eva had never felt any sense of danger during her time in Dubai. Furthermore, the newspapers do not report much on deadly crimes, contributing to the overall perception of security. There are extensive measures in place to ensure Dubai remains a safe city, he explained to her.

She asked the head of police about criminals, inquiring whether the police conduct checks before allowing people into the country. To her surprise, he said, "All criminals are welcome here if they have done nothing wrong in our country. We know where they are, and of course, keep them on our radar." He continued, "Criminals like it in Dubai too."

"Really?" she replied.

"Yes," he nodded. "Like you, they love the safety and security of Dubai."

She burst out laughing, appreciating his sense of humour.

During the iftar, the head of police mentioned how the prisons in Dubai are great. "Prisoners prefer going to prison in Dubai to other countries, mainly because the weather is much better here. They can enjoy the sunshine during their breaks instead of standing in the pouring rain."

"Yes," she added. "Being out in the rain is no fun."

It was a highly entertaining conversation.

A couple of years ago, she read about the police in Dubai arresting the suspected head of a cocaine trafficking gang, described as the most wanted man in the Netherlands, even though the Netherlands and Dubai have no extradition treaty.[93] He controlled about one-third of all cocaine trafficking in Europe. According to an article and video published by Gulf News, he was also known for ordering killings as if they were cups of coffee. He was hard to catch as he would change his looks every few months and used fake passports and visas.[94]

The alleged criminal entered Dubai through DBX airport using a fake passport and visa. He lived in a residential area in Dubai, where he was not engaged in criminal activity. He kept a low profile, living in his villa with the lights off. He did not make any purchases under his name in Dubai. There is, however, only so much Netflix you can watch, and eventually, he got caught.

Dubai Police said it took them five days to arrest him after Interpol issued the arrest warrant.[95]

Eva would like to have interviewed the most wanted man in Holland to ask him what his considerations were for moving to Dubai. Last she heard, he was on trial and held at a maximum-security prison in Holland. He allegedly said, "Dubai police must be the best because I have been on the run for years." Let this be a warning to any criminals contemplating a move to Dubai.

In 2021, the global police agency Interpol elected an Emirati as President of Interpol for a four-year term.

According to an article in the Khaleej Times, advanced surveillance technologies play a significant role in arresting some of the world's most wanted criminals. Between 2020 and 2022, Dubai police arrested 597 international fugitives, often part of organised criminal syndicates, charged with money laundering and drug trafficking from more than 101 countries. As part of the department's cooperation with international agencies, Dubai police provided 9,012 intelligence and criminal tips to the governments of 195 countries and 60 law enforcement agencies and organisations, part of Interpol, leading to the dismantling of international criminal syndicates. Dubai police have also repatriated 85 people involved in crimes like forgery, theft, and embezzlement.[96]

Her conversation with the head of police smoothly transitioned to other anecdotes. In a light-hearted discussion, she shared her amusing "confessions" of perceived wrongdoings during her stay in Dubai. Surprisingly, the head of the police debunked a common urban legend and reassured her that the notice in the lift of her apartment about not hanging laundry on her terrace was not a legal stipulation but a suggestion. Jokingly, she expressed her relief upon receiving this clarification.

After finishing her confessions, she asked him, "Do others do this with you? Do they all come to confess their wrongdoings?"

"No, they do not," he replied. "But it must feel good, doesn't it? You must feel relieved."

"Yes," Eva responded. "I feel extremely relieved having shared all my sins with you!"

The conversation continued past midnight, with Eva seated between the good-looking head of police with a great sense of humour and the charismatic, highly entertaining head of airport security. The contrasting yet harmonious blend of their personalities made for an unforgettable night. She was fascinated by both men, and she learned a lot from them. She thoroughly enjoyed the playful banter, which kept the conversation engaging. It was a night she will never forget, and she is grateful for the opportunity to have experienced it. As the night wound down and the clock approached 3:00 a.m., she bade farewell in tandem with her Saudi friend's departure. She still had a lot of questions, a testament to the richness of the exchange they had.

The head of police expressed his intent to inquire about Eva's life. "Can I ask you a question?"

"Surely, with your advanced surveillance systems," she replied, "you already know everything there is to know about me, more than I probably know." Artificial intelligence systems may have a better understanding of us than we have of ourselves.

Years later, Eva met a European who had spent time in jail in the UAE. She got to hear an inside view. It had been a traumatic experience, especially for his family. He told Eva that the prisoners are put in a section with others who have committed similar crimes. The murderers are grouped together. Another section may have all prisoners who committed financial crimes. When they are let outside into the yard, everyone is mixed up. He explained that the nationalities in prison reflect all nationalities in Dubai, including Emiratis.

After iftar, Eva continued to have random encounters with high-ranking government officials, further solidifying her belief in the serendipitous connections she experienced in Dubai.

Over a casual breakfast at her favourite local spot, Baker & Spice, in Souk Al Bahar, she was pleasantly surprised when an Emirati gentleman, dressed in a dish dash and a baseball cap, a look she found cool, kindly offered to cover her meal. The waiter approached her and said, "The gentleman over there would like to pay for your breakfast." She felt flattered. She was having breakfast on my own and welcomed a chat.

He joined her at her table. He was an advisor to His Highness Sheikh Mohammed Bin Rashid Al Maktoum on maritime affairs. Embracing the opportunity for conversation, they delved into the maritime industry and shipbuilding. The Dutch are renowned for their shipbuilding expertise, so they had plenty to discuss. Dubai is a city of serendipitous encounters. It thrives on connections, shared stories, and the blending of diverse perspectives.

Retreat to the Farm: A Tranquil Escape

Some Emiratis own 'desert farms,' one might liken to vacation homes. On a memorable occasion, Eva was invited to a farm in the desert outside of Dubai. A Michelin-starred chef had been hired to prepare a feast for the event. The food was exquisite, perfectly complementing the desert setting. Eva had the opportunity to speak with prominent Emiratis in business during dinner. They were gracious hosts and shared their insights and perspectives on numerous topics. Eva was impressed. They were intelligent, articulate, and passionate about their country. They will play a key role in shaping the future of the UAE.

The evening's special guest was Awad Mohammed Majri, Dubai's intrepid adventurer, fresh from his conquest of Mount Kilimanjaro. He had just returned, and although he was still exhausted, he told them enthusiastically about his expedition. The narrative of his journey was nothing short of captivating. They had wanted to etch their nation onto the global stage for something beyond awe-inspiring skyscrapers by becoming the world's pioneers in ascending Mount Kilimanjaro – by camel. Their aspiration was initially met with resistance, as permits were denied for the use of animals, camels included, in their ascent. But Awad and his team were determined to succeed. They appealed the decision and eventually received the necessary approval for their camels.

The journey was long and arduous. The team had to contend with extreme weather conditions, rugged terrain, and the threat of altitude sickness. But they persevered, and on January 18, 2023, they became the first people ever to ascend Mount Kilimanjaro by camel. Awad's accomplishment is a testament to his grit, determination, and love of adventure. It is also a testament to the UAE's reputation as a global centre for exploration[97].

In the subsequent weeks, Eva was privileged to attend the inaugural screening of "Climbing Kilimanjaro by Camel," a documentary about the trials and triumphs faced by these men and their intrepid camels. The film cast a spotlight on their struggles and underscored their unwavering determination. The premiere film was captivating, celebrating the human spirit and adventure.

During the premiere, Eva spoke with a Saudi gentleman who had travelled to Dubai for the event. He spoke with her but avoided making direct eye contact. He came across as being uninterested and quite rude. Having been invited, she politely kept the conversation going. She thought he might be hesitant to make eye contact with her because he was uncomfortable being seen talking to a woman in public. It was noisy as the music was loud, and she could not hear him properly. She did not want to lean closer to him as she felt he would feel even more uncomfortable.

Eva had not experienced this treatment before in private conversations with Muslim men. She later understood that some Muslim men, for several reasons, including shyness, cultural norms, or a desire to uphold personal values, may choose not to make direct eye contact with women, especially in public. Keep in mind that in Saudi for decades, men and women have been segregated in society. Saudi men still feel and act awkward when talking to women.

Chapter 18.

Camels and Horses: Local Celebrities

Camels: Beyond the Desert Icon

Camels have been a part of Dubai and the broader Middle Eastern culture for centuries. They hold a special place in Emirati traditions and heritage. Camel racing is one of the most popular sports in Dubai, where camels compete against each other, guided by jockeys on their backs. Child-sized robots have since been built to replace the jockeys. These robots have built-in walkie-talkies, which allow the owners to deliver commands to the camels during the two-mile race. A small, automated whip is operated via remote control. Camel races can range from short sprints lasting a few minutes to longer races that can go on for several kilometres and take around 10-15 minutes to complete.

Should camels captivate you, visiting a camel farm and camel market in the UAE is a must. The farms give you an up-close look at these amazing animals. It is an excellent opportunity to learn more about their role in Emirati culture.

Back in London, I met up with a guy who had worked at a modelling agency. As we chit-chatted, he told me about his memorable experience in Oman. He received a call asking him whether he would agree to be part of a jury of a beauty contest there. Given his modelling agency background, he thought it was to give prizes out to girls. They wanted him to be part of the jury to judge the beauty of their long-legged *camels* in a camel catwalk beauty contest!

It was taken seriously. Camels were divided into juniors, 4-7 years old, and seniors, 8-12 years old. The judging panel of esteemed elders, camel experts, and beauty connoisseurs sat beneath a luxurious canopy. The camels were prettily dressed up with accessories, jewels, and tassels. Each camel was meticulously evaluated. The winners were presented with cash prices of millions of dollars and certificates of excellence.

Beauty is in the eye of the beholder. Some things make a camel stand out. Their big, soulful eyes with long eyelashes are known to steal hearts. Also, their pouted lips, size, shape, body condition, knees, how they move, the shine and colour of their coat and unique hump(s) can all add to the overall charm and play a role in assessing their beauty. No hair colouring, tattooing, or other cosmetic modification like Botox is allowed. Before the competition, the camels are kept out of the sun and fed a strict wheat, milk, honey, and dates diet.

Camels are not only about looks. They are also known for their ability to survive in harsh desert environments, extreme heat and cold. People often think camels' humps store water. This is factually incorrect. Camels are not able to store water. They do have the ability to survive without water for a long time. They can lose up to 30% of their body weight in water, far more than most other mammals. Whenever they have an opportunity to drink, they will gulp vast amounts of water down, enough to rehydrate themselves.

Their humps are made of fat. Their fat store can be converted into energy when they cannot access food in the desert. They also have heat-resistant pads on their feet and other body parts so they do not get burnt when sitting down for a break in the desert.

Camel meat has been a part of Emirati cuisine for centuries. It is considered a delicacy and holds cultural significance in the region. Oman was the place where I had my first taste of camel meat in an Omani restaurant with authentic Omani cuisine, next to the stunning opera house.

From the Middle East to North Africa and even parts of Asia, camel meat dishes have been a part of traditional cuisines for centuries. Camel meat is lean and slightly gamey, like beef, but with a unique twist.

I could not stop thinking about the camel in my stomach for the rest of the week. I felt guilty like I had eaten horse meat. I love my meat, but camel meat seemed somehow different. And no, I do not think I would eat horse meat. Some say Australian camel meat is better than the camel meat in the Middle East because their camels tend to be fatter and tastier. You will find camel milk in camel chocolate and soap, just two by-products. They make great gifts for friends at home.

Equestrian Elegance: A Deeper Look at Horses

Horses were introduced to the Middle East much later than camels by various invading armies and nomadic tribes, bringing a new mode of transportation and warfare. Horses quickly became prized for speed and strength, changing the region's travel and trade dynamics.

My passion for horses took root during my early years as a young girl. A quaint stable nestled in the heart of our village stood proudly next to the dunes bordering the coast of Holland. The irresistible allure of riding through the dunes and along the sandy stretches of the beach captivated me. Embracing the thrill of competition, I enthusiastically participated in dressage and jumping competitions from an early age. I used to come back home with cups and rosettes, proudly displaying my achievements. I would wear a button of my favourite horse pinned on my t-shirt, and my bedroom walls were adorned with horse posters. I would also read books about horses, including captivating stories about Arabian horses originating from the distant lands of the Middle East.

Little did I know that these stories would plant the seeds of curiosity. It is my earliest memory of the Middle East. Horses are in high demand in the racing sector. Holland is known for its great cows, but Holland is also a horse exporter. The Netherlands is the third largest exporter, after the UK and the US. The high demand for Dutch horses is because the breeds raised are considered high quality.[98]

Sheikh Mohammed bin Rashid Al Maktoum is a prominent figure in horse racing and equestrian sports. He is deeply involved in various equestrian ventures. He founded Godolphin, a global thoroughbred racing and breeding stable.[99] Godolphin has become one of the world's most successful and well-known racing stables. It operates in multiple countries and participates in major horse racing events worldwide.

Alongside Godolphin, His Highness Sheikh Mohammed Bin Rashid Al Maktoum also owns Darley Stud, one of the largest and most influential thoroughbred breeding operations globally.[100] The stud farm is responsible for breeding top-quality racehorses and stallions. His Highness Sheikh Mohammed Bin Rashid Al Maktoum is passionate about horses and equestrian sports. His interest in horses goes beyond business. He is said to have shared his love for horses with the late Queen Elizabeth II. Their shared interest in equestrian activities led to collaborations and interactions over the years, particularly in the context of horse racing and breeding. His racehorses have been consistent contenders at Royal Ascot, one of the UK's most prestigious horse racing events. The Royal Ascot meeting is renowned for attracting top racehorses, trainers, and owners worldwide.

I was privileged to attend Royal Ascot in the UK, a prestigious event steeped in tradition and elegance. I was fortunate to be invited to the Royal Enclosure, a desirable section at Royal Ascot reserved for those with an exclusive invitation. This honour traces its roots back to when the enclosure was a sanctuary for distinguished guests of the King himself. It is where the British social season comes to life. [101] Individuals mingle and share stories over champagne and afternoon tea with scones, cream, and strawberries on the immaculate green lawns. The atmosphere is one of refined luxury, with guests dressed in formal attire. The women wear beautifully decorated hats, adding to the delightful spectacle.

At Royal Ascot, there is also enormous excitement in the paddock area where the horses trot around. Horse enthusiasts and casual spectators congregate, keenly focused on the horses parading before them. Every nuance, every hint of strength, is meticulously assessed. The spectators evaluate the horses' form, their preferences for hard or soft ground, and other details which may contribute to them being a winner. The anticipation reaches its climax as bets are placed, with each bet serving as a testament to the belief in a chosen horse's ability to conquer the course. With mounting excitement, the races unfold, creating a spectacle of speed, power, and strategy. Cheering voices meet the thundering hooves as the contenders surge toward the finish line. The energy is palpable, creating a fusion of shared excitement and individual hopes.

Dubai has an iconic racetrack called Meydan. The grandeur of the establishment was undeniable, and my visit was a delightful experience. I wandered around the track, taking in the splendour of Meydan. As I soaked in the atmosphere and observed the majestic horses, I could not help but feel something was missing.

It was then that I realised the thrill of gambling was missing. In stark contrast to my experiences in other parts of the world, such as Royal Ascot in the UK, Meydan had no betting.

The anticipation that comes with placing a well-calculated bet was notably absent. I was surprised by this, as gambling is often seen as an integral part of horse racing. The Dubai government has emphasised promoting horse racing as a sport and a social event rather than a platform for betting. As the UAE has a predominantly Muslim population, and Islamic law prohibits gambling, the government has chosen to respect these cultural and religious norms by not incorporating gambling into the horse racing experience. Gambling is illegal in Dubai. As a result, there are no physical platforms available for horse race betting at Meydan. Yet behind the curtain of official restraint, I have been told gambling does take place online, removed from the public eye.

The Meydan racetrack is designed to offer a luxurious and world-class experience. The focus is on enjoying the races, socialising, and appreciating the beauty and athleticism of the horses rather than the gambling aspect. While gambling might not be a part of the horse racing experience at Meydan, the track still hosts high-profile races like the Dubai World Cup[102], one of the richest horse races in the world. Whether amidst the opulence of Meydan or the refined tradition of Royal Ascot, the essence remains the same – a celebration of equine majesty.

Although gambling has always been illegal, rules on gambling have recently been relaxed. Ras Al Khaimah has announced that Wynn Resorts, a luxury hotel and casino operator, will launch a new property on Al Marjan Island in 2026 featuring a "gaming area," paving the way for gambling. UAE's first legal casino is scheduled for 2027[103]. It will be 18,500 square meters, making it the largest in the world, further diversifying the UAE economy and catering, amongst others, to the Chinese.

In addition to Meydan Racetrack and the Dubai World Cup, I saw a fantastic production in Abu Dhabi, part of the 2014

Qasr Al Hosn Festival: Cavalia at Qasr Al Hosn, an equestrian production created by Normand Latourelle, one of the co-founders of Cirque du Soleil[104]. It was spectacular! My friend secured front-row seats right in front of all the action. The remarkable production showcased a dazzling array of talents, uniting 41 magnificent horses with 36 skilled riders, aerialists, acrobats, performers, and musicians. Against the stage's backdrop, the horses galloped with breathtaking grace, their hooves splashing through water, creating a symphony of movement and spectacle. The captivating performance held an allure that transcended mere equestrian admiration, inviting all, whether captivated by horses or not, to partake in its grandeur. I was particularly impressed by how the horses and riders worked together in such perfect harmony. The horses were well-trained and seemed to enjoy performing. The riders were skilled and athletic. The aerialists and acrobats were also exceptionally talented, and they added a touch of magic to the show. The music was excellent, helping to create a sense of excitement and wonder. The overall effect was magical, and I highly recommend Cavalia at Qasr Al Hosn when it is put on again.

My love for horses taught me how to play polo in Tidworth in 2002. I then spent time in Argentina, where I played at several farms and watched the famous Adolfo Cambiaso[105], one of the best polo players in the world, in action at the Palermo Open in Buenos Aires. The Palermo Open is one of the most prestigious polo tournaments in the world. It is held annually and attracts the best polo players. The tournament is played over two weeks in November and December, and the final is always a sell-out event. The Open Division is the highest level of competition, and it is made up of the best polo players in the world. I was even lucky enough to play a chukka with Salvatore Cambiaso, an accomplished polo player, at one of the farms I stayed at. It was an amazing time, and I became quite addicted to polo.

Therefore, I was thrilled to receive an invitation to a dinner party in Dubai, graciously extended through a Swiss business connection, Juliette. Like me, she has dual nationality – half-Swiss and half-British. We get along well, and I thoroughly enjoy her company. One of her friends hosted the dinner at an exclusive private residence in a gated villa, a sanctuary reserved for those fortunate enough to be part of the polo community. I was extremely grateful for the invitation and excited and keen to visit their stables.

As I stepped onto the grounds, I was greeted by a breathtaking panorama. The grounds were wonderful. Visiting the stables was an experience. They had around fifteen meticulously cared-for polo ponies. What struck me were the air conditioning units tirelessly humming day and night to maintain a cool and comfortable environment for these magnificent polo ponies. The upkeep of these prized ponies was a commitment beyond the ordinary, particularly in the scorching desert heat. I spent the evening enjoying the company of the newly introduced family. We talked about polo, business, and life in general. I learned about the polo community in Dubai and made new connections.

In polo, each player is assigned a handicap rating ranging from -2 to 10, with 10 being the highest skill level. The handicap rating is determined by a committee or organisation based on a player's proficiency, experience, and performance in previous matches. The handicap system allows for competitive games between teams of different skill levels without compromising fairness. To get to a handicap of ten, you must acquire exceptional ponies, necessitating considerable investment. A stable of powerful and agile horses is the key to unlocking the next echelon of achievement.

Reflecting upon my early years in Dubai, I recall being invited to a leisurely picnic on the Al Habtoor Polo Club grounds. The weather was perfect, and the grounds were breathtaking. I met new people and enjoyed the picnic. Polo is a great way to connect with people from all walks of life. It is a sport enjoyed by people of all ages and cultures. It reminded me of hanging out at Guards and Cowdray in the UK in my thirties. Guards Polo Club is in Windsor Great Park and Cowdray Polo Field in West Sussex, one of the UK's most beautiful places. The grounds are vast and green, and the polo field is immaculately maintained. I loved spending time there, taking in the scenery and the atmosphere.

Chapter 19.

Learn how to Haggle!

Upon moving to Dubai, asking for a discount was utterly foreign. I considered it improper and would have been mortified if I were shopping with a friend who dared to request a lower price. I have since developed a systematic approach to securing discounts. Learning how to negotiate is crucial to your survival in the Middle East. The best place to learn is at the souks.

Emma, CEO of a media company, explained that when she is keen on a product and believes the price is steep, she initiates the process by expressing genuine interest. She allows herself to be educated on the product. Then, she explains her rationale for deeming the price too high. Subsequently, she proposes a counteroffer, one she considers equitable, and remains poised to engage in further negotiations if necessary. In her negotiations, she found several phrases to be particularly effective. In a department store, she may ask, "Is there any room for flexibility in the price?" In a souk, queries such as "Could there be a discount for purchasing two items?" and "Can you improve upon this figure?" often yield positive results. The pivotal inquiry frequently follows these probing questions: "What would be your best price?"

Demonstrating a discerning eye by identifying imperfections or emphasising one's status as a returning customer are valid reasons for seeking a concession. Additionally, citing budget constraints can be a credible basis for requesting a more favourable deal. Her experiences in the vibrant souks of Dubai provided many opportunities for refining negotiation techniques.

She shared an amusing anecdote. While browsing in a high-end jewellery section at a prestigious London department store, she told her companion about "closing a deal" in the context of a business transaction they were orchestrating. To their surprise, their conversation caught the attention of a vigilant shop assistant who promptly extended a discount on a splendid diamond bracelet and ring she had admired. The term "deal" appeared to have been singled out, bypassing the rest of their dialogue. The assistant inferred a discount request, possibly influenced by Emma's friend's Middle Eastern appearance.

Emma also shared her shrewd insights into Dubai's jewellery scene. She advised me not to be overly fixated on the marked prices prominently displayed at Dubai Gold & Diamond Park or the renowned Gold Souk. Emma, a seasoned diamond enthusiast, taught me to always inquire about the best possible price. Once the phrase "I need to consult my supervisor" enters the conversation, she says you are close to coming to a deal.

Further enlightening me, Emma revealed an intriguing facet of Dubai's jewellery retail landscape. Behind the array of distinct shop names lies a revelation. Many of these establishments are owned by a select group of companies. They like customers to think there are many merchants, but they are in the hands of a couple of firms. It is like the washing powder brand in Europe. It seems the customer has a lot of choices, but the brands are in the hands of just a couple of large corporates.

This revelation underscores the convenience of not needlessly sifting through all the stores in pursuit of a superior deal. You will pretty much get the same pricing everywhere.

In Dubai's bustling and diverse marketplace, negotiation becomes a dynamic interplay, a dance of words and expressions. The journey towards acquiring an item, whether in the glittering halls of high-end stores or the labyrinthine alleys of traditional souks, transforms into a captivating tale of engagement, connection, and the pursuit of value. Each piece I own has its anecdote of my interaction with the tradesman. I have my favourites on WhatsApp, and I love it when they try to sell me more.

Chapter 20.

Religion and Law

Unveiling Dubai's Diverse Religious Landscape

Religion plays a significant role in people's lives, with Islam being the predominant faith. The GCC countries, including Saudi, UAE, Qatar, Bahrain, Oman, and Kuwait, uphold Islamic traditions and values. Books have been written on Islam for you to delve into. I will give you the basics. An Arab is any person who adopts the Arabic language. Most Arabs are Muslims, but many Muslims are not Arabs. Iran, for example, is a Muslim country but not Arab. They speak Persian, also referred to as Farsi. Around 23% of the world's population is Muslim. Interestingly, the country with the world's largest Muslim population is found in Indonesia.[106]

Arabic is the official and original language of the *Qur'an*, the Islamic holy book, and Muslims believe it to be the word of God, Allah, as revealed to the Prophet Muhammad. Muslims worship in a building called a mosque, and the most important weekly service is held on Friday at noon. When Muslims pray, which can be anywhere, they face Mecca in Saudi. Some Muslim men wear a small cap called a *taqiyah* when they pray.[107]

One of the first things you will hear about are Sunnis and Shias, two major branches of Islam. They both agree on the fundamentals of Islam and share the same Holy Book. However, differences arise, mainly from their distinct historical experiences, political and social developments, and ethnic composition. These differences arise from the question of who would succeed Prophet Muhammad as the leader of the emerging Muslim community after his passing. In summary, Sunnis believe the *caliphs* (leaders) who succeeded Muhammad were legitimate. In contrast, Shias believe that only the descendants of Prophet Muhammad, through his bloodline, specifically Ali ibn Abi Talib (Prophet Muhammad's cousin and son-in-law) and his descendants as spiritual leaders, are rightful successors. [108] There can be some debates between Sunnis and Shias about who is right or wrong.

Sunnis make up most of the Muslim population. Only about 10% of all Muslims are Shias, with most Shias in Iran, Iraq, and Bahrain.[109] Most Muslims do not allow their differences to divide them, but there can be animosity and polarisation between them. This can be a sensitive topic, and it is best to avoid it in conversation.

Practising Islam involves following the Five Pillars, which include:

1. *Shahada:* The Testimony of Faith, which is performed upon becoming a Muslim
2. *Salat:* Performance of the five daily prayers
3. *Sawm:* Fasting during the month of Ramadan
4. *Zakat:* Donating 2.5% of your income to people experiencing poverty and needy
5. *Hajj:* Once in your lifetime, if you are able, a pilgrimage to the Holy City of Mecca. [110]

It is recommended for believers to perform five daily prayers. These prayers are spread throughout the day and help Muslims connect with Allah and seek His guidance and blessings. It is a way for Muslims to find peace and spirituality in their daily lives. Remember that prayer times are fixed, and plan meetings and calls around these prayer times.

Mosques are not only places of worship but also serve as community centres. Prayer rooms can also be found in other public places, such as airports, train stations, and shopping malls. Religious practices and observances are deeply ingrained in everyday life, influencing everything from social customs to business practices.

Ramadan is a period of fasting and spiritual growth. It is like a marathon of fasting, lasting about a month, where Muslims show off their willpower and dedication. Muslims abstain from food and drink (even water) from dawn till sunset. However, they make up for it with feasts called iftars at sunset. Ramadan is also about giving back to the community through charity and kindness. Muslims are all about spreading love and compassion during this holy month. Avoid eating, drinking, or smoking during the day in front of someone who is fasting. In some countries, you can get arrested for this. The greeting to use is *"Ramadan Kareem."*

Expats may join in during Ramadan or set a personal goal to achieve. One year, I gave up coffee. Thinking of all those fasting gave me the strength to do so.

In the past, restaurants and coffee shops would be covered up. More recently, I have found it much less conservative in Dubai, and business continues as usual during Ramadan.

There is the Islamic New Year. "Happy New Hijrī Year!" is what you can say. Al-Hijra is the first day of the month of Muharram. It marks the Hijra (or Hegira) in 622 CE when the Prophet Muhammad moved from Mecca to Medina and set up the first Islamic state. It is a low-key event. Unlike the secular New Year, it is not a firework-filled fest. For those who observe it, the Hijrī New Year serves as an annual reminder of the passage of time, the rich history of Islam, and the resilience of Muslims.[111]

Other Islamic holidays include *Eid al-Fitr*, which marks the end of Ramadan, and *Eid al-Adha*, which involves the communal sacrificing and eating of animals to commemorate

Prophet Abraham's willingness to sacrifice his son. The dates for Eid al-Fitr and Eid al-Adha change each year, so checking when they occur before booking meetings is essential.

You will find the holidays go on forever, especially around Ramadan. If you try to do business, things will be slower than usual. Remember that fasting is a challenge. During the first week, people are usually still available for business, but you will find them less available as Ramadan continues. They may also attend iftars and socialise with friends and family, leaving everyone exhausted during the daytime.

Once, on a flight to Jeddah, the second largest city in Saudi, I suddenly noticed all the men were going into the toilets on the flight. They came out with just white towels wrapped around them. I was baffled by what was going on. It looked like a bachelor party. Also, I thought their outfits seemed inappropriate for Saudi. I had no idea. Then I learned this is what they wear when they go to Mecca on their pilgrimage, symbolising humility or purification. However, this is not a universal practice.

Every year, millions of Muslims from across the world journey to Mecca from wherever they live. Pilgrims may fly to Jeddah and then travel to Mecca by bus. Once they get to Mecca, there are two rituals which they can perform: the lesser pilgrimage or *Umra* and the main pilgrimage or *Hajj*.[112] Women are also allowed to perform the pilgrimage to Mecca, known as the Hajj, and no longer need to be accompanied by a male guardian. Today, women make up about 40% of all pilgrims to Mecca.[113] The Hajj is typically undertaken during *Dhu al-Hijjah*, the last month of the Islamic calendar.[114] The women have their section. I can see why. Mixing with men wearing only a white towel is not a good idea anywhere around the world.

Non-Muslims are not allowed to enter Mecca. Signs on the roads leading to Mecca warn non-Muslims not to do so. The signs also state that doing so is punishable by law. There are always rogues that break the rules. Construction workers may slip through the net. If a non-Muslim is caught entering Mecca, they may be arrested and deported.[115]

Saudi expects you to have a religion. So, if you are planning to travel there, make sure you embrace a religion. It does not matter which one, but you must have one. Atheism can be viewed as quite controversial and even taboo in the country. Most Saudis consider atheism incompatible with their cultural and religious values, leading to a negative view of atheists and even legal consequences. The same holds for agnostics, who believe that the existence of God or a higher power is unknown or unknowable but not excluded.

A management consultant, Sophie, made the mistake of being too particular on her first trip. She looked at the form but found nothing matching her religious convictions. The document listed Buddhism, Christianity, and another six or so religions. She ticked the "non-Muslim" box. She said the guy at the counter looked at her in horror and said, "No, no, you are Christian." Then, she discussed why she did not fit the Christian category, although she had attended a Christian school. She felt "non-Muslim" had more flexibility as a category to capture the full nature of her belief system. All his colleagues were staring at her and cringing. Sophie started to realise she may have said something wrong. This was not a conversation to be had at the visa application desk for Saudi. After he insisted she was Christian, she finally said, "Okay, fine, I guess you could say I am Christian. My value set is Christian."

She met up with a boyfriend who was a Middle East veteran. "Listen, Sophie," he said to her, "going to Saudi for the first time is not the right time to be stubbornly sticking to your principles. It is illegal to *not* have a religion in Saudi."

On her second trip to Saudi, Sophie had the same guy helping her at the visa counter. Once again, he asked her, "Religion?" she dutifully answered, "Christian."

Saudi follows a strict interpretation of Islamic law, which states all citizens must adhere to and publicly practice a religion. The government enforces this restriction, and those who openly declare themselves non-religious or atheist might face persecution, imprisonment, or even execution. In total, 43 countries punish blasphemy with imprisonment. In 22 countries, apostasy is criminalised; in twelve, it is punishable by death.[116]

Sophie wanted to document her adventures and took a photo of the Saudi Visa Application Section in Wafi Mall. A security guard promptly approached and politely asked her to delete the images. She learned taking photos of strategic and military locations, government organisations, or political buildings is illegal for security reasons.

You also should not take photos of people without their permission. Taking someone's picture without their consent is considered an invasion of privacy. So, no photos of women or families in public places. The UK Government on their website warns tourists that men have been arrested for taking photos of women on the beach.[117] Also, you cannot take pictures of accidents or even hang around places where accidents have happened.

The UAE is known for its open-mindedness and tolerance towards other religions. I have seen more Christmas lighting and decorations in Dubai than in London. The UAE does not miss any chance to celebrate and embrace diversity while seizing every commercial opportunity, including Christmas. One of the most expensive Christmas trees, costing around $11 million, was constructed in the centre of Emirates

Palace in Abu Dhabi in December 2010.[118] Every year, Emirates Palace still puts up one of the world's most impressive and luxurious Christmas tree displays.

Dubai's Legal Terrain: Constantly Evolving

Dubai's cultural norms and strict laws may differ from what expats and tourists are accustomed to in their home countries. They may not always be aware of all the local laws and regulations, which can inadvertently lead to trouble and legal issues. Dubai's legal framework is complex, and keeping up with the latest changes is difficult. Make sure you always double-check what anyone tells you. Dubai is known for its strict enforcement of laws, and violations can lead to severe consequences, including fines, legal action, or even deportation. The strict rules contribute to a safe environment, reducing crime and ensuring a high standard of living.

There are internet access and content restrictions, ensuring that communication and online interactions align with local norms and standards. The government blocks specific types of content, such as political discussions.

Dubai has laws prohibiting defamatory or damaging statements about all individuals, not only public figures. This applies to both locals and expats. You will not find expats in Dubai saying anything negative about the Rulers. Honour and respect in Arab culture are key factors in understanding the restrictions on harmful speech. Shame plays a significant role in Arab culture, and insults and criticism should be avoided at all costs as the family's honour should be defended. Engaging in slanderous or offensive speech can lead to legal consequences. Harmful or defamatory posts online can also result in legal consequences, so individuals must be cautious about what they share publicly.

Although it is against the law to protest, during COP28, the UAE will make "space available for climate activists to assemble peacefully and make their voices heard."[119] This is a positive development in terms of freedom of expression.

One friend asked me, "Can I leave a negative review about a restaurant in Dubai, or will I be sued?" According to my lawyer in Dubai, you will not be at risk of being sued unless it contains insults or swearing.

Swearing can land you in jail. It may also lead to deportation. In the UAE, swearing can be punished by up to three months in prison and a fine. If you are caught swearing, apologise immediately and explain you did not mean to offend anyone. If you are arrested for swearing, cooperate with the police – and do not argue.

Skype, Facetime and WhatsApp calling are blocked in Dubai for security reasons. Along with other internet restrictions, this can pose challenges for individuals who rely on these platforms for personal or business communication. WhatsApp texting is permitted. The prohibition of VPN usage can also limit options for bypassing these restrictions. One friend quoted Skype not working in Dubai as a reason for her not setting up a company there. I explained to her that while certain communication platforms like Skype, Facetime and WhatsApp (calling functionality) are restricted, alternative platforms like Zoom and BOTIM allow individuals and businesses to continue their online meetings and interactions.

You are free to do anything you want if it does not infringe on a third party's rights or cause public disorder. If you do the latter, you will get into trouble. Always remember you are a guest in the country.

Chapter 21.

Empowerment and Equality

Perception of the Middle East

Stereotypes and judgments often cast a narrow lens on both men and women in the Middle East, perpetuating misconceptions – and oversimplifications. Arab men are unfairly typecast as either terrorists, extravagantly wealthy Sheiks, or dictators.

This caricatured perspective is illustrated through a joke about a Middle Eastern student at Oxford. He wrote to his father that everything was great, but he did not feel comfortable travelling to his university in his golden Ferrari. He told his father that his fellow students, even his professors, travel by train. The next day, his father replied, "Sorry, son, I did not know. I transferred 20 million dollars to your account so you can buy yourself a train, too." This joke underlines the stereotype that everyone is wealthy in the Middle East.[120]

European women's views of Muslim men's behaviour vary widely. Some have positive experiences, describing Muslim men as respectful, kind and family-oriented. They appreciate the Muslim men's commitment to their faith. Others, however, have negative experiences, including harassment, or feel they are treated like second-class citizens.

A friend in London, Jane, said she was surprised at how friendly the people she met in the Middle East were on business. Before going to the Middle East, she did not expect anyone to be nice. She thought Islam meant no fun and a lack of spontaneity. After her trip, she called me full of excitement. She had so much fun and had countless stories to tell.

Negative portrayals in the media may contribute to stereotypes, portraying Muslim men as violent and oppressive. This can lead women to believe all Muslim men are dangerous and sexist. One business partner in the Middle East recalled being in Italy and noticing the women he was talking to were apprehensive and even scared of him. Their views were based on negative stereotypes about Islam or Muslims they had heard or seen on TV. He found that dressing in European clothing, which he did anyway out of respect for the Europeans, instead of turning up in his traditional dress, made an enormous difference when forging relationships.

Talking to women who have never been to the Middle East, they are sceptical. "When there is a headline in the newspaper about women being treated badly, it impacts my view on all countries in the Middle East. The headlines about Iran do not leave a good impression of women's treatment."

Women who have not been to the Middle East before may worry about being harassed or having trouble networking at conferences. Sonia, working for a hedge fund, said, "I travel for business on my own to conferences, but I would not feel safe travelling to the Middle East. The UAE may be the only exception." I felt safe travelling alone in the Middle East and had no issues travelling through the region and networking at conferences. Although unmarried, I always wore a wedding ring to avoid unnecessary attention in business.

Not all women are treated equally in the Middle East, and it does matter where you are from. When I was at the Euromoney Conference in Riyadh, Saudi, a Moroccan businessperson, Fatima, said she felt discriminated against. I asked her why. She had spent time in New York in investment banking and was worldly. Although she always referred to herself as French, the Saudis could tell she had Moroccan heritage. They, therefore, treated her differently and had different expectations. Fatima added, "Saudis think all Moroccan ladies are hookers." She decided to keep her head covered at the conference, even though all other women had their head scarf draped around their necks. Fatima's experience did not discourage her from travelling to the Middle East again. She continues to be successful and is doing a lot of business.

Women are often inaccurately depicted as veiled, oppressed, and subjected to abuse by their husbands. While it is true women in some Middle Eastern countries face certain challenges and restrictions, it is important to avoid generalisations. In Saudi, women were granted the right to drive in 2018, allowing them to go to work. This was a major victory for women's rights in the country.[121]

While certain countries in the Middle East still impose restrictions on women's movement and travel, and instances of domestic abuse persist, women are challenging the *status quo* and achieving remarkable progress. Governments and organisations in the Middle East are implementing policies to bolster women's rights and promote gender equality, allowing them to participate in society actively.

Women are increasingly pursuing education, entering the workforce, achieving financial independence and assuming more prominent societal roles. They are also setting up successful businesses. Today, women actively participate in politics, education, and business. They lead some of the largest companies in the region, with some also making their mark internationally.

Forbes Magazine publishes an annual list of the region's most powerful businesswomen[122], ranking the female leaders championing business success in the Middle East and beyond. Social media has proven to be a powerful tool, empowering women to share their experiences, voice their opinions, and raise awareness about gender inequality[123].

The UAE has made substantial strides in advancing women's rights. It has mandated that women must hold 50% of seats in Parliament[124] and wants listed companies to have at least one woman on their board.[125] There is still much to do to build gender diversity on boards and management levels.[126] Additionally, when women do have a seat at the table, they want their voices to be heard. However, they are not waiting for a seat at the table but building their own.

Initiatives also target education improvements for girls, elevated female representation in leadership roles, and addressing crucial issues like domestic violence. This shift reflects a broader momentum toward a more inclusive and equitable future for both men and women in the Middle East. Female political leaders are driving positive transformations within their communities.

There is no single "Middle Eastern woman." Women in the region come from different countries, cultures, and backgrounds. Their experiences and perspectives are diverse. It is also essential to understand that, like in Europe, not every woman wants a career. Many women, especially of the older generation, are perfectly happy in the home, looking after their family.

I recall an animated conversation with Salma, a Saudi businessman's wife, during a dinner at the magnificent Ritz Carlton Hotel in Riyadh. She asked me if I felt lonely being separated from my friends and family. She could not imagine leaving her family behind in Saudi to settle in a foreign country. Her devotion to her family was unwavering. She deeply yearned to spend every precious moment with her loved ones.

In Arab societies, the family is the foundation of society. It is the primary source of identity, support, and security. People are expected to put the needs of their families first, even before their own needs. In European societies, the family is not as central to people's lives as in Arab societies. People are more independent, and they are free to make their own choices about where to live and work. They are also more likely to move away from their families to pursue their goals.

The cultural difference in the importance of family can also be seen in how people raise their children. In Arab societies, children are expected to obey their parents and respect their elders. They are also taught to put the needs of their family first. In European societies, children are more likely to be raised with a sense of independence and self-reliance. They are also taught to be tolerant of different cultures and beliefs.

Not all women in the Middle East or elsewhere have career aspirations. In Dubai, *'Jumeirah Janes'* is a label attributed to expatriate women who invest their time in their families. The Jumeirah Janes are often portrayed as being wealthy and privileged. Some are simply women who have chosen to focus on their families and live a more leisurely lifestyle. Women would like to have the choice to stay home or work.

In conclusion, the global evolution of women's roles continues to shatter stereotypes and forge new paths of significant contribution across various sectors. We can focus on the negatives, but we should celebrate the progress. However, the ultimate destination remains far on the horizon.

It all starts with education. With the availability of education and the implementation of empowerment initiatives, the possibilities expand for women, enabling them to engage actively across all echelons of society. As the journey towards gender equality continues, it is evident that societies worldwide, including those in the Middle East, recognise the transformative potential of women's contributions. The ongoing evolution of women's roles is a testament to their resilience and a driving force behind positive change and progress.

What I found intriguing was an insight from a Dutch Ambassador, who revealed the Dutch Government intentionally appoints women to Ambassadorial positions in the Middle East. Women can engage with both the female and male segments of society. Moreover, certain male, ego-driven challenges are less of an issue with women. Other nations have adopted similar practices, recognising women's strengths in diplomatic and leadership roles. I also heard of private banks in London appointing women as relationship managers for the Middle East.

Social Hierarchies Unveiled: Pecking Order

Like anywhere else, Dubai has a social hierarchy or "class system." 85% of Dubai's population comprises expats from all over the globe. At the top of the order are Emiratis, who make up around 10-15% of the population. Emiratis are given special privileges, such as access to government jobs and education, and they tend to have a higher standard of living than expats. Within the Emirati community, there is also a pecking order, with Royal families and members of well-known tribes at the top.

People believe the local Emiratis are pampered, with generous perks to discourage political dissent. Like kids whose parents shower them with gifts, they may feel entitled, which can take away a sense of purpose. Others say they hold top positions while the expats do the work. This may be the case for some, but plenty of well-educated and motivated Emiratis are happy to roll up their sleeves.

The next tier comprises foreign nationals working in professional or managerial positions. These expats tend to be well-paid and have a comfortable lifestyle, but they are still considered outsiders by the Emirati. This group includes, for example, British, American, and European expats.

The third tier comprises Muslims from other Arab countries, followed by Muslims from non-Arab countries, including, for example, Pakistan. These expats are often seen as more culturally like Emiratis and tend to be treated more respectfully.

Manual labourers and service sector workers are at the bottom of the pecking order, mainly from Southeast Asia. You see many workers from India, Bangladesh, and the Philippines. These workers make up the majority of the UAE's total population. They often face discrimination and exploitation.

Sana shared two stories highlighting how the pecking order influences life in the UAE. A British man had a couple of drinks at a conference in Dubai. He called for his driver to take him home to his villa in Emirates Hills but then decided to drive himself. As he was backing out, he hit a pillar. He got out of his car to assess the damage and was ready to take responsibility, but the police officers who arrived did not want to blame him. Instead, they blamed the Philippine driver, who received a small fine and a suspended sentence.

Sana also told me a story about her father, a high-ranking man in Dubai. He dressed in simple, traditional clothing when praying on Fridays. Sana was meeting with him after prayers to go to a restaurant, but the restaurant turned him away because, based on his appearance, they thought he was a construction worker. "You cannot change a place, Sana," her father told her. "If you do not like it, you can leave, whether it is a restaurant or a country."

People's experiences are often shaped by their perceived social rank. It can be frustrating for those who feel they are not treated with the respect they deserve. Dubai is a rapidly changing city, and the pecking order is not set in stone.

The social hierarchy will become more fluid as the city becomes more diverse and cosmopolitan. However, it is also likely that social status will continue to play a role in daily life for many years.

Confronting a Global Issue: Domestic Violence

Whenever I am at a dinner party in Europe, someone at the table will bring up domestic violence and "honour killings," the murder of women deemed to have shamed either a specific man or their family by contravening societal norms and familial expectations. Men account for around 80% of all homicide victims worldwide. In the public sphere, women account for only one-tenth of all homicide victims. However, they bear a disproportionate burden regarding deadly violence within the home. In most of the killings committed by intimate partners or other family members, the victim is a woman or girl, which suggests the most dangerous place for women is the home.[127] Domestic and gender-based violence seriously affects women globally, including in the Middle East. We see reports of such incidents in Europe, too.

It is crucial to address this persistent problem through comprehensive global efforts involving legal reforms, awareness campaigns, support services for survivors, and education to challenge harmful gender norms. Governments, organisations, and activists worldwide work tirelessly to combat domestic violence and create safer environments for women.

While challenges persist, progress is being made to raise awareness, provide resources, and enforce laws protecting the rights and well-being of women. It is essential to have open conversations about these issues and support initiatives promoting gender equality and women's empowerment. By doing so, we can collectively create a world where all individuals, regardless of gender, can live free from violence and discrimination.

Domestic Staff and Construction Workers Protection

One individual from Sri Lanka, Amaya, who currently resides in London, shared with me her strong reservations about relocating to the Middle East due to concerns over the treatment of domestic help. She specifically pointed out the female workers from Sri Lanka who migrate to the Middle East to serve families. Many countries in the Middle East, she said, lack robust labour laws or regulations to safeguard the rights of domestic workers.

These workers sometimes find themselves exposed to exploitation and mistreatment by their employers. They depend on their employers for their livelihoods. Regrettably, this power imbalance sometimes leads certain employers to believe they can mistreat domestic workers. In certain cultural contexts within the Middle East, domestic workers are denied the same rights and safeguards extended to other workers. Domestic workers, often unable to communicate effectively in the local language or unfamiliar with local laws, become more susceptible to abuse and are often hesitant to report mistreatment due to fears of deportation.

I explained to Amaya that regional governments are taking note of these issues and are trying to address them.

For instance, in December 2022, Dubai introduced a new law for domestic workers. It grants them essential protections, including a minimum wage, a weekly rest day, paid annual leave, and the right to change employers. A dedicated hotline has also been established for domestic workers to report abuse or exploitation. This hotline is managed by the Ministry of Human Resources and Emiratisation (MOHRE).

Furthermore, Dubai offers various support services for domestic workers, including legal assistance, counselling, and housing aid. Dubai has extreme wealth, but it also has poverty.

Amaya also pointed to the construction workers and their poor living conditions, overflowing labour camps and people living in tiny rooms having to share the room and one shower with many people. Her husband joined the conversation, pointing to the reported deaths of migrant workers in Qatar during the World Cup. He added he had heard employers confiscate their passports, so there is no way for them to escape, and even if they could, they would not be able to afford a ticket to their home country.

Poverty exists everywhere around the world. I told him that Qatar had denied the reported deaths and told Amaya that Dubai has been introducing reforms and regulations to enhance workers' rights and conditions.[128]

This includes measures to improve accommodation, wages, and access to healthcare for migrant workers. Efforts have also been made to improve transportation for construction workers, especially during extreme weather conditions. Providing air-conditioned buses and ensuring mandatory breaks during hot weather are positive steps toward safeguarding workers' well-being. Dubai has implemented labour laws and regulations to protect workers' rights, including provisions for minimum wages, working hours, leave, and other benefits.

While Dubai and the UAE have taken steps to reform the *kafala* sponsorship system, which has been criticised for enabling potential exploitation and abuse, aspects of this system still exist. It ties workers' residency permits to their employers, creating vulnerabilities.

Critics argue that labour practices, such as recruitment fees paid by workers to secure employment, can lead to debt bondage and exploitation. Workers may become trapped in unfavourable conditions due to financial obligations. Despite improvements, there are concerns about enforcing labour regulations and monitoring mechanisms' effectiveness to ensure compliance. Cases of contract violations and delayed payments have been reported. While Dubai has established labour courts to address disputes, workers, mainly migrant workers, may face challenges accessing these channels due to language barriers, lack of awareness, or fear of reprisals.

I told Amaya and her husband ongoing challenges are being addressed. I agreed with them that continued reforms, increased transparency, and a solid commitment to workers' rights are crucial to ensuring fair and ethical labour practices in the Emirate.

Chapter 22.

The Future and Security of Dubai

Powering the Future

Dubai is a marketing powerhouse, skilfully weaving dreams into reality. I vividly recall standing on my apartment terrace, gazing at the horizon, and gesturing towards the ongoing construction sites to my friends visiting Dubai. "There," I said, "that is where the opera house will be!" I turned to them, excitement in my voice. "You do not see it yet, do you? You only see a construction site, don't you?" They nodded in agreement.

Dubai has a unique talent for enticing you to invest in its future, providing visual glimpses of what is coming through posters on building facades. They sell you a brighter future. One of Dubai's recent landmarks is the Museum of the Future[129] in the Financial District. The museum boasts an architectural design in the shape of a human eye. It is a structure for a visionary city. The building is an accomplishment. It has no conventional corners and no columns. It has recreated the experience of a cosmic voyage featuring a space station.

Dubai's ability to market itself as a prime tourist destination sets a remarkable example for the world to follow. The city's ability to create focal points, from the Burj Khalifa to the Palm, engages visitors and tells a compelling narrative of growth and innovation. Every visitor is a potential marketeer — their snapshots, shared with friends and family, shape perceptions. Dubai's stunning architectural marvels, particularly the Burj Khalifa, have become iconic symbols captured through countless lenses. It is one of the most photographed buildings in the world.

Border Security and Order

The UAE has avoided terrorist attacks and civil unrest in recent years. I cannot recall a single incident in my ten years in the UAE. It has implemented an effective approach to border security and handling civil unrest. The UAE is always aware of risks and continues allocating resources to strengthen its security forces and intelligence network. The UAE's security and safety are essential priorities for the government, and it will continue to invest in its security forces and intelligence network to protect its citizens and residents.

The UAE has several key entities maintaining security and safety, such as the Council for National Security, Ministry of Defence, Ministry of Interior, local police authorities, Civil Defence, Ports, borders and free zones, and the National Crisis and Emergency Management Authority (NCEMA).[130] These forces are responsible for preventing and responding to crime while protecting critical infrastructure and government facilities.

The UAE military is one of the most advanced in the Middle East. It has a strong air force, navy, and ground forces. It is also well-equipped with modern weapons and technology to defend against any threats to its borders. The armed forces are one of the leading militaries in the region.[131] The priorities and performance of the UAE military highlight its government's goals to protect the country's role and influence and develop itself as a force within the broader region.[132]

The UAE also has a sophisticated intelligence network capable of gathering and analysing information, using AI, regarding potential threats to the country's security, enabling the government to mitigate risks proactively. This intelligence network prevents terrorist attacks and other crimes within the UAE.

A large and visible police force helps to deter crime and make people feel safe. Police officers in the UAE are visible in cars, horses, and motorbikes. This police presence has undeniably made people feel safe.

Charting the UAE's Path Forward

The UAE is seen as a stable country with a strong government. The key to prosperity for any society, regardless of its form of government, is the ability to protect its borders and wealth from external threats, including military ones. It is also crucial for a society to manage and control internal power struggles to prevent them from escalating into civil war. A smooth transition of power to the next leader is of utmost importance. Without a successful transition of power, a society risks the destruction of its wealth and resources. Additionally, a society can face existential damage without a solid military to guard against outside interference.

The future of the UAE will depend on the choices made by its rulers and whether they can maintain the country's stability and prosperity.

Saudi versus UAE: The Battle for the Future

Some argue that the UAE and Saudi are two ambitious and dynamic economies in the Middle East on course for collision. Both countries are investing heavily in innovation, infrastructure, and tourism. Which country is better positioned to succeed in the long run?

The UAE has been positioning itself as a testbed for innovation. The Emirate is strategically located in the heart of the Middle East. It is a central hub for trade and commerce between Europe, Asia, and Africa. This prime location has made it an ideal destination for businesses looking to expand their reach globally. Dubai has been smart about diversifying its economy. It could not rely on oil revenues like Abu Dhabi.

Abu Dhabi is also diversifying. They have invested heavily in tourism, real estate, finance, and logistics. The government has done a fantastic job creating an environment that attracts local and foreign investors with tax incentives and streamlined procedures. They have made it super easy for companies to set up shop.

The UAE, including Dubai, is currently experiencing boom times. Dubai is constantly evolving and pushing boundaries, with impressive skyscrapers, luxurious hotels and restaurants continuously popping up. Moreover, the startup community is thriving. Is Dubai about to embark on its Golden Age with its best years ahead? Or will the UAE be taken over by Saudi, which has ambitious plans?

Saudis used to go to Dubai for pleasure. This is changing. Saudis can go to London, Geneva, and Paris and now find entertainment on their doorstep in Riyadh.

Saudi has advantages. The country has a large population and a young workforce, which is precisely why it is under pressure to create jobs and a future for the new generation.

It is not all oil and desert in Saudi. It has natural attractions, such as the Red Sea and the mountains of the Tabuk region, which not many people know about. It also has mountains with snow, where the Winter Olympics will be hosted in 2029. As Saudi is pushing to diversify its economy and reduce its reliance on oil, as outlined in Vision2030[133], it is finding itself in direct competition with the UAE.

Saudi is also looking to attract tourists. Technology centres are being established, and it is challenging Dubai as a logistics hub. It intends to provide experiences to attract tourists. Like Dubai, Saudi is launching enormous projects. For example, with construction underway, they are building a super ambitious USD1 trillion project called NEOM, creating a cutting-edge, futuristic city from scratch.

One of NEOM's first projects is "The Line" in the Tabuk Province. This is an incredibly ambitious initiative to redefine urban living by creating a new futuristic city, prioritising sustainability, connectivity, and quality of life. Designed as a 170-kilometre linear development, like a big glass and mirrored wall. It plans to house up to nine million people. There will be no cars, no streets, and no carbon emissions. The plan is to power the city entirely with renewable energy. It will be showcasing Saudi's commitment to innovation and progress.

Like Dubai, Saudi has made it easier for foreigners to obtain visas to attract expats and tourists. It has set a target to increase tourism's contribution from 3% to 10% of GDP and attract 100 million visitors to Saudi by 2030. It recently announced the launch of two new airlines: Riyadh Air and Neom Airlines.

India is Saudi's number one target market. A cricket federation has been established in anticipation of their arrival. Saudi considers tourism a catalyst for other industries to flourish. Connectivity, therefore, is essential.

If you pitch for lucrative government contracts in Saudi, you must establish your regional head office there[134]. A couple of exceptions to this rule have been made, according to an article in The National[135]. It has been rumoured that around 500 companies have already moved their regional headquarters from elsewhere in the region to Saudi.[136]

The Saudi population of over 30 million people currently makes up over 50% of the GCC population. More expats are expected to move to Saudi. Dubai's single-digit corporate tax[137] is still lower than Saudi's double-digit corporate tax rate. However, Saudi is offering tax exemptions. Dubai's Jebel Ali port has competition coming its way. Saudi has unveiled its first integrated economic zone, which gives companies a tax exemption for up to 50 years.

Despite all the privileges offered by Saudi, the UAE is still the location of choice for the headquarters of many international companies. As well as favourable laws, the UAE is preferred for its openness and its easy visa policies, as well as its entertainment, which allows alcoholic beverages, parties, and other advantages Riyadh does not yet offer in the same way.

Some say Saudi cannot afford to be as liberal and open as Dubai. It may allow bikinis, but only on designated expat beaches. Dubai is still the major transportation hub connecting Europe, Asia, and Africa. The UAE and Saudi's success will depend on attracting foreign investment. The UAE has a head start in this regard, but Saudi is changing to make it more attractive to foreign investors.

As the Saudi economy strengthens, the UAE economy will also strengthen. Relocating several regional companies to Saudi will not harm the UAE economy much. Thousands of companies will maintain their presence in Dubai, which is still considered the financial and business centre in the Middle East. They will open regional headquarters in Riyadh to keep up with Saudi laws, but it will be an expansion, not a transfer.

I would compare it to Hong Kong versus China. Although it may be best for business in China, many would rather live in Hong Kong. The key difference between Saudi and the UAE is that Dubai allows alcohol.

So, which country is better positioned to succeed in the long run? It is too early to say for sure. Dubai and Saudi both have ambitious plans. It will be interesting to see how each country achieves its goals. The more significant trend is the Middle East versus the rest of the world.

In the Fire of Capital

PART II

DOING BUSINESS IN THE MIDDLE EAST

In the Fire of Capital

Chapter 23.

My Business in the Middle East

In 2003, I founded a placement agent business and initially assisted fund managers in raising capital, but later expanded to include private companies. The services also included advising on marketing materials, conducting dry runs with management teams to help them optimise their investor pitches, rehearsing potential investor Q&A, and developing strategies for targeting appropriate investors.

I am constantly expanding my network. This involves maintaining existing relationships, attending conferences, and cold calling. I enjoy networking, and it comes naturally to me.

From an early age, I was already networking beyond borders, even though I did not know what "networking" meant. When I was six years old, after meeting everyone at my school, I started hanging out with kids from the school next door, leaning over the hedge separating us. Soon after, I cycled an hour to attend a party at another school further down the road.

I created a business out of networking, and my talent for connecting people, backed up by deep knowledge of the markets and industry sectors, picked up over the years working in investment banks in London. Although my core focus has been introducing investors to investment funds and private companies, I also worked in business development, selling technology solutions.

I have also been involved in M&A transactions, which is different from raising capital for a company. In an M&A transaction, the shareholders of a business want to sell the company or buy another company. If there is a buyer and a seller, there is potential business to be done. This business can be done anywhere in the world.

Placement agents are crucial in connecting companies and investment funds with potential investors. They work tirelessly behind the scenes to bridge the gap between companies seeking capital and investors looking for promising investment opportunities. By leveraging their extensive networks and industry expertise, placement agents are vital in helping businesses secure investment, propelling their growth and success.

Investors often do not realise how much work a placement agent has put into a transaction. It is not only about connecting two parties. It may sound easy to connect a buyer and a seller, but there can be a lot of challenges, especially when the selling cycle takes a long time. There are many stories about what can go wrong during a transaction.

The Middle East adds a layer of complexity. There is no issue for women to pitch in the Middle East, and speaking Arabic is unnecessary. The allocators are often a mix of expats and locals, with Chief Investment Officers and analysts being expats and the final decision maker at the top being a local. However, other cultural issues can make closing transactions in the Middle East challenging.

Chapter 24.

Dress for Success

The first question any woman needs answered is what to wear for the occasion. Saudi was the only place where I needed to wear an abaya. I always stuck to black to be on the safe side. To add a dash of colour, I would wear my Hermes scarf. I did not want to be mistaken for a local. The expat men are not required to wear the local dress code, a dish dash, for business meetings in the region. I could not help but feel they were missing out. I had so much fun shopping for an abaya. I understand why the local women are proud to wear their abayas.

I remember being in Dubai Mall and chatting with an elegant Saudi lady in a high-end furniture shop. She introduced herself as Rasha. I told her I was going to Saudi for the first time and wanted to ensure my abaya was appropriate. I asked her advice on shops offering high-quality abayas suitable for a professional setting. She smiled warmly and imparted her wisdom with a touch of humour: "Men are the same all over the world. They barely notice what you wear."

Following her suggestions, I explored a couple of her recommended stores. I will never forget my experience shopping for abayas at a boutique in Dubai Mall. The designer guided me in selecting the perfect abaya; his expertise and attention to detail were impressive. I took the time to learn about abayas' different styles and designs and found one I felt comfortable and confident in. Once you explore the abayas, you will discover a wide range of designs. As an outsider, you might initially assume they are all the same black togas. However, there is a significant difference in the materials' quality. They felt like ball gowns to me, so elegant.

I was so impressed by the designs – and the service. I returned to the boutique to purchase more abayas. Over time, my collection expanded to include a variety of styles. I had one abaya specifically for air travel, with a convenient throw-over style and snug sleeves to avoid entanglements, an issue I learned about when lifting my suitcase into the baggage compartment in the aeroplane. Another abaya, adorned with sparkling black Swarovski crystals down the front, became a cherished favourite for evening outings.

Similarly, an American expat friend in Saudi loved the abaya, emphasising its remarkable practicality. She told me how she would throw her abaya over her pyjamas when taking her children to school in the morning!

I am so grateful for the opportunity to have experienced the beauty and diversity of Middle Eastern culture through the abaya. They can be both practical and stylish. They are a way to cover up and express oneself and one's cultural identity.

Originally, the abaya was a simple and practical garment designed to provide modesty and protection from the harsh desert environment. It was often made from lightweight fabrics like cotton or linen, allowing for breathability in hot climates. Over time, it evolved both in terms of design and cultural significance. It became more elaborate, with intricate embroidery, beading, and ornamental details. Different regions developed their unique styles of abayas, reflecting local customs and traditions.

For example, abayas in Saudi are typically black and long, with a loose fit. They may be made from cotton, silk, or polyester. Some abayas have intricate embroidery or beading. Abayas in the UAE are like Saudi ones but may be more colourful and elaborate. Some abayas have gold or silver threadwork. In Qatar, they are often made from high-quality materials, like silk or cashmere. They may be decorated with lace or other embellishments. Abayas in Oman are typically long and loose, made from cotton or silk, with a plain design.

Recently, interest in the abaya as a fashion statement has been resurgent. Today, you can find abayas tailored to individual preferences with diverse colours, patterns, and cuts. High-end designers in the Middle East and Europe make elaborate abayas. They can be costly. The marriage of luxury and tradition, evident in these intricate pieces, showcases the abaya's transformation from a modest protective garment to a canvas for artistic ingenuity and self-expression.

There are different dress codes in Saudi, depending on the city. Jeddah is a more relaxed city than Riyadh regarding the dress code for women. At the same time, I would wear my abaya with the long headscarf draped around my neck in Jeddah. I would only cover my hair when visiting government entities in Riyadh.

Visiting the Saudi Aramco compound in Dammam was a surreal experience. The entrance protocol was particularly striking. At the gate, I was required to take off my abaya. Fortunately, I was aware of this and wore a business suit underneath. Everyone inside the Saudi Aramco building was dressed in Western clothing. Then, when leaving, I could put on my abaya again. It was windy, so wearing the abaya was a relief and protected me from the desert sand being swept up by the winds. Saudi Aramco's expat compound was not an anomaly but representative of a broader trend.

In Saudi, expats often reside in Western compounds, where a more relaxed dress code prevails. Another lesson is always to ensure the clothing under your abaya is presentable in case you are required to take the abaya off.

I was invited once to a private party at the villa of a prominent Saudi family outside of Riyadh. I was the only woman there, unsure if taking my abaya off was appropriate. I had dressed conservatively underneath. It was still hot, even at night, and I wanted to take the abaya off. However, I did not want to make a *faux pas* by taking off my abaya without being sure if it was okay. I was too shy to ask the host, so I kept my abaya on, though it was uncomfortable. Luckily, after the drinks in the garden, dinner was served indoors. At the end of the evening, the host said, "I had told Abdullah this evening would be casual." I was unsure if he was referring to my long glamourous earrings or my abaya, but I think he was trying to tell me I could have taken it off.

During my time in Iran, the dress code required me to adhere to stricter regulations than in Saudi. While an abaya was not obligatory, a headscarf was a non-negotiable part of my attire. Long jackets from Dutch designer Pauw, falling above the knee, became my staple. Paired with black trousers, this ensemble balanced modesty and modernity while keeping my style. To avoid ambiguity and convey my status as a visitor, I would tie a Hermes scarf around my neck in addition to the headscarf. It made me feel confident and put together. One person commented, "You look more official than the government officials in Iran." I took it as a compliment.

There is a diversity of opinions and perspectives on the dress code in Iran, and not everyone agrees with the strict regulations. In the evenings in restaurants, young people are often more likely to push boundaries and challenge the *status quo*. I noticed young girls rebelliously revealing more of their bodies than they should, provoking the local police.

In all other countries in the GCC, I would wear a loose-fitting black trouser suit and match it with my Hermes scarf. I would keep my makeup light and use natural-coloured nail polish, avoiding bright colours. I would always bring my Prada handbag to meetings, as I had been told it was necessary to show success in emerging markets. I had not thought about it before, but designer goods are desirable in countries with high levels of economic inequality. They can be a way to show you have achieved a certain level of success.

On the flight from Riyadh to Dubai, I would see younger Saudi women go to the bathroom in an abaya and come out in flashy European clothing. This is a clear example of how women can use clothing to express themselves differently in different contexts. With stricter dress codes in Riyadh, these women may feel more comfortable and obliged to wear an abaya. However, they seemed to prefer wearing European clothing on the flight to Dubai.

Chapter 25.

Setting up for Business

Finding and Keeping Employment

I run my own business, but I often get asked how to find a job in Dubai. While many places prioritise merit and candidates' skills, personal connections play a significant role in Dubai. Securing a job often depends on knowing someone within a company who can vouch for you. This networking-based approach can benefit those with friends or relatives working in reputable organisations.

If you have no connections and are looking for a job in Dubai, your best bet is to come to Dubai with a pack of resumes and start knocking on doors in person. Go to the free conferences and networking events. In parallel, you can use online job boards and contact recruitment agencies. The salaries in the UAE are like those in Europe, but the lack of income tax is a huge benefit, as income tax back home can be as much as 40% or more. There are indirect taxes, such as VAT, on consumption. However, you need to factor in the cost of living in Dubai, which may be higher than in other countries.

Emiratis put importance on education and often pursue their studies in the US and Europe. The focus on education is made clear in a quote by His Highness Sheikh Mohammed Bin Rashid Al Maktoum: "Education is the cornerstone of progress and the key to unlocking human potential. Investing in youth is investing in the future of our nation."[138]

A degree from a renowned European or US institution signifies a standard of excellence in education and enhances one's prospects of securing a desirable employment opportunity. This sentiment extends to their recruitment practices, as Emiratis often prefer individuals with degrees from reputable institutions in Europe or the US. These institutions are seen as more rigorous and demanding than their counterparts in other parts of the world. As a result, graduates from these institutions are often considered to be more competent and well-rounded.

In the past, there were cases of fraudulent practices in Dubai. It was uncovered that some expats were obtaining fake degrees. The government subsequently cracked down on such activities in 2019 with new regulations imposing imprisonment or penalties if caught faking degrees.[139] This is a positive step, as it will help to ensure that only genuine degrees are accepted in the UAE.

Not all Emiratis are automatically impressed by a degree from a Western university. They will still want evidence of your skills and experience and ensure you fit the company culture well. However, a degree from a reputable institution can undoubtedly give you a leg up in the job market in Dubai.

When you go for an interview, companies may require evidence of your wife's consent to relocate to the Middle East. To assess her willing acceptance of the move to the UAE, the company may arrange a visit for her to explore the city, residential areas, and schools. This allows for a thorough evaluation to ensure she will enjoy the relocation. The hiring company is concerned that the wife may become miserable once the family moves over and asks her husband if they can return home.

Regarding pay, the best jobs are government jobs, where Westerners are mostly treated well. Western corporates, the brand names setting up branches, are next, followed by Indian companies, which tend to pay the least. Indian companies are often smaller and have less money to spend. For example, an Indian analyst getting paid AED7,000 monthly at an Indian-run company could upgrade to AED25,000 for the same job at a Western company.

People often are paid what the employer thinks the employee needs. The commonly held view is that women do not need the money versus men who must look after a family. Charlotte, unmarried, works for a family office. She explained that women structurally get paid less than men in the Middle East. A man with 5 children will most certainly get paid more than an unmarried woman even if they have the same job. She told me there was even an official cap on pay to women in her firm.

She said it is hard to increase your salary in a family office setting, which leads to high turnover in staff as people feel the only way to get a promotion is to switch companies.

Sylvia, the CFO of a retail company, informed me you have a lot of holidays. When she joined the company, her boss had clarified that although her contract stated she had 30 days of holiday, the actual number was closer to 90 days. He explained, "You will not be doing any work when I travel, and nothing happens during Ramadan. That is an additional 60 days on top of your 30 days."

A mistake you should avoid when taking a job in the Middle East is thinking the company is unsophisticated and that you will tell them how things work in Europe. Companies in the Middle East are not unsophisticated. Each company will have its own culture and way of doing things. Be respectful of the company's culture and be willing to learn about their way of doing things. If you come in with the attitude that you know better than everyone else, you will not succeed.

Be patient. It takes time to build relationships and to make a difference. Do not expect to change everything overnight. Start by quietly settling in and getting to know the people. Then, after a few months, you can offer value-added direction. Remember that you will never be in charge. The social contract is that you are paid well, but you must understand that you will always be an advisor to the locals, not a decision-maker.

Your ability to live and work in a foreign country often hinges on sponsorship and a visa. Unfortunately, individuals are often at the mercy of their sponsors, allowing employers to exploit their power and mistreat employees. Although not all sponsors are bad, I have heard complaints. Employees often do not dare to complain and accept much more than they otherwise would because they risk being fired. And when you get fired in Dubai, you will have to leave the country if you do not find a new job soon after. In the UAE, an employer will cancel the employee's work permit once the employee is terminated or resigns. In the past, this meant you needed to leave the country immediately. These days, you can reside in the UAE for up to 60 days without exiting the UAE.

Choosing the Right Business Structure

Before you start setting up a business in the UAE, do your research. Several types of companies can be registered. You must decide whether to register a free zone, mainland, or offshore company.

Free zone companies are in special economic zones, separate from mainland Dubai. They offer a variety of benefits, such as 100% foreign ownership and relaxed visa requirements. Free zone companies are typically cheaper to set up than mainland companies. However, free zone companies are not allowed to trade with the UAE, so they are only suitable for businesses operating internationally.[140] In the past, if you wanted complete control over your company, setting up in one of Dubai's free zones was the way to go. These zones, located in special economic zones, were created by the government to attract foreign businesses looking for 100% ownership. More than 30 free zones are operating in Dubai. Free zones have been created around industries. For example, DIFC (Dubai International Financial Centre) caters to the financial industry.[141] A joke amongst expats is that DIFC stands for Dubai International Food Court because of its many restaurants.

Free zones have relaxed visa requirements. People previously set up a company solely to obtain a residency visa. People used to set up business in a free zone and then do business across the UAE. They would even contract with the government. The service providers tell them this is fine, and the government looks the other way. It may be fine today but could be used against you.

Mainland companies are located on the mainland and are subject to all UAE laws and regulations. They are more expensive to set up and operate than free zone companies, but they have the advantage of being able to trade with the UAE. Mainland companies are also more suitable for businesses targeting the local market. In 2020, the UAE scrapped them for a UAE national to sponsor a mainland company. Expats can have 100% ownership of mainland companies, making it a more appealing option. Abu Dhabi and Dubai released a list with over 1,000 activities allowed 100% foreign ownership.[142] Reasons for not opting for a Mainland company with 100% control would be because the activity is not on the Permitted activities list, deemed an activity with "strategic impact," and therefore ineligible for 100% foreign ownership.

Emirati partners must own at least 51% of the shares in specific industries like banking and insurance. Regardless of the new rules, you may decide it is operationally and strategically beneficial to set up your business with a UAE shareholder. Offshore companies are not subject to UAE laws or regulations. They are typically used for holding assets or intellectual property.

Offshore companies are not suitable for businesses wanting to trade in the UAE. To operate a business in the UAE, you must apply for the necessary permits and licenses.

Which structure is best for you will depend on your business activities. If you target UAE mainland clients, then a mainland company is the best option. A free zone company may be better if you are only interested in operating internationally. Additionally, if you want to hold assets or intellectual property offshore, you may want to go with an offshore company. Once you have obtained the necessary permits and licenses, you must open a bank account for your business. This will allow you to receive payments from customers and make payments to suppliers.

Opening a bank account cannot be taken for granted. The UAE is possibly the only country where service providers ask for a fee to set up your bank account. If you need to hire employees, you must obtain the necessary work permits and visas from the government. The process for obtaining work permits and visas can be complex.

I merely provide a high-level glimpse of the possibilities as a starting point. Once you have done your research, you should consult a qualified advisor before setting up a company in the UAE to help you navigate the legal and regulatory landscape and ensure your company is set up correctly. I would advise you to get quotes from multiple advisors before deciding which route to take. There are factors to consider, and the wrong choice could have serious consequences for your business.

Finding a qualified advisor can be challenging. Some are more qualified than others. Ask for recommendations from colleagues who have set up businesses in the UAE. Ensure the advisor you choose has experience setting up the type of business you plan. Get everything in writing, including the fees, the timeline, and the services provided. Make sure their quotes are all-inclusive.

Nathalie, a florist, shared an experience where her company received written advice from an advisor stating they could use their company to do a certain commercial transaction. However, when they started trading, the advisor did a complete U-turn and said they could not use the company for that purpose. This happened after the advisor had previously said it was fine.

Advisors may promise quick turnaround times, but it always takes longer, especially when setting up a bank account.

Melissa, a high-end jewellery designer, had a similar experience. When she set up a company in one of the Emirates, her advisor told her she needed to file a particular document immediately at a high cost to avoid being fined an even higher amount. However, when she read the law, she thought the filing did not apply to her. She called the Emirate direct, and they confirmed it was not mandatory. She felt the consultant had been extorting her into paying for an unnecessary service. Melissa explained that there is a high turnover in staff. The advisors are not always up to speed. If something does not sound right, it helps to read the laws yourself and verify the information you are given. You should always contact the relevant authorities directly if you have any concerns.

Doing business across the Emirates can be complex and costly. Setting up in one Emirate does not allow you to conduct business in all the other Emirates. Each Emirate requires a specific license for each business activity. Michelle, who set up an assembly plant in one of the Emirates, received an order from a company in another Emirate. She thought she could use the company truck to deliver the goods to the buyer, but it would not be that simple. She discovered that she was only allowed to deliver the goods using a truck registered in the Emirate of the buyer. Companies set up an additional six companies, with empty offices, in each Emirate to enable business across the UAE.

Embracing Emiratization: Workforce Diversity

'Emiratization' is a term used to describe increasing Emirati nationals 'participation in the UAE workforce. It is a strategic initiative to promote sustainable economic growth and ensure citizens can access employment opportunities within their country. The goal is to eventually reduce reliance on expatriate workers and build a skilled and diverse local workforce. In other GCC countries, similar policies are called by different names, such as Saudization, Qatarization, Kuwaitization, Bahrainization, and Omanization.

Through various policies, programs, penalties and incentives, Emiratization aims to empower Emiratis by providing them with education, training, and job opportunities across different sectors. The National newspaper reported, "Companies with 20 to 49 employees who fail to employ at least one Emirati in 2024 will face a fine of Dh96,000."[143]

Emiratization has been met with mixed reactions by the expat business community. The government believes it is necessary to protect Emirati citizens' interests and ensure they have a stake in the country's economy. Others think it is unfair to discriminate against expats. Emiratization has positively impacted the Emirati workforce in Dubai and has created opportunities for Emiratis to gain valuable work experience and develop their skills.

It has created challenges for businesses setting up, as they may have to pay higher salaries to Emirati employees and provide additional benefits. Not all Emiratis have the skills and experience required for jobs in the private sector. The government has traditionally offered most employment opportunities for Emiratis in the public sector, which do not require the same skills and experience. As a result, some Emiratis are not prepared for the demands of the private sector. Therefore, Emiratization can be expensive as Emiratis must be trained for private-sector jobs.

One CEO preferred to hire foreign workers as they are often cheaper and more willing to work long hours. He said it can be expensive to train nationals for jobs in the private sector, as they require workers with skills and knowledge. He felt the government should invest in programs to train Emiratis for employment in the private sector or provide more support to businesses hiring Emiratis, such as providing subsidies.

Not all Emiratis want to work in the private sector. Some prefer government jobs, which are considered more sociable. Despite these challenges, Emiratization is a necessary step for the UAE to achieve its goal of becoming a knowledge-based economy. By increasing the participation of Emiratis in the private sector workforce, the UAE can build a more skilled and diverse workforce, better equipped to compete in the global economy. Many examples of hard-working, successful Emiratis are now in the private sector.

There is a divide between the older generation and the younger Emiratis, often educated abroad. An Emirati man in his early 30s returned to the UAE after studying in the US and working in Germany for many years. He had adapted to the direct communication style of his German colleagues and was surprised to find that this was considered too blunt back in his home country. He often clashed with his Emirati colleagues and superiors in his first job. He would be told he was disrespectful, even when simply trying to be direct and efficient. Emirati style is more indirect in the UAE. He faced a period of readjusting. Instead of firing him, which was not an option, his boss moved him to another department. This happened several times.

I can relate to his experience. When I first arrived in the UAE, I felt like an elephant in a porcelain cabinet, akin to how I felt when I moved from the Netherlands to Belgium. I can be quite noisy and enthusiastic. I had to tone myself down. I first observe people to find out where the boundaries are and how things work. Once I establish what is acceptable and what is not, I revert to operating within the limits.

Chapter 26.

Banking Hurdles

The head office of the Central Bank, the primary financial regulator of retail and wholesale banks, is in Abu Dhabi. The Regulatory authority in DIFC (Dubai International Financial Centre) is called the Dubai Financial Services Authority (DFSA), and the regulatory authority in Abu Dhabi Global Market (ADGM) is called the Financial Services Regulatory Authority (FSRA). In the UAE, deposits are not insured, but in the past, the government has intervened to ensure depositors did not suffer a loss. UAE banks stand out with their technological sophistication, providing mobile apps and internet banking services.

The key banks on the high street are Emirates NBD, Abu Dhabi Commercial Bank (ADCB), First Abu Dhabi Bank (FAB), and Dubai Islamic Bank (DIB). Some expats assume Islamic banks with "Islamic" in their name are exclusively for Muslims. This is not the case. The Islamic banks welcome non-Muslim clients, offering a full range of banking services and providing Islamic products. In addition to local banks, numerous foreign bank branches operate. The foreign banks often demand substantial initial deposits.

Residents can open personal bank accounts. Thorough preparation is crucial. Familiarise yourself with the required documentation and minimum deposit. Be prepared for the process to take time, as obtaining a bank account in one day is unlikely. Typically, you will need a local SIM card, Emirates ID, proof of address, and possibly a salary statement.

Banks can decline to open accounts, even for residents, mainly if you are from what is perceived as a high-risk country. Rigorous compliance and due diligence on new clients are priorities as banks navigate regulatory and inspection pressures. Previously, non-residents could easily open accounts, but this has become more challenging. Banks are much stricter than they used to be. If you come with millions, banks may be more flexible.

Opening corporate bank accounts is especially arduous, prompting some to acquire companies with established bank accounts. I went through the process. This process hinges on demonstrating substance, which comes down to having a real presence in the UAE and often takes months. A local residential address, UAE visa, and Emirates ID will increase your chances of acceptance. Local service providers with expertise can expedite the process. High minimum opening balances for corporate accounts, ranging from AED50,000 to 250,000, can pose hurdles for startups. Though corruption has been minimalised, you may encounter questionable practices at banks. I maintain confidence in local banks, but a degree of vigilance is prudent.

Fiona told me about an interesting experience while attempting to open a UAE bank account for a company abroad, involving extensive paperwork and numerous stamps, which proved cumbersome. The last step was unexpectedly expensive, as they charged per page rather than for the entire document. The bank called her, and she explained the last step was quite expensive, so she had decided not to proceed. The bank assured her they could open the account. She thought there may have been a change in the rules and arranged to meet with the two bank officials at a hotel in Downtown. For half the price of what was charged in the UK, she could skip the final step in the process, and they would get it directly approved in the UAE.

There is always a solution in Dubai, but being educated in a compliance-focused investment banking environment, she could not accept this offer.

UAE banks are considered secure. A bank clerk told Fiona, "After an account has been dormant for a year, the funds are transferred to the central bank." This measure is held to prevent employees from stealing money from dormant accounts. Around 30% of people queuing up at the local bank were there to unfreeze an inactive account due to inactivity. He had said to Fiona, "It used to be even higher, around 50%, when we had a six-month trigger to qualify an account as dormant. We had to change it to a year."

Living in the UAE can result in European banks closing accounts held in Europe. I experienced this firsthand when my account with a European bank in Monaco was unexpectedly closed. This occurred after I used my debit card for a transaction at the Dubai Gold and Diamond Souk. The bank sent me an abrupt email announcing the closure of my 15-year-old account. Furthermore, I faced a similar situation with two other European bank accounts. Both banks told me they deemed the UAE a high-risk country and had decided to no longer service residents in the UAE.

The Financial Action Task Force (FATF) placed the UAE on the grey list in March 2022.[144] The FATF is an international body that sets standards for combating money laundering and terrorist financing. The grey list is a list of countries with AML/CFT deficiencies. The UAE was placed on the grey list because of concerns about its AML/CFT regime. In particular, the FATF was worried about the UAE's ability to effectively combat money laundering and terrorist financing involving shell companies, non-profit organisations, and alternative remittance providers. The UAE has been working to address the FATF's concerns.

In June 2022, the UAE government announced measures to strengthen its AML/CFT regime. It has changed the AML/CFT law to enhance customer due diligence and record-keeping requirements. Also, the resources of the Financial Intelligence Unit (FIU) have been increased to improve analyses of suspicious transactions and to enhance its collaboration with international partners, sharing information about money laundering and terrorist financing threats.[145]

The FATF will review the UAE's progress in addressing its AML/CFT deficiencies in October 2023. The UAE could be removed from the grey list if it can demonstrate it has made significant progress. However, if the UAE cannot show such progress, there is a risk it will be moved to the FATF's blacklist, which is a list of countries non-compliant with AML/CFT standards. This would not be a desirable outcome. Fiona joked, "If they were to end up on the blacklist, then it would allow them to do business which they may currently be declining." It would cause more problems for those who wire money in and out of the UAE.

Arabian Business recently reported that the UAE achieved record-breaking financial crime confiscations in 2023 and is hopeful to be removed from the grey list.[146]

Remain vigilant. Research by Middle East Economy found that 66% of UAE residents have received messages from fraudsters posing as their bank. Furthermore, 44% of UAE consumers claimed to have received more SMS messages from scammers than from their family and friends.[147]

Chapter 27.

Culture of Business in the Middle East

The Middle Eastern Pace of Doing Business

As one of my dear friends, who unfortunately recently passed away, always used to say, "No one makes any money in the Middle East, but it's so much fun, isn't it?" While many individuals have achieved remarkable success, conducting business in the region can be challenging but rewarding in other ways.

Raising capital can be complex and time-consuming, marked by countless variables constantly in flux. Instances of unforeseen setbacks are common, yet occasionally, everything falls into place seamlessly. Nevertheless, collecting payment can present challenges even when a deal is successfully closed. Business etiquette in the UAE places a strong emphasis on respect. Additionally, patience is crucial when engaging in business dealings, as timelines and processes may not always align with one's expectations. If you do not have time on your hands, the Middle East is not the best market for capital raising.

Before you step foot in the region, research and learn as much as possible about the local culture, business practices, and laws. This will help you avoid making cultural faux pas or breaking laws. The Middle East is a region with a rich history and culture. Dress appropriately, avoid public displays of affection, and be mindful of your words and actions. Awareness of the religion's role in the region is essential. By understanding the cultural differences, religious values, and practices of the people you will be doing business with, you can avoid making unintentional mistakes that may damage your business.

Business in the Middle East is often based on relationships. Take the time to build rapport with your business partners. This can be done by meeting with them in person and entertaining them. The building of relationships can take a long time. Things move more slowly in the Middle East. Be patient. Do not expect everything to happen overnight. When things do not go according to plan, be flexible, adaptable, and prepared to change your plans. Delivering results is imperative, but with a good relationship, there will be patience from your business contacts in the Middle East, too.

Wasta and Integrity: Influence and Corruption

Wasta is an Arabic word for using personal connections to get things done. It is often used in business, where it can give individuals and companies a competitive advantage – for example, having a friend who can help you with introductions to secure a job opportunity. Wasta plays a significant role in Emirati society and is deeply ingrained in their social fabric. It is not much different from what is called the old boys' network in the UK. Connections are helpful anywhere around the world.

My Italian friend, Sofia, told me she had a vision to establish her luxury sustainable handbag brand. With years of experience in the handbag industry, a knack for design and an understanding of the latest sustainable technologies, she believed she could create pieces that would stand out in the competitive market. However, she knew succeeding in the business world required talent and the right connections.

She had a distant relative, Aisha, who was well-connected in Dubai's business circles. Aisha had a vast network of influential contacts, often called *wasta* connections. One evening, over a cup of traditional Arabic coffee, Sofia shared her aspirations with her. As they sipped their coffee, Sofia expressed her desire to launch her sustainable luxury bag brand. Still, she mentioned her concerns about navigating the complexities of the market and gaining visibility among the established players. Aisha listened attentively and smiled after reflection, saying, "I might have a few contacts who could help you."

One of them, Fatima, was a well-known businesswoman with influence in the retail sector. Fatima had a chain of high-end boutiques and was always looking for unique and exclusive products to feature in her stores. Sofia's eyes lit up with excitement. She realised her wasta could open doors that would have otherwise taken her years to access.

With Aisha's recommendation, Sofia secured a meeting with Fatima. During their meeting, Sofia showcased her sustainable handbag designs, spoke passionately about her vision, and accentuated exclusivity and craftsmanship. Fatima was impressed by Sofia's dedication and the elegance and sustainability of her creations. She agreed to feature her handbags in her boutiques.

The power of wasta had come into play, connecting a talented entrepreneur with a prominent businesswoman. Sofia's luxury handbags started appearing in Fatima's boutiques, and the exposure brought attention from handbag enthusiasts across the Middle East. In a matter of months, Sofia's brand gained recognition for its quality and unique design, attracting a loyal customer base.

The initial boost from her relative's Wasta had set the wheels in motion for Sofia's business success. Over time, Sofia's brand expanded beyond Dubai's borders, reaching international markets. While Wasta might raise questions about fairness and meritocracy, it is an integral part of Middle Eastern business culture, often employed to bridge gaps and expedite opportunities. My friend's story demonstrated how leveraging personal connections could propel a talented entrepreneur forward, leading to a flourishing business.

There is a fine line to navigate between wasta and corruption. Corruption is the abuse of power for personal gain. As defined in Investopedia, "Corruption occurs when someone in a position of power is using their authority to influence decisions, or conducts any other dishonest or fraudulent behaviour, like giving or accepting bribes or inappropriate gifts, double-dealing, under-the-table transactions, manipulating elections, diverting funds, laundering money, and defrauding investors."[148]

Corruption exists in various forms in all countries, but doing business in the Middle East is perceived to be higher risk. To safeguard your company's reputation, it is always wise to conduct reputation due diligence.

Zainab, a seasoned and influential businesswoman in the Middle East, was pivotal in a construction project that would be an amazing addition to the skyline. The project involved the creation of a luxurious high-rise tower, a multimillion-dollar project. A consortium of local and international companies had united to breathe life into this visionary undertaking. Zainab's stature provided access to key decision-makers within governmental and regulatory spheres. Renowned for her effectiveness in achieving results, often through the employment of *wasta*, she had gained respect within the business community.

As the construction project progressed, issues began emerging, such as delays in permits, approvals, and inspections. One evening, Zaineb was approached by a representative of a smaller subcontractor, I shall call him Farid. He had been grappling with the arduous task of securing essential permits. Farid discreetly slid an envelope containing a substantial sum of cash into Zainab's hand. "I have heard of your amazing connections and believe they could facilitate our project's progress."

Zainab recognised that accepting the bribe could lead to a convoluted web of corruption, tarnishing her reputation and the project's integrity. With unwavering resolve, she returned the envelope to Farid, affirming, "While I empathise with your predicament, I cannot engage in such practices."

Without needing any envelopes, they initiated discussions with regulatory entities and government officials and alleviated the delays. The project regained momentum with time, and the tower began ascending towards the sky. The collaborative effort of the consortium members led to a successful completion, leaving the project with a legacy of quality and transparency. Zainab's resolute decision to reject corruption and champion the project's integrity constituted a pivotal juncture.

While both concepts, wasta and corruption, involve using influence, the key difference lies in the intention and legality of the actions taken, as demonstrated by another story. Jenny has worked as a management consultant in the financial industry in Dubai for years. She has seen firsthand the challenges of doing business in a country where corruption remains a problem.

Jenny was asked for a bribe by a Chief Investment Officer at a family group. Such individuals may be called "gatekeepers." For him to invest in a particular investment proposition, she would need to offer to pay him a fee. She could not agree to what might be construed as a bribe. The Chief Investment Officer then tried to justify his request by claiming the family group was aware of and approved of this practice. He barely received any salary, and the family understood he could take money from the sales side. Jenny asked him if the family group could send an email expressing their backing, but he refused. The situation was not as transparent as he had claimed.

Jenny also told me about a meeting she had with a CFO at a company in one of the GCC countries. The CFO told her he had a real problem. He had been brought in to streamline the investment division but found that everyone was stealing from the company. No one would share any financials with him about the investments made, as it would become clear they had been diverting money to their bank accounts. The company's owner was friends with all the people stealing from him. The CEO found it difficult to discuss his findings with the owner. The owner did not want to acknowledge that his friends might be stealing from him. Unfortunately, a lack of governance and control systems can lead to abuse by employees.

I heard from a local that it is known and, to some extent, accepted that employees would steal from the company, but exactly how much theft is acceptable is not put in writing, which can lead to disputes down the line.

Jenny's stories highlight business challenges in countries with problematic corruption and fraud. Foreign companies must know these risks when doing business in the region.

In the past, the only route to setting up a business in the UAE was through a local partner, tapping into his wasta or connections. This business was lucrative for local partners, who could use their influence to get things done for foreign companies. However, sometimes, a local partner would employ bribes or other favours.

The change in the UAE from a system of local partnerships to one of 100% foreign ownership has been a positive development. It is easier for foreign companies to set up, and the once widespread corruption has been reduced. However, there have also been challenges associated with the change, such as not having access to the connections of a local Partner. Local Partners are now employed as advisors instead.

Trust versus Competence

The story of a chauffeur employed by an Emirati Royal highlights the significance of connections and, more crucially, the element of trust prevalent in the Middle East. The Royal asked his chauffeur for his opinion on an investment in the UK. The chauffeur, who did not know much about the company, said he would research it and get back to him. The chauffeur contacted his contacts in the UK and told the Royal they thought it was a worthwhile investment. The Royal invested in the company and made a profit. He was so impressed with the chauffeur's advice he gave him money to invest on his behalf. However, the chauffeur lost all his money. Unfortunately, this story ended in financial loss.

This twist serves as a reminder that financial decisions carry inherent risks. It emphasises the intricate balance between information, expertise, and chance in investment. The chauffeur's interaction with the Royal about an investment opportunity in the UK is also an example of how relationships and insights can intertwine to shape major decisions. In any transaction, the principal taking the final decision will be influenced by the people around him, which may lead to a change of heart in the final hours of a transaction.

Unpacking the meaning of Inshallah

You will often hear the phrase "inshallah" being tossed around in conversations, especially when interacting with people from Muslim backgrounds. "Inshallah" is an Arabic term translating into "if Allah wills it" or "God willing." It is a way of expressing hope or acknowledging that something is in the hands of a higher power. It is one of those phrases used in conversations beyond the Muslim community. "Inshallah" can be used in a variety of contexts. For example, a Muslim might say, "Inshallah, I will be there tomorrow" or "Inshallah, I will get a good grade on my exam." *Inshallah, it* is not a guarantee something will happen. It is simply a way of expressing hope or making a wish.

The meaning of *inshallah* in business can be controversial. Expats may believe it is a way of avoiding commitment and an excuse for not delivering on promises. Others believe it is a way of expressing hope but should not be taken literally. If someone says, "I will deliver the goods inshallah," it is safe to assume they are not making a guarantee. However, if someone says, "I hope to close the deal inshallah," it is safe to think they are serious about making it happen. Getting dates out of people in the Middle East can be quite a challenge. Having always worked for American investment banks, Fiona told me "inshallah" has taken time to get used to as she prefers dates she can put in her calendar. She had to learn to go with the flow.

In Iran, I came across the proverb: *'Khastan, Tavanestan ast"*, akin to the Dutch saying *'Waar een wil is, is een weg'*, which translates into "When there is a will, there is a way."[149] Louisa May Alcott, a 19th-century American novelist, would say, "Nothing is impossible to a determined woman."[150]

Chapter 28.

Formalities are Necessary

The Importance of Status: Navigating Names and Titles

Dealing with the lengthy names in the Middle East proved to be quite a challenge for me. Remembering the first names was typically straightforward.

Depending on the country, the most common male names include Muhammad, Ali, Ahmed, Omar, Abdullah, Hassan, Hussain, Ibrahim, Ismail, Yusuf, and Bilal.

Female names you will often encounter include Fatima, Aisha, Zainab, Maryam, Halima, Amina, Sumayyah, and Asma.

First names are often chosen because they have religious or historical significance. For example, the name Muhammad is the name of the Prophet Muhammad, the founder of Islam. Ali is the name of the Prophet Muhammad's cousin and son-in-law, the first caliph of Islam. The name Fatima is the name of the Prophet Muhammad's daughter.

I heard an interesting story about Abdul, a common Arabic name meaning "servant of the Most Gracious." People might think that it is inappropriate to use the name Abdul in front of names as the word "slave" has a negative connotation in many cultures, and it is often associated with oppression and inequality. However, I was told the name Abdul has a different meaning in Islam. In Islam, all people are slaves of Allah, regardless of their social status or background. This is because all people are created equal in the eyes of God. Therefore, using Abdul in front of names is not necessarily inappropriate.

The real struggle came with the longer parts that followed. I always admired those individuals at conferences who effortlessly pronounced the extended names of prominent figures as they stepped onto the stage. My greatest fear was always getting it wrong.

To aid in recalling names, it is helpful to understand the logic behind the long names. It begins with the first name, followed by the father's name prefaced with "bin," and concludes with the family name. On rare occasions, the grandfather's name may also be included. For example, the name "Mohammed bin Rashid Al Maktoum" is the name of the current ruler of Dubai. Addressing individuals as "Mr." or "Ms." during initial meetings is the preferred approach in business interactions.

Interestingly, Debra, head of business development at an engineering company, told me she experimented with addressing people using their first names in cold emails. She noticed a significantly higher response rate when opting for the simple "Hi Mohamad" than the formal "Dear Mr. Mohamad." Especially the younger generation, who had spent time abroad, were content with being addressed on a first-name basis. However, with the older generation, it is advisable to stick to using titles unless they prefer informality.

An analyst working at a family office in the UAE shared an insightful tip with me – she suggested adding "Ms." in front of my name. Sometimes, it is not immediately clear whether a first name belongs to a Ms. or a Mr. She had noticed her colleagues on the investment team giving women priority over men.

Status is important in Emirati culture, evident even in the order in which individuals enter and exit rooms – based on rank. Using the appropriate titles and greetings when addressing people is crucial. This practice demonstrates respect and understanding of their cultural norms. When interacting with a government official, the standard terms of address are 'Excellency' or 'Your Excellency.' In a country like the UAE, where members of the Royal family often hold influential positions in both business and government, addressing someone as 'Your Highness' or 'Your Royal Highness' might be necessary.

The titles 'Sheikh' for males and 'Sheikha' for females are reserved for Rulers and members of the Royal Family. When meeting with a Sheikh or Sheikha, it is crucial to pronounce it correctly as 'Shake' rather than 'Sheek'. Hearing a newcomer say Sheek is painful to my ears.

Respecting Personal Space

As outlined earlier, when it comes to greetings, Emirati men might offer a handshake that is less firm than what is customary in the West. And be prepared – Emirati women may opt for a bow or a nod instead. Therefore, waiting for women to initiate a handshake before extending your hand is best.

In Emirati culture, individuals may make physical contact during conversations by touching your hands, arm, or back, more likely between men and, usually, at the end of a good meeting. This gesture is a sign of warmth and friendliness. You can avoid any unintentional offence by maintaining a relaxed and open response. Do not recoil, as this will be seen as offensive.

It may come across as confusing. On the one hand, you must not shake hands with women, but you may find a hand on your back. I suggest you go with the flow and follow their lead.

The Etiquette of Name Dropping in the Middle East

Relationships are essential in the Middle East, like in other places. Having good relationships can be helpful in business, as it can open doors and give you access to opportunities you might not otherwise have. There is a lot of hot air in the Middle East. People may try to impress you by name-dropping or claiming to have connections they do not have. They may say they are best friends with one of the Royals. Even if this is true, they may have the links in a personal context but not a business one. For example, someone may be great friends with a Royal, skydiving together, but that Royal may not take their call regarding investments. Be aware and do your research. There is no way to verify the validity of these claims. So do not be fooled by people who try to impress you with their connections. Make sure you are dealing with someone legitimate.

A head-hunter in London, Jemma, was interviewing candidates for a private banking position in the Middle East. She told me 12 out of the 16 candidates were called Mohamed, spelt in many different ways, and all candidates claimed they had an excellent relationship with a Royal.

Ariana told me that she began to populate her website with photos, aiming to substantiate her extensive travels across these countries. Her motivation was partly driven by the emergence of competitors who were quick to name-drop. However, she opted not to name-drop. Instead, she focused on capturing her travels to countries, including photos of landmarks. By doing so, she aimed to provide potential clients with tangible evidence she had of being present in these locations. In its simplest form, her website is a testament to her presence outside the offices of sovereign wealth funds and influential family groups. She believed this held more authenticity than mere claims of knowing Royalty. The extent of her interactions within these offices remains concealed from the client's perspective, maintaining discretion in the specifics of her meetings and encounters.

I want to emphasise the importance of refraining from name-dropping during investor meetings, which could lead to unintended consequences. It is crucial to recognise that not all investors hold the same opinions or level of respect for the names you may bring up in a meeting. Furthermore, by invoking someone else's name, you might inadvertently be subjecting your name to similar scrutiny as lacking discretion.

A more effective approach is to create an environment where the investor feels they are the primary focus of your attention and efforts. In certain countries, collaborative investment is favoured among families, while in others, such as the UAE, investors may prefer exclusive deals. To navigate these nuances successfully, it is wise to maintain ambiguity regarding the specific individuals or entities you are in discussion with. This approach ensures your interactions remain respectful, unbiased, and tailored to the preferences and dynamics of each investor and country.

Praise and Prosper

Formality holds a distinct place in the Middle East, introducing a unique cultural nuance. Honouring rulers or other prominent leaders is imperative. Bestowing a "floral compliment" before engaging in conversation carries profound significance. This gesture is highly regarded, a courteous and respectful prelude laying the foundation for dialogue. Whether forging an initial acquaintance or engaging in casual banter, do not overlook the art of adorning your words with kind sentiments before delving into the heart of the matter.

This custom proved to be a lesson Debra grappled with, as her natural style leans towards directness. While she was always in the habit of expressing gratitude and enjoyed conversing, she had not fully embraced the elaborate introduction. Over time, she has come to appreciate the value of initiating discussions with an appreciation for the opportunity given by her host and a genuine compliment on their hospitality. This complement may extend beyond the brief 15 seconds she might allocate in other cultures and instead take several minutes.

Attending regional conferences amplifies this trend, with attendees generously dedicating time to laud the host for orchestrating a successful event. To those seeking an example, I suggest keenly observing conference dynamics as participants make introductions, elegantly threading compliments and yielding harmonious opening speeches. They should be giving out prizes for the best introduction. I often listen, mesmerised.

Personal relationships are key. Debra said she was inclined to establish business relationships before cultivating friendships. However, in the Middle East, the sequence is reversed. Nurturing a personal bond takes precedence, paving the way for business interactions. As in Southern Europe and South America, roughly 30 minutes of the conversation is dedicated to chit-chat. Conversations can revolve around local culture, artwork adorning the walls, indigenous culinary delights, or related topics. Politically charged matters and religious discussions are best sidestepped. Debra would continue the chit-chat until the host inquired about the purpose of the meeting.

The critical lesson is to fly out to the Middle East to forge relationships. If you fly out with the view of returning with a bag of money, you will inevitably end up disappointed.

Chapter 29.

Establishing new Connections

Networking: Building Bonds Beyond Borders

I networked at conferences held in Dubai and throughout the GCC. I would playfully joke with friends, saying, "I used to attend balls, and now I go to business conferences." Some of these conferences were nothing short of spectacular.

Middle Eastern business culture places immense importance on trust and relationships, significantly influencing business pace and success. So, while conferences offer a starting point for connections, managing expectations and understanding the actual work and relationship-building happening beyond the conference setting is essential. These gatherings served as exceptional platforms for venturing into the Middle East by offering insights gleaned through casual conversations in the corridors. During these moments, advice and anecdotes were exchanged, and connections were forged. The on-stage discourse remained subdued, perhaps to avoid contentious subjects. However, during the off-stage moments, away from the spotlight and cameras, I had meaningful discussions with speakers and participants, gaining invaluable insights.

I especially enjoyed the conferences put on by the Dubai Chamber of Commerce. The Chamber of Commerce organised country conferences, such as the Latin America and the Africa conferences, attracting high-level politicians and people in business. Attendance at these conferences was a privilege, extended exclusively through invitations. Naturally, the focus was on how Dubai could create bonds and reap the rewards. These events were meticulously arranged, infused with local flair, and renowned for their exceptional culinary experiences.

Most conferences included a performance. The Emiratis have a great love for their traditional dance. As someone who loves music and dancing, I thoroughly enjoyed watching their captivating performances and listening to their chants. Men typically perform these dances with a minimum of 25 participants. The dancing is slow and rhythmic, almost hypnotic. They usually use canes. In other dances, swords and guns are used, which are jostled around. I have been told they are staging the battles they fought against their attackers.

At the Chamber of Commerce Latin America Conference, the Latin American crowd also gave a taste of their local culture and sang "La Bamba, La Bamba," a catchy melody with a lively rhythm. The guests were moving and clapping to the beat, and the hosts were appreciative and happy to see their guests enjoying their time. The Latin American delegation put on a lively performance. It brought back memories of the months I had spent in South America. It was great that the Latin American delegation took the time to thank the hosts in their local tradition.

It is always polite to arrive early, but it is imperative if there is a key opening speaker at a conference, in which case you should come extra early. One year, the opening speaker at the Euromoney conference[151] in Qatar was late. The whole conference had to be put on hold. It would have been disrespectful to have started without his opening address. We ended up having a three-hour networking session over coffee until finally, he arrived, and the opening session could take place. It was great for business. All the important people in

Qatar were present in the room. When there is a speech by a high-ranking government official, which is the case with all conferences, family groups are often asked to attend his speech. However, many only stay for the opening address; you will see them all leave at the end. So, networking in the morning is the most precious time during these conferences for forging new connections.

Another tip – if a conference is several days, expect Day Two to have few attendees. People often only attend the first day, so it is better to go on day one if you can only participate one day.

There are hundreds of conferences organised in the UAE every year. Conferences may be free to attend. Some are invitation-only, and others require payment. Do your research and find out what the better ones are. Go to any conference and ask the attendees what they have found the best conferences.

The World Trade Centre[152] in Dubai also organises continuous trade shows. Some of the ones I attended include GITEX (technology), Arab Health, WETEX (renewables), Gulffood and Paperworld. The exhibitions are often free to attend. You usually only need to pay if you want access to the presentations. Trade shows are great opportunities to meet local family groups. Typically, they will have a booth, and the key principals will be present on one of the days. Additionally, you can establish connections with various government departments, allowing you to have a casual conversation and providing valuable insights into regulations helpful for businesses looking to operate in the region.

Family Office conference organisers create an atmosphere of optimism and potential. They promise that business is straightforward and the region has plenty of liquidity. Securing investments or deals in the Middle East can be more complex than it seems during these events. While conferences can provide a platform for initial networking and introductions, building trust, understanding the market, and finalising business transactions takes time. The initial conference meetings begin a longer journey towards potential partnerships or investments. Following up with one-on-one sessions in a more private and focused setting allows for deeper discussions, due diligence, and negotiation. During these follow-up meetings, parties can genuinely assess the compatibility of their goals and strategies.

Shady Business: Dealing with Dubious Characters

Like any other city, Dubai is not immune to the presence of individuals operating in the grey areas of legality. During my initial year in Dubai, I encountered people who seemed engaged in questionable activities. It became apparent they were targeting newcomers, possibly because newcomers might be more susceptible due to their lack of familiarity with the local environment.

Drawing from her experiences dealing with dubious people in business, Chantal, an investment banker, developed a keen ability to identify inconsistencies and red flags. Interestingly, the suspicious individuals she encountered were consistently foreigners rather than Emiratis.

Chantal shared a story with me about an intriguing encounter she had in Dubai. A meeting was set up by a man who was an Olympic showjumper. They bonded on their shared love for horses. Despite the apparent wealth and prestige associated with the meeting venue, a luxurious hotel suite on Sheikh Zayed Road, Chantal was not easily impressed. Appearances could be deceiving. Standing outside the hotel room, she felt a sense of caution. Going into a hotel room alone with someone she did not know for long might not be sensible.

The man who greeted her had unusually bulging arm muscles, resembling a bouncer at a nightclub. To her surprise, he was the principal rather than a bodyguard. The meeting occurred in a grand suite, with everyone seated three meters apart. Although the discussion revolved around the sugar business, their answers to Chantal's inquiries about industry trends were evasive and unconvincing.

"What are the trends in the marketplace?" she asked.

"Everyone uses sugar," they replied, pointing to the sugar on the table. "It's a big market."

They then presented a business opportunity in Greece, highlighting a joint venture with a reputable Greek family and government concessions. Chantal's intuition signalled doubt about the authenticity of the individuals she was dealing with.

After the meeting, she reached out to her contacts for a background check. A Brazilian friend with connections in the sugar industry confirmed the two men were not recognised figures in Brazil. A Greek acquaintance provided a vague warning about prominent families getting involved with dubious partners during times of crisis.

When she met him a year later in person, he said to her, "Unfortunately, in crisis, some respectable families sometimes get involved with the wrong people."

Chantal's suspicion grew as she investigated their online presence. Profiles on their website, purportedly belonging to key figures, lacked credibility. All profiles on LinkedIn had one connection only, appearing fake. She noticed one lady from Asia with a genuine profile on LinkedIn, with more than one connection. She was associated with another company. Interestingly, that company's website shared a similar frilly Russian design to the company Chantal had been talking to. This company appeared filled with individuals skilled in martial arts, which she thought might explain the man's exceptional muscular build. They could all be part of the same black belt network. The Italian man she met, described as 'a businessman,' was featured in a society magazine, going out with a famous model.

Although she did not have anything concrete to point to, her investigation revealed potential ties to criminal activities, prompting her to question the true nature of the business proposition and the individuals behind it. Could they have ties to the Russian and Italian Mafia? Chantal concluded she could not do business with them and promptly communicated her inability to do so. The encounter left her feeling uneasy, with a lingering sense of caution. For a week, she kept looking over her shoulder.

I have learned from such stories that dodgy criminals tend to move in when a country is in trouble. They exploit the situation to launder money while the distressed government looks the other way and grants them concessions. Since no other investor has the risk appetite to enter, they become the investor of last resort, effectively an investor focused on distressed opportunities.

After the criminals have invested, other families notice the activity and enter the market. The institutional investors are the last ones to enter, while the criminal gang has already exited and moved on to the next troublesome country. The dodgy crowd, or those operating in the grey zones, are all eager to tell you about their scheme, but of course, they cannot. Criminals stay close to the truth, leaving what I call a 'footprint in conversation.' Listening carefully to what they say lets you figure out what is happening.

We have been taught the good guys are good-looking, fit, clever, and charming, like James Bond, while the bad guys are ugly, overweight, and not very smart. It is often the opposite. The good guys are overworked bureaucrats without time to go to the gym. Dubai Police is an exception. They keep themselves in great shape. The bad guys are often super charming, clever, and fit. I mean, they must be able to outrun the police. Being fit is a necessity. Their charm convinces people to agree to things they should not agree to. And they tend to be super bright in structuring seriously complex structures. The not-so-clever ones end up in jail.

Chantal also told me a story about the time she was having a drink with a charming guy on the terrace of the Palace Hotel in Downtown, and then afterwards Googling him, only to find out he had been ripping off grannies in the UK. She told me the baddies are often highly charismatic and great to hang out with for fun but not fit to do business with, especially if you are a regulated business. She calls it the parallel universe. They could have been legitimate, successful investment bankers but operate on the other side of the track.

Chantal's experiences in Dubai took her into even more unexpected and intriguing situations, including a meeting with a hitman. One evening, a British ex-army friend invited her to join him for a drink at Zuma, a well-regarded restaurant in DIFC (Dubai International Financial Centre). As they were on their way to the restaurant, her friend casually mentioned that one of the individuals they were meeting, an American, was a hitman by profession. This revelation was shocking and unsettling, as Chantal found herself in a world utterly unfamiliar. Despite her anxiety, she attended the meeting and met with the American hitman.

To her astonishment, his appearance was quite the opposite of what she had expected. He had the demeanour of a gentle and approachable person, resembling a cuddly teddy bear rather than someone involved in such a lethal profession. He looked like he would not be able to harm a fly. Hitmen are often portrayed as cold and calculating in movies and TV shows but can be as ordinary-looking as anyone else. This encounter was a stark reminder that looks can be deceiving, and one should not underestimate the complexity of the people and circumstances one encounters in unfamiliar territories like Dubai.

There are many military people in Dubai. Expats refer to Dubai as "spy central," a base camp for the region. I remember meeting a Britt in Dubai, admitting he was a spy in charge of collecting intelligence. He said he was allowed to say what he did for a living as it was simply gathering information.

Another friend of mine, Karen, a private equity fund manager, was invited to a meeting to meet a guy and check him out to see if he was legitimate. She was happy to do so. However, looking at the investor deck, she sensed something was off. The presentation mentioned he had studied architecture. This is not how academic achievements are presented in the country he came from. They would always mention the city and year of graduation. So, she quickly realised it did not bode well. Karen said, "He likely had merely walked through a hotel and concluded he had studied architecture."

Karen also told me a story of a meeting organised by an older, soft-spoken American gentleman who invited her to discuss Iran-related transactions. She entered a hotel suite to find herself in the presence of three individuals, each with a puzzling background. The first person she noticed was a man who exuded a military presence, giving her the impression that he might have been part of special forces or a similar elite group. The second individual introduced himself as a pain management expert. After listening to the first two descriptions, I joked with Karen whether he was into torturing. The third person, who had arranged the meeting, revealed an even more astonishing background. He claimed to have planted bombs under bridges in Russia and was now a businessman active in the hotel sector. The combination of characters and their diverse histories made the meeting feel incredibly unusual and out of the ordinary.

As the conversation progressed, the American gentleman suggested Karen should connect with someone at Walt Disney. This proposition raised her suspicions, as she believed Walt Disney was associated with covert methods of influencing people's minds. The proposed introduction made her uneasy about the nature of the meeting and the motivations of those involved. She told me that while she maintained contact with the American hotel specialist, she remained uncertain about the intentions of the other two individuals, finding the entire experience unsettling. She never got to the bottom of their intentions.

The experiences of Chantal and Karen in Dubai were a blend of intriguing and bizarre encounters that challenged their perceptions and beliefs.

After listening to their stories, I started to insist on getting the name and a copy of the person's deck before agreeing to meet them so I could do a simple Google search to check them out. This is especially sensible when you move to a place like Dubai, where you do not have the same social network to rely on for referrals and background checks. The introducer may be legitimate, but they may not have done their due diligence on the person they introduce you to. They may simply be relying on what they have been told.

It is always better to be safe than sorry, so I always research before meeting someone new. I Google their name and other identifying information, such as their company or job title. I will look for news articles or social media posts about them. Also, I will check their online profiles on platforms such as LinkedIn or Facebook and am wary of those with a handful of connections. A friend said running a reverse image search on their photos is possible to see if they are using someone else's pictures. I am going to do that next time.

What some do in business is to ask to see a person's visa in their passport and ask if they are a resident. If someone is living in a hotel without a visa, it is a red flag. They may not be allowed to work or live in the country. You can also approach it more subtly by asking, "What is the purpose of your move?" "Where do you live?" and "Are you a resident?" By asking the right questions and doing the necessary checks, it may help you avoid any shady characters. I learned to trust but verify before signing on the dotted line. I learned this by doing, and I have learned to listen to my gut. If something does not feel right, it probably isn't. Trust your instincts and walk away from a deal if you have a bad feeling about it. It does not mean I am always right about my positive feelings. When I am positive, I gather more data before forming an opinion. It is essential to see how someone acts over time rather than relying on their first impression. People can be good at putting on a front, so getting to know and seeing how they behave is important.

After hearing all the stories about shady people in business, I called Caroline, the CEO of a multi-family office in London. She told me, "Rebecca, London has changed too. You should see the sketchy characters passing by our office."

Caroline's reassurance helped put the experiences of Chantal and Karen into context and even normalised them to some extent. Different cities and environments can have their share of unusual encounters and characters, and these experiences can sometimes be a part of the landscape, regardless of the location. Sharing stories and comparing notes with others can provide valuable insight, helping you navigate such situations with a better understanding and a sense of perspective.

When people feel disconnected from their neighbours and community, they are more likely to act in unethical ways. This may be because they feel like they do not answer to anyone and do not feel like they are part of something bigger than themselves.

Dubai is constantly growing and changing, making it difficult for people to feel like they belong. This may lead to isolation, making people more likely to engage in unethical behaviour, especially if they have mouths to feed.

We should not get down, believing the world is a cutthroat place. There is still a lot of good in the world, and we should focus on the positive so the negative does not consume us. My friends have told me their worst war stories. There are many legitimate people to do business with.

Chapter 30.

GCC Business and Cultural Insights

I travelled across the GCC, meeting with investors and family groups. The GCC (Gulf Corporation Council), established in 1981, is a political and economic alliance. The six GCC countries include Bahrain, Kuwait, Oman, Qatar, Saudi, and the UAE. The main objective of the GCC countries is to enhance cooperation and integration among its members.[153] The locals in the GCC were always highly respectful. Surprisingly, I had more issues with the expats than with the locals. The country's borders are not aligned with tribal families crossing borders. The following chapters will share my experiences and friends' stories in the region. No one strategy works when doing business in the region. There are distinct differences between each of the countries in the GCC, which I hope to bring out in the following chapters.

The Bahrainis: Confused between Saudi and Iran

The current King of Bahrain is King Hamad bin Isa Al Khalifa, a Sunni. The population of Bahrain, officially called the Kingdom of Bahrain, is about 1.8 million. The capital is Manama. Bahrain was under British administration until 1971 when it gained independence. The Bahrainis seem caught between Iran and Saudi. Bahrain quickly ran out of oil after its independence, and the King has since been receiving Saudi funding. However, over 65% of the population is Persian.[154]

Bahrain is an island nation connected to the mainland east coast of Saudi by the King Fahd Causeway, a 25-kilometre roadway opened in 1986, joining the two countries. Due to a ban on women driving in Saudi, the causeway was the only bridge in the world where women could go on the bridge on one side (Bahrain) but not the other (Saudi). The border runs the length of the bridge, right through the centre.

Louisa told me an amusing story. In a business meeting with a Bahraini, he told Louisa his wife wanted to shop at IKEA in Saudi. She had to dress up in an abaya to cross the bridge into Saudi. "It's a nightmare," he said. "When we are in IKEA, I cannot find her, as everyone is wearing the same black abaya!" Louisa joked, "Clearly, men struggle to recognise the differences between these exquisite abayas."

The Bahrainis have a sense of pride in their past glory. The country transitioned from being an ancient trading hub to embracing modernisation. Bahrain is where you will find intermediaries managing money for Saudi Ultra High Net Worth Individuals. While Bahrain has long been considered a leading financial centre in the region, Dubai has managed to steal its thunder in recent years.

Initially, Bahrain was innovative and relaxed by allowing alcohol and prostitution without openly promoting it. This allowed them to attract visitors and establish themselves as a regional hub. One of my acquaintances used to be an accountant and told me that he audited the accounts of a Madam who catered to the Saudis with 'pleasure.' Her client list was extensive. The Saudis would party in Bahrain and indulge in activities forbidden on home territory.

As time passed, Bahrain's lack of innovation started to take its toll. It lost its status as a regional financial hub, highlighting the importance of continuous innovation to stay ahead.

Bahrain felt like a wonderful, quiet beach resort to me. I loved my trips to Bahrain. There is not the same intensity as in

Dubai, allowing you to unwind. The expats who used to live in Bahrain and then moved to Dubai say they preferred Bahrain. And the Bahrainis say they would not want to swap Bahrain for the UAE or Dubai. The expats describe Bahrain as homely, with more mingling between the locals and the expats than in Dubai. Bahrain is one of the few countries in the GCC, like Oman, where you find the locals work for a living. They do not see themselves as privileged. Jobs carried out by taxi drivers and secretaries are all filled by Bahrainis. It is easy to meet locals.

Do not leave Bahrain without watching the flamingos in Manama. Greater Flamingos are large, pink birds native to Africa and Asia. They are attracted to Bahrain in the winter when the weather is warm and plenty of food is available. It is worth heading to the Ritz-Carlton to watch the flamingos from the hotel's pool. Hard to miss is the Bahrain World Trade Centre, a skyscraper with wind turbines integrated into its design.

Bahrain has become an increasingly popular tourist destination in recent years. Time Out Bahrain lists many tourist sites, including historical locations like the Bahrain Fort and Qal'at al-Bahrain Archaeological Site (a UNESCO World Heritage Site)[155]. Relax on delightful beaches, visit modern attractions like the Bahrain National Museum and Bahrain International Circuit (home to the Formula 1 Grand Prix), or enjoy traditional markets like the Manama Souk.

Another landmark is "The Tree of Life," believed to be over 100 years old. This ancient tree defies the harsh conditions and continues to thrive despite the apparent lack of water sources. It has become a symbol of resilience and strength in the face of adversity.[156]

The Kuwaitis: Straight to the Point

The Emirs of Kuwait are members of the Al Sabah dynasty. Sheikh Nawaf Al-Ahmad Al-Jaber Al-Sabah is the current Emir. The population of Kuwait is about 4.6 million. The capital is Kuwait City. The currency is the Kuwaiti Dinars.[157]

A friend in Kuwait described the current Emir Sheikh Nawaf Al-Ahmad Al-Jaber Al-Sabah to me as a very peaceful family man. He is famous for publicly weeping when discussing the Gulf War as Crown Prince. He told me, "The Emir won people's hearts and minds and came across as very genuine, which he is. He has had health issues and is not as involved in running the country as he used to be. He has fully delegated, giving full executive powers to his brother, Sheikh Mishal, the Crown Prince. Although officially deputy commander, Sheikh Mishal is known for serving around 30 years as the *de facto* commander of the National Guard. The National Guard, during his tenure, was known to be incredibly strict with the enforcement of its rule set. Corruption was minimal, and all power was centralised."

When I first landed in Kuwait, I thought Kuwait was *as flat as Holland*. Kuwaitis embrace different cultures with open arms. I loved the personal touch on arrival. At the border, you are welcomed to Kuwait and informed about the number of times you have previously visited the country. "Good morning, Ms. Meijlink. Welcome to Kuwait. This is your fifth visit to our country."

I found Kuwaitis the most international among all the GCC countries. It is easy to bond with them. They are known for their global outlook. The Ministry of Higher Education has a Scholarship Program to promote studying abroad. Many Kuwaitis studied in the US, with engineering as one of their favourite disciplines.

The Kuwaitis are hospitable. On my first visit to Kuwait, I was given an amazing reception. Whilst I was finishing my first meeting, the CFO of the local bank asked me about my transportation plans and how I intended to get to the next meeting. I replied I would hail a taxi. He found this unacceptable and promptly instructed the company driver to take me to my next destination.

At the next meeting, the investor asked me how I had arrived. I explained that the CFO of the previous company had been extremely generous by providing me with his company car. As I was about to say goodbye to the investor in the second meeting, he said, "Hang on, I will get my company driver to take you to the next meeting."

In many countries in the Middle East, it is customary to provide guests with transportation and other forms of assistance. I must have had "First time in Kuwait" written in capital letters on my forehead.

The Kuwaiti investors diversified their investments early on. They have one of the longest histories of investing, making them the more mature investors in the GCC, like the Dutch pension funds. The Kuwaitis are also extremely direct and, like the Dutch, fierce negotiators. They also like to laugh. I remember a joke told to me by a Kuwaiti investor: "Why are the Dutch all so tall? Because all the others drowned." It made me laugh. It is a bit of a bad joke, but quite funny anyway. (For those who did not get the joke: Holland is below sea level, so the risk of being flooded is high).

Karen agreed they like to laugh, and she recalled a joke made by a business owner active in the healthcare sector: "Of course, we do not want people to be healthy. We make the most money when people are sick." She understood the irony but could not help feeling a little shocked, too.

The Kuwaitis can be direct in meetings. Again, it made me laugh and realise how rude the Dutch can be. I concluded the Kuwaitis beat us to it. After someone was forthright in a meeting, I remember laughing and saying, "You are worse than I am!"

You will know where you stand in business. They will tell you if they like your proposal and give you constructive feedback. The Kuwaiti directness may seem assertive. The intention, however, is not to be confrontational. Instead, it reflects Kuwaiti communication, where clarity and efficiency are valued.

In Kuwait, I got the feeling I was in a frontier market. It is a bit tatty on the streets – and I loved it. To further indulge, I visited the Souk Al Mubarakiya, one of the oldest souks in Kuwait. It also used to be the centre of trade before the discovery of oil. Some say not much has been done to renovate Kuwait after the war. Office buildings can still have bullet holes in their walls. Every Kuwaiti has a suitcase beside their bed, with a backup plan, ready for a quick escape.

While the government has taken steps to streamline processes, bureaucracy can be a challenge. The country's bureaucracy can be slow and inefficient. Kuwait has a complex regulatory environment, with different agencies involved in the approval process for businesses. This can make it difficult and time-consuming to get things done. Getting a business license in Kuwait can take months or even years. Due to the decision-making process, local partners or sponsors are often necessary, and patience is vital.

Alcohol is not allowed in Kuwait. Hotels and restaurants will not serve you alcohol. There are also no bars and nightclubs. In private settings, you may, to your surprise, be presented with a drink. Jenny, who attended a wedding in Kuwait, said she asked for a gin and tonic and got a whole glass filled with gin. Drinking alcohol privately is not illegal. Still, buying and selling, bringing alcohol to a public place, or being intoxicated in public areas, including in a car as a passenger, are all serious crimes. So, when offered a drink in a private setting, you can graciously accept. But do not take a bottle to the party. Anyone caught possessing alcohol for personal use will be slapped with a fine of up to KD100.[158]

The Omanis: The Zen Diplomats

The Sultans of Oman are members of the Busaid dynasty, which has been the ruling family of Oman since the mid-18th century. Haitham bin Tariq is the current Sultan. He was proclaimed Sultan on 11 January 2020 upon the death of Sultan Qaboos. The population of Oman is about 5 million. The average age in Oman is 30 years. The capital is Muscat. The currency is called the Omani Rial (OMR), pegged to the US dollar.[159]

A friend in Oman told me that Sultan Qaboos was also known as the 'Father of Oman.' He was the longest-serving ruler in the Middle East and the Arab world, having governed for half a century. He successfully executed a modernisation agenda that ended Oman's international isolation. During his reign, the country experienced significant improvements in living standards and development.[160]

Oman's official religion is Islam. Most Omanis follow the Ibadi branch[161], distinct from the Sunni and Shi'a branches of Islam. Other religions are represented by foreign nationals who have relocated to Oman for trade and jobs. Oman is known for its religious tolerance and openness, allowing people to practice their faith freely.

Oman's economy is heavily dependent on oil, making the price of oil a crucial factor that significantly impacts both the economy and the currency. The Sultanate's vision is outlined in Oman Vision 2040.[162] Like other oil-rich nations, Oman is actively working towards diversifying its economy to reduce its reliance on oil. Due to its strategic maritime location, Oman specialises in industry, tourism, and logistics.

Oman's credit rating has seen upgrades in recent years, spurring an increased inflow of foreign investment. The credit rating is critical, as it serves as a barometer for investors to assess Oman's creditworthiness, significantly influencing the nation's borrowing costs. A higher credit rating translates into more favourable borrowing terms, a catalyst for fresh infrastructure initiatives. The upgrade reflects the considerable improvements in Oman's fiscal measures, reduced external funding pressures, and ongoing efforts to overhaul the country's public finances. Higher oil revenue supports its budget surpluses while significantly reducing government debt/GDP to below the 'BB' median.

In business, the influence of religion is noticeable. Omanis' emphasis is on fostering a harmonious and inclusive work environment. Their ability to balance the need for creative thinking with cultural sensitivity exemplifies the Omani approach to business communication, which values teamwork, respect, and maintaining positive relationships within the workplace.

Things do not move fast. "Tomorrow!" is usually the answer if you ask someone to do something. Do not be surprised if someone tells you that something that should typically take five minutes in Oman takes two hours.

Omanis have gained a reputation internationally for their masterful diplomacy. They are known as "diplomatic peacemakers." At the heart of their culture lies a deep commitment to cultivating harmonious relationships with other nations and communities. Their dedication to peaceful coexistence and a preference for dialogue over confrontation have significantly influenced their diplomatic approach. Moreover, Oman's strategically advantageous geographical location at the crossroads of Asia, Africa, and Europe positions it as a proficient mediator in resolving regional conflicts.

Per data from the National Centre for Statistics and Information (NCSI), the UK remains the principal source of Foreign Direct Investment (FDI) in Oman, contributing to nearly half of the total FDI in the first quarter of this year (2023), followed by the US. The UK is Oman's second-largest trading partner.

The national attire for men is the dish dash, usually white, but they can be more colourful than in other GCC countries. Men can wear a variety of accessories, including the *muzzar*, a turban, the *assa*, a cane or stick worn primarily for formal events, and the *khanjar*, a ceremonial curved dagger worn during formal occasions and is sometimes referred to as "a symbol of male elegance." The dagger you will see everywhere. It is an essential part of the Omani flag and is featured on Omani banknotes. Once a weapon for self-defence, it has become a symbol of national pride.[163]

Their distinctive daily headwear can quickly identify an Omani. A *kumma* is the traditional Omani men's headwear. It is carefully sized and includes little holes all over the embroidery to keep the head cool in the hot Omani sun. The cap is flat on top. Most women in cities wear the *abaya* and the *hijab*.

Two borders connect Oman to the UAE. My first trip to Oman was on a visa run to the Hatta-Al Wajajah Border crossing. The journey from Oman to Dubai was 400 kilometres long and took about 5 hours. It is a trip up and down to Oman on the same day, effectively resetting the visa period. Oman has a streamlined visa procedure. Whether by car or bus, the journey is straightforward. I opted for a mini-bus, catering for the visa run. The shifting scenery, transitioning from sandy UAE to the rocky landscape of Oman, made an enjoyable day out in the countryside. I loved the desert terrain and rough mountains.

Omanis are renowned for their warm and inviting manner. During a meeting at the Ministry of Finance, I sat across from an Omani official, sensing an aura of tranquillity. It made me feel like a stressed-out investment banker. He was just so chilled out and relaxed. And it was not just him. All Omanis had this Zen way of being, very easy-going, unlike anyone else in the GCC. My roadshow experiences in Oman felt akin to returning from a spa after a rejuvenating massage.

I tried to understand the secret of Omani tranquillity. Initially, I thought it might be something in the water. But then I learned that Omanis burn frankincense under their dress. It not only smells nice, but it is also said to foster inner serenity. Dhofar, a region in Salalah, Oman, is well-known for being the Land of Frankincense. Oman extracts this precious resin from the *Boswellia sacra* tree. Frankincense has been used for centuries in perfumery, medicine, and religious rituals. I now have a vial of frankincense at home and add drops to my bath to achieve the "Omani Zen." I have found that burning frankincense or adding it to my bath does indeed have a calming effect on me. I recently had dinner in London with an Omani friend who gave me a large pack of Frankincense that will last me another year.

If you want to add a touch of Omani Zen to your home, I encourage you to use frankincense. To learn more about Frankincense, take a tour that includes Al Balid archaeological sites, the Frankincense Land Museum, Sumhuram Old City, the Frankincense Trail, and Wadi Dawka.

The Omani kitchen is excellent. Omani cuisine combines flavours from various cultures, including Arabian,

Indian, Persian, and African influences. Traditional dishes are *shuwa* (a slow-cooked lamb dish), *mashuai* (roast lamb), and *harees* (a porridge flavoured with cinnamon and sugar before serving). I recommend starting with shuwa. This Oman national dish is the best. Preparing takes a long time because the meat is marinated in Arabic spices before being wrapped in banana leaves and then cooked in an underground sand oven for one or two days.

Many traditional dishes are available at Al Angham Restaurant, a local Omani restaurant near the Royal Opera House. At the restaurant, I enjoyed a delicious camel dish. It is an upmarket restaurant. If you are in Muscat, you should go – a pleasant place to visit, whether for work or pleasure.

Oman has great forts and castles reflecting its grandeur and traditional mud-brick houses. It was an influential maritime power during ancient times and played a significant role in global trade routes. Historical sites such as Bahla Fort and Nizwa Fort provide insights into Oman's past.

The country is also home to the Al Hajar Mountains, the mesmerising Wahiba Sands desert, and the pristine beaches of Salalah. Expats from Dubai love to enjoy the mountains, the beaches, the dunes, and refreshing *wadis* with crystal-clear waters to swim in. Oman is a paradise for outdoor enthusiasts. You can go mountaineering, rock climbing, canyoning, scuba diving, camping in the desert, or off-road driving. It is one of the favoured weekend escapes from Dubai.

The Qataris: Play Hard to Get

Qatar (pronounced *Kuh-TAR*) is a small country with a big personality. Since the mid-1800s, Qatar has been a wealthy nation with a strong economy ruled by the Al Thani family. The current Emir is Tamim bin Hamad Al Thani. The country's population is over 2.8 million, but only about 300,000 are Qatari citizens. The rest are expats from all over the world. The population is concentrated around the capital, Doha, a modern city with a skyline dominated by skyscrapers. The currency is called the Qatari Riyal. The Qatari Riyal is among the world's strongest currencies. It has a stable exchange rate and is backed by Qatar's rich natural resources like oil and gas.[164]

The blockade against Qatar was lifted in January 2021 after a three-and-a-half-year boycott by Saudi, the UAE, Bahrain, and Egypt. The blockade was imposed in June 2017 after Qatar was accused of supporting terrorism and having close ties to Iran. Qatar denied the allegations. The blockade had a significant impact on the country's economy. The blockade damaged relations between the countries in the GCC and raised concerns about the stability of the Gulf region. As a result, I spent less time in Qatar than in other GCC countries.

The lifting of the blockade had a positive impact. It was a significant victory for Qatar, improving relations between Qatar and its neighbours. Saudi and UAE companies can now engage in direct commercial dealings with Qatari counterparties, as the previous prohibition has been lifted.

Lifting of the blockade does not mean all tensions between Qatar and its neighbours have been resolved. The countries still have disagreements, and the blockade could be re-imposed. However, it has been a positive step, a sign the countries are willing to work together to resolve their differences.

Getting to know the Qataris can seem challenging. It is difficult for outsiders to break into small communities, like anywhere in the world. Karen found Qatar the most challenging nut to crack. When she attended conferences, she used to take out her stopwatch to see if she could set a new personal record of maintaining a conversation with a Qatari. It was the most challenging place to network with the locals. She tried not to take it personally. They did not seem interested in meeting foreigners. She told me, "In their minds, conferences are an opportunity to mingle with each other and catch up." Initially, she attributed it to the village mentality. One way she learned to break the ice with Qataris is to talk about their culture and heritage.

However, she found it easier to chat with Qataris outside of Qatar. She was introduced by a lawyer to a Qatari Royal in a tiny coffee shop in Knightsbridge in London. He was incredibly friendly, unlike the reception she had in Qatar. Their rich cultural heritage and traditions play a significant role in shaping their social interactions. They value privacy and tend to be more reserved when meeting new people. Additionally, the close-knit nature of their communities means trust and mutual connections are highly valued. "Qatar also has so much money," she said, "they do not need anyone else. It is the world's largest exporter of liquid national gas."[165]

A friend's brother working in Qatar in the Energy sector said, "You feel they *need* you, but they do not *want* you. They would like to be able to do it themselves, but then they do not want to roll up their sleeves, so they end up reluctantly asking us in again."

Charlotte, working in IT services, mentioned that the premises of Qatar Investment Authority (QIA) were fortified with a level of security surpassing that of other sovereign wealth funds. Within the organisation, a select few had an overview of its investments. Stringent protocols governed the data accessible to QIA employees, outlining strict boundaries on the information they could interact with and transport in and out of the building. Service providers were obligated to establish localised servers to manage data servicing, further enhancing the fortress-like security measures.

Previously, individuals required an exit letter endorsed by their employer for each departure from Qatar. In 2020, the Qatari government abolished the stipulation for an exit permit. This change ushered in a new era of unrestricted travel to and from Qatar, liberating individuals from the constraints imposed by their employers.

Most people internationally have heard of Qatar, either through their investments abroad or, more recently, because of the World Cup being hosted in Qatar.

Broadcaster Al-Jazeera[166], an international news television network owned by the Qatari government, raised Qatar's media profile. The country is also known for investing over USD 40 billion in the UK, including the Shard Building, Harrods, Sainsbury, Ritz Hotel, Savoy Hotel, and the HSBC Tower.

Sport is used as a political tool for Qatar to improve its foreign relations. The FIFA World Cup was an excellent opportunity for Qatar to showcase its country to the world. To host the World Cup, you must be wealthy and have a large population. Qatar was the first Arab nation to host the tournament. Qatar is unique, having hosted it with its small population. People doubted they could manage the event, but they pulled it off.

Hosting the World Cup accelerated Qatar's infrastructure development, including constructing state-of-the-art stadiums, transportation networks, and accommodation facilities. The tournament has brought significant economic benefits to Qatar, including increased tourism, job creation, and business opportunities. The World Cup served as a platform for cultural exchange among nations. Fans worldwide came together to celebrate their shared love for football, fostering connections among diverse cultures.

As alluded to in an earlier chapter, the construction of World Cup infrastructure in Qatar raised concerns internationally regarding workers' rights and labour conditions. Steps were taken to address these concerns, with ongoing efforts to ensure fair treatment for all workers involved.

What annoys some Qataris is that some Europeans do not understand the difference between Qatar and the UAE. Even those who went to the World Cup in Qatar still think they went to the UAE, one Qatari jokingly shared with me.

The Saudis: End to Segregation of men and women

Saudi is the largest GCC country. It is known for its vast deserts, including the Rub' al Khali (Empty Quarter), one of the largest sand deserts in the world. Saudi has a population of about 33 million people. The currency is called the Saudi Riyal. Saudi is home to Islam's two holiest shrines in Mecca and Medina. The country follows a conservative form of Sunni Islam, which heavily influences social norms and laws. The country has a rich cultural heritage deeply rooted in Islamic traditions and customs. In recent years, Saudi has implemented various reforms to modernise and open its society.

The Al Saud dynasty held a monopoly of political power. Mohammed bin Salman, also known as MBS, a member of the Saudi Royal family, serves as Crown Prince and Prime Minister of Saudi. Mohammed bin Salman was born in 1985. Few people outside Saudi knew Mohammed bin Salman Al Saud before his father became king in 2015. The young Crown Prince is now considered the *de facto* ruler of Saudi.[167]

Riyadh, Jeddah, and Dammam are the three largest cities in Saudi Arabia. Riyadh is inland. It is the largest city, the capital and financial centre. It is bustling and fast-paced, with a skyline of towering skyscrapers and modern shopping malls. Riyadh is also home to many important government institutions.

Jeddah is a port city on the Red Sea coast. It is known for its more relaxed atmosphere, diverse population, and beautiful beaches. Jeddah is also a major centre for business and trade and a gateway to the holy cities of Mecca and Medina. In Jeddah, people are less conservative than the people of Riyadh. It will take around 8 hours to get from Riyadh to Jeddah by car. I recommend taking flights between the cities.

Dammam is an industrial city in the Eastern Province, home to many oil and gas companies and the military. Dammam borders Bahrain, and driving from Dammam to Bahrain is possible. These two cities are connected by the King Fahd Causeway, a 25-kilometre bridge that spans the Persian Gulf. The drive typically takes around an hour, depending on traffic conditions.

Saudi Aramco, the national oil company, is headquartered in Dharan, a smaller city 20 kilometres from Dammam. Saudi has significant oil reserves and is one of the world's leading oil producers. Now, Saudi is known for more than oil and sand.

The country's Vision 2030 plans to diversify its economy by reducing its dependence on oil. It is developing other sectors such as tourism, entertainment, and technology to attract foreign investment to create new jobs for a booming young population.[168]

Non-oil revenues have been steadily increasing. He has opened the country to foreign tourism and investment. We see investments in sectors such as tourism, technology, and healthcare. Sports has also become a big thing, which I will expand on in a later chapter. He is localising the defence industry.

Saudi is deploying incentives and ultimatums to persuade multinational companies to locate their regional headquarters in Riyadh instead of Dubai.[169]

The pace of change has been quite astonishing. His emphasis on social reforms has brought about significant changes, promoting inclusivity and empowering women.

Women have been appointed in senior roles in the government and the private sector as part of a campaign to empower women. The landmark decision in 2015 to grant women the right to vote and stand for office marked a significant stride towards gender equality.

MBS abolished the male guardianship system. The guardianship system was used to forbid women from travelling and even from leaving the house without a male family member. Women can now travel alone.

Women are no longer required to wear the abaya. Wearing the hijab has now become a personal choice.

Until recently, men and women were segregated in society. For example, restaurants had separate entrances for women. Many restaurants are now quietly allowing men and women to mingle.

The Saudi government has also reined in the religious police, mutawa. The mutawa had broad powers to stop and question people, arrest suspects, and detain them without charge. They were known for strictly enforcing Islamic dress codes and gender segregation rules. They would patrol public spaces to ensure that men and women were not engaging in immoral behaviour, such as holding hands or kissing. They used to raid businesses to ensure they were closed during prayer times and not selling alcohol or other prohibited goods. They would monitor social media for any content they deemed offensive or un-Islamic. The mutawa plays a significant role in

Saudi but can no longer detain people or arrest suspects without a warrant.

Additionally, MBS has been cracking down on corruption, gaining a popular vote. This campaign aimed to improve transparency and accountability in the Saudi government.

I have been told he is very "task-oriented." Through stories shared by friends, I have learned that anyone offering to help him accelerate his timelines for the execution of Saudi's grand plan will get his ear. He is interested in solutions. It is much easier to meet with him in person than getting a meeting with someone of his level in any other GCC country.

Nathalie, whom I met at the Capital Club in Dubai, told me about her vivid memory of her first meeting with a Saudi individual. The prospect of meeting someone in traditional Saudi attire filled her with excitement. The meeting had been arranged for her in Dubai through a business contact. Anticipating a conservative encounter – she had been informed that he rarely travelled beyond Saudi – she decided to have a chaperone accompany her.

Interestingly, to her surprise, he had also brought a female chaperone along. The meeting was completely different from what she had been expecting. He arrived in a short-sleeved polo shirt while she had dressed conservatively in wide trousers, a matching long shirt, and a draped Hermes scarf. He delved into his enjoyable experiences in the US, sharing details of his American girlfriend. This was so different from the briefing before the meeting. It surprised her and left her slightly disappointed, as it did not align with her anticipated conservative image.

When she shared her experience with the person who had introduced her to him, he was equally taken aback by the disparity between the Saudi individual's described demeanour and the encounter she had described. This disconnect made them both realise Saudis can exhibit distinctly different personalities, depending on whether they are in Saudi or abroad.

In the West, this phenomenon may appear difficult to comprehend. A public facade in Saudi often exists, quite different from the persona displayed abroad. This duality stems from the complex interplay of cultural norms and personal expression. Observing Saudis engaging in lively activities abroad, such as partying in nightclubs in London, might lead to a greater understanding of how these behaviours could be driven by a desire to compensate for the more restricted social atmosphere they experience in their home country.

The memory of her inaugural journey to Saudi also remains vivid in her mind. It was a period of intense activity, as she had orchestrated a roadshow for one of her former bosses from one of the investment banks she had worked at in London. Their primary objective was to build relationships, engage with investors and educate them on the services that could be provided. Their ambitious itinerary included visits to Riyadh, Jeddah, and Dhahran.

With this being their first voyage to Saudi, she had spent weeks preparing her ex-boss, John, on cultural norms and etiquette. Following a lunch meeting with a former private plane flight attendant who had resided in Saudi, she reached out to John to share a piece of advice she had gathered. She had recommended she exercise caution around the religious police, suggesting a rather unconventional response if ever confronted by them. She said, "In the event of an encounter with the religious police, swiftly cover your face with the headscarf and run."

These stories may have triggered a sense of unease in John. She had accentuated the more thrilling anecdotes, presenting an imbalanced perspective. The tales of intrigue and suspense certainly made for a more captivating narrative.

En route from Kuwait to Saudi, a curious incident unfolded as they awaited their departure at the airport. John turned to her and remarked, "Nathalie, I can see your bare feet peeking out." This observation seemed perplexing, given she was draped in a full abaya. Upon closer inspection, a sliver of skin was inadvertently visible as she stepped forward. Was he trying to be amusing and teasing her, she wondered? To her surprise, his concern was genuine, and he insisted they buy a pair of socks for her right there and then at the airport to conceal her exposed feet. Socks? The temperature outside was a scorching 40°!

John was harbouring some apprehension about their impending flight to Saudi and needed reassurance. To put his unease to rest, she approached a group of local women at a shop within the airport. She said, "My companion here believes I should be wearing socks inside my shoes."

They chuckled and responded by lifting their abayas, revealing their bare feet in their sandals. "You look immaculate," they said, "and are bound to have a splendid journey!"

Turning to John, she asked, "Did you hear what they said?"

While his scepticism persisted, he relented, allowing the matter to dissipate.

However, fifteen minutes later, he noted a strand of hair was showing from beneath her headscarf. Her long blond hair was snugly tucked away within a discreet black cap, further concealed by the draped headscarf. She was meticulously and comprehensively veiled. She tucked in the strand of hair and calmed him down again.

Upon arrival at Riyadh Airport, a palpable tension hung in the air, casting a sombre mood over the scene. The atmosphere was very tense. As they took a taxi to their hotel, Nathalie started to chat with John, intending to provide him with additional insights into navigating Saudi customs.

John was distant, his gaze fixated straight ahead. With a measured but resolute tone, he curtly requested, "Please refrain from speaking to me. It is not advisable to converse while in the taxi."

It dawned on her that he had taken her earlier counsel to heart too earnestly. She had previously informed him that a man and a woman sharing a taxi was deemed inappropriate and against local norms, potentially leading to legal issues. Additionally, she mentioned that societal norms dictated limited interaction between men and women, even extending to settings like restaurants and cafés, where segregation was often practised. He was repeating these rules back to her, to her surprise and bemusement.

Upon our arrival at the offices of a well-known institutional investor, tensions were running high. Before the meeting began, Nathalie needed to intervene assertively, "John, please understand that while I have dressed respectfully, fully adhering to the guidelines, I am not a local."

This candid exchange led to an apology from John, who later confided that his heightened sense of responsibility for her well-being had driven him to act obsessively. Nathalie told me they often share a laugh over this incident. He playfully jokes, "If people start referring to me as 'Nathalie's cleric' when I return to the UAE, I will know you have been talking about me." This humorous reference has become a recurring joke between them.

A friend of Nathalie, an expat, was picked up at Riyadh Airport by his Saudi partner in a Ferrari. As they were driving to his hotel, they were stopped on the road by the police. "Why are you not praying?"

"We flew in together," he replied. "My friend is not a Muslim. I already prayed on the aeroplane."

They let him go. He said he would have been in big trouble if he had not made that story up.

I was told another amusing story by a woman, Salma, CEO of an Omani company. She went on business to Saudi, joined by an expat who had organised the meetings for her. She had a GCC passport and went through border control faster than the expat. In those days, it was a ritual which took at least an hour, as fingerprints and photos all needed to be documented and verified. She agreed to go ahead as they were running late for their meeting.

When she arrived at the hotel in Riyadh, the investors were waiting for her. They immediately started the meeting.

Suddenly, the police arrived. "Why are you meeting here?" they asked.

They explained it was a business meeting.

Pointing at the men, the police said, "You go and have a business meeting with other men." Then they told Salma. "And you, go and have a meeting with other women."

The hotel receptionists had called the police to report improper behaviour.

They continued the meeting the next day at the office of the investor.

Saudi's social landscape has evolved notably in recent times, adopting a more relaxed ambience. The most memorable moments were captured during the earlier days, characterised by the tension in the air. Back then, no one would meet your gaze, and smiles were a rarity. Strangely, I found myself secretly relishing this edgy atmosphere. It was a unique environment, charged with a distinct energy.

The transformation became evident at the airport on my recent Saudi trips. A warmth and friendliness welcomed me at the airport in Riyadh. The previous staff had been replaced with a sales team. Similarly, hotel staff members would laugh and exchange playful banter with me. I forgot I was in Saudi. It could have been Dubai. Also, the arrival of Uber alleviated the early-day challenges of getting around, with not many taxi drivers speaking English.

Among the most remarkable moments of Karen's investor meetings was the visit to the offices of Prince Al Waleed bin Talal Al Saud, a Saudi businessman, a legend, although not without controversy.[170] He was part of a group of prominent Saudi businessmen locked up in the Ritz Carlton and subjected to a corruption crackdown.

He was one of the only Saudis she had heard of before moving to the Middle East, mainly because of his association with polo. She still remembers him appearing in a polo outfit on CNN to discuss his holding in Citigroup. He serves as the founder and chief executive officer of Kingdom Holding, an entity with extensive investments spanning financial services, tourism, hospitality, mass media, entertainment, retail, agriculture, petrochemicals, aviation, technology, and real estate sectors.[171]

Karen told me his investment office, situated adjacent to the Four Seasons in Riyadh, is like a museum. It shows his awards and photographs, posing next to politicians. The display exudes a sense of power and legacy, leaving a profound impression. Her male client felt a little intimidated. Meeting with this investment group was an experience, even if an investment was not secured on this occasion.

Prince Al Waleed bin Talal Al Saud was known for advocating women's rights. He spoke out despite living in a country where women could not drive or vote. He encouraged his female employees, who comprise 65% of his workforce, not to wear the veil in his offices. He also took to Twitter to express his support, writing, "It is time for women to drive!" He financed Hanadi Zakaria al-Hindi, the first Saudi woman commercial airline pilot.[172]

When she visits Saudi, Karen continues to wear the abaya, though it is no longer mandatory for foreigners. She believes it is a gesture of respect and consideration of the values held by the older generation. Some still find it difficult to adjust to the changes in Saudi. They may be confused and even angry. It will take time for habits to evolve. Remember that change has been fast, and men are still learning to interact with women.

She noticed a certain air of pride emerging among expat women in Saudi who also opt to continue to wear the abaya. As their approving nods meet, it felt like they were the torchbearers of a previous era, having experienced Saudi before the sweeping changes.

She will be missing her abaya. Just like the older generation, she must get used to the change and rearrange her wardrobe for her travels to Saudi. Saudi is undergoing a rapid and profound transformation, likely to persist in the years ahead.

Following the abolition of mandatory segregation, the entertainment industry blossomed. In 2018, Saudi unveiled its first cinema in over three decades, a pivotal moment for the entertainment landscape. Subsequently, more cinemas have opened. Saudi has hosted international concerts, and even raves have taken place. The Saudi lifestyle is not much different from life in the UAE. The Saudi government is concurrently investing in bolstering tourism infrastructure. This includes establishing hotels and resorts and more lenient visa regulations for international tourists.

Karen warned me to be careful in Saudi and stick to the rules. Saudi has stringent penalties, including public beheadings. I told her this occasionally comes up in Europe when discussing the Middle East. She explained that the crimes that warrant death sentences in Saudi are murder, drug trafficking, apostasy, and armed robbery. Beheadings are enacted in public squares, serving as a deterrent to crime.

In 2022, Amnesty International reported at least 65 executions in Saudi, a decrease from the preceding year's 81. While this figure reflects a decline, it remains significantly higher than other nations. The practice of public beheadings in Saudi is fraught with controversy. Human rights organisations vehemently denounce the practice, branding it as barbaric and inhumane, stressing its cruel and degrading nature. The Saudi government maintains that this practice aligns with Islamic Law and crime prevention.

In the West, some argue Saudi is safer than other countries. Recently, there have been calls to abolish the death penalty in Saudi. In 2020, the Saudi King issued a decree limiting the death penalty to the gravest of crimes, yet it did not altogether abolish the practice.

Chapter 31.

Insights beyond the GCC

The Middle East is larger than the GCC. You may also hear reference to MENA, which includes the Middle East and North Africa. I will touch on some of the countries in the following chapters.

The Egyptians: A Proud Nation

The current president is Abdel Fattah el-Sisi. The population of Egypt is 100 million. The capital is Cairo. The currency is called the Egyptian pound.[173]

Suzanne, someone I met at a networking event in Dubai, moved to Egypt to work as a CIO for a family group. On her first day, she tried to impress her new boss, a Coptic Christian, emphasising her familiarity with the Arab culture. Her boss looked shocked. She then tried to adjust what she had said. "Well, you are African, of course."

Her boss did not look amused at all. "We are Egyptian," he said sternly.

Suzanne clearly understood from this incident the Egyptians have a strong sense of national identity. Their pride is attached to the history of their country.

After the awkward exchange with her new boss, Suzanne researched Egypt. Egypt boasts a rich history and culture going back thousands of years. It is home to ancient civilisations like the Pharaohs, renowned for their monumental constructions like the Pyramids. Egypt's contributions to mathematics, architecture and literature are also noteworthy.

Modern Egyptians take pride in their country's heritage, landmarks, and achievements. The Nile River, the Sphinx, the Great Pyramid of Giza, and the temples of Luxor are examples of iconic sites evoking a sense of national pride.

Egypt's diverse cultural traditions, cuisine, and language further strengthen its connection with their nation. Nationalism and a sense of belonging are deeply ingrained in the Egyptian identity, so Egyptians often express their pride in their country and its rich past.

Egypt is predominantly a Muslim country, with Islam being the state religion. Egypt's Christian heritage is deeply intertwined with its historical and cultural identity. Ancient churches, monasteries, and religious sites can be found throughout the country. [174]

The Coptic Orthodox Church is one of the oldest Christian denominations, and its roots in Egypt date back to the early centuries of Christianity. Despite the religious differences, there is a long history of coexistence between Muslims and Christians in Egypt.[175] Tensions and incidents have arisen only occasionally over the years.

You will encounter many Egyptians in positions of influence in the Middle East. It is an easy move for them, as they speak Arabic.

Muriel recalled being in a meeting in Dubai when suddenly half the attendees left. They all were Egyptian. She found out a revolution had broken out in Egypt. The Egyptian Revolution of 2011, also known as the January 25 Revolution, was a series of anti-government protests that commenced in Cairo on January 25, 2011.[176]

The protests were sparked by the death of a fruit vendor beaten by the police. They quickly grew into a broader movement, demanding the removal of President Hosni Mubarak. Mubarak resigned on February 11, 2011, following

18 days of protests. This revolution established a democratically elected government but also brought about a period of political instability in Egypt.

Muriel had just returned from Cairo. We had a Zoom video call. She told me Egypt is currently full of people from the Gulf. Egypt has nice weather and is incredibly cheap after the devaluation of its currency over the last year.

She told me some Egyptians feel superior to the Gulf, even though the Middle East is propping them up during their economic crisis.

Government and businesses had been overleveraged, which had an especially catastrophic impact on those who had borrowed in dollars. The Egyptian pound devalued from 15 to 39 against the dollar.

Suzanne, who has lived in Cairo for years, told me Egypt is often described as a patriarchal society where men hold positions of power and authority. Traditional gender roles assign women to domestic and caregiving roles. It starts at an early age. A five-year-old boy will be told how amazing he is, while the five-year-old girl may be ignored.

She mentioned she does yoga with Cairo's super-elite females. Chatting with them, she found their lives are dominated by their family, especially their fathers and brothers. I mentioned internationally that women are more oppressed in Egypt than elsewhere in the Middle East. She agreed the sense of entitlement among men in society is evident. They hold most positions of power. She said, "Even though there are female spokespeople in government, this is a male-dominated society. Women are often excluded from decision-making processes."

Muriel was constantly bumping into Egyptians across the GCC. She shared with me one of the earlier experiences she had in Bahrain with an Egyptian. She had only been a year in the GCC and was still heavily influenced by stereotypes. She had scheduled a meeting with an asset manager in Bahrain.

As soon as she walked into his office, she realised within five minutes that the Chief Investment Officer, who was Egyptian, did not speak a word of English. She had reached out to him over LinkedIn, so admittedly, she could not test his English beforehand. She gave up on any sensible conversation and said, "I will follow up with your team." She was ready to finish the meeting but was politely trying to fill time.

He then asked her if she would like a special coffee.

Muriel graciously accepted, thinking he would order his assistant to bring them a coffee.

He grabs his coat. He starts waving his hand, telling her to follow him. *Hmmm, things were not exactly going as planned at this stage.* She was looking to wrap up the meeting, and this was taking another turn.

They ended up at a local coffee shop, where he told her about his personal life and how often he went to the gym weekly. He seemed lonely in Bahrain and was happy to have someone to talk to. After a couple of hours, she thought things were getting too personal and realised she needed to make a move to ensure she would be on time for the next meeting at her hotel.

He offered her a lift by car, which was exceptionally kind. She, however, was quite nervous about his offer because she felt the whole conversation was too intimate for a business meeting, and she was concerned about his intentions. Muriel told him it was a generous offer, but she would take a taxi.

"Let me at least take you to the road and help you find a taxi," he said.

Anyway, there were absolutely no taxis coming. None. He insisted on driving her to her next meeting. She could say nothing more after standing at the side of the road for thirty minutes, so she agreed to get into his car. Muriel felt she was entering the danger zone. In her mind, this was not sensible. She had her hand on the lever of the vehicle, ready to jump out at any moment.

While on the highway, she noticed they passed a sign indicating directions to her hotel. She turned to him and said, "Oh, shouldn't we be taking this exit?"

"No, no," he said, "it is the next turning."

She got more anxious. In her mind, she envisaged being transported to the desert and never coming back alive. She had watched too many thriller movies.

After taking the second turn, he dropped her off at her hotel.

Muriel admitted she felt incredibly guilty about all her thoughts, clearly having stereotyped him.

He turned out to be a charming and kind man, although a bit too personal for what was a business setting.

Muriel told me that she would not have been in this situation if she had a driver. She would advise all women in business to make sure they have a driver for the day and not rely on taxis.

The Indians: Struggle to say No.

India's Prime Minister is Narendra Modi. The population of India is about 1.4 billion. The capital is Delhi. The currency is called the Indian rupee.[177]

The Indians arrived in Dubai centuries ago. Back then, Dubai was a humble fishing village. Indians began to settle in, bringing their entrepreneurial spirit and bargaining culture to Dubai. Over time, the Indian community grew exponentially and contributed significantly to Dubai's development. They played key roles in the trade, construction, finance, and hospitality sectors. From operating bustling spice markets to building towering skyscrapers, Indians have left a mark on Dubai. Dubai has excelled in attracting people from India. A light-hearted joke by an expat: "Dubai is the nicest city in India." Others call Dubai a province of India. More and more Indians are moving to Dubai.

In 2023, over 1.5 million Indians lived in Dubai and over 3.5 million in the UAE. Indians represent over 35% of the UAE population, representing one of the largest Indian communities worldwide outside of India.[178] About half are represented by labourers.

The Indian community in the UAE also includes prominent Indians, including billionaires. They made their money by playing a significant role in the economic development of the UAE. Of all visitors travelling to Dubai, Indians make up the largest segment.

The presence of Indian professionals, including Chief Investment Officers and analysts, in family investment groups across the Middle East is notable. There are reasons for this. One reason for the prevalence of Indian analysts in investment teams is cost. Hiring Indian professionals can be cheaper for companies compared to hiring Europeans, given differences in labour costs. India has a large pool of well-educated and skilled professionals in various fields, including finance and investments. Indian analysts bring strong analytical and technical skills, making them valuable assets to investment teams. Many Indian professionals are fluent in English, which is widely spoken in India. This is a plus and helps effective communication between international investment teams and external global counterparts. I found the Indian community to be incredibly well-networked. They know how to work the system.

Julia, the founder of a jewellery business, told me she observed a couple of traits in her interactions with individuals from India. Firstly, there can be challenges when receiving timely payments and deliveries. I told her about my experience working with incredible Indian clients who paid me retainers and consistently honoured their payment commitments. I discovered that when a deal was a one-time arrangement, there was a higher risk of not receiving payment than when it was part of an ongoing relationship.

Secondly, she told me directness can be elusive, making it difficult to obtain a clear and straightforward "yes" or "no" response. She joked it has been suggested the British have influenced these characteristics.

Julia told me an amusing story about doing business with India. She would go to India to choose stones to put into rings. In her first year, she asked for blue stones and was sent a different colour, pink. Then Julia learned to ask, "What colour stone do you think would look good in this setting?" By asking a more open-ended question, she engaged collaboratively and indirectly. This way, the suppliers provided recommendations based on their available stock. This enabled her to make an informed decision as to whether any of the available colours suited her needs.

Her story underscores the importance of understanding and navigating different communication styles in the business world. Being open to alternative ways of expressing ideas and using creative strategies can lead to smoother interactions and successful collaborations, even where there might be initial challenges in communication. If it does not work one way, try it another way.

Addressing superiors in Indian corporations with the appropriate title, such as "Sir" or "Madam," reflects the hierarchy observed in many workplaces in India. This formal mode of addressing people acknowledges the status and authority of the individual. Using titles like "Sir" or "Madam" helps create a sense of professionalism and courtesy in the workplace. It shows that you recognise and appreciate the hierarchical structure and authority within the organisation. Additionally, it can contribute to building positive relationships with colleagues and superiors by demonstrating your understanding and adherence to local customs and norms.

Before we go on to the Iranians, I must tell a story. In a meeting, I told someone from India I was doing business in Iran.

"I would never do business with Iran!" he firmly told me.

"Why not?" I asked.

"They never pay!" was his answer.

"That is a bit much coming from you, as India is not exactly known for paying on time."

Luckily, he had a good sense of humour and laughed.

"So, you are telling me the Iranians are one step up from India?" I asked.

"Yes!"

The Iranians: Tough Intellectual Negotiators

The Supreme Leader of Iran is Ali Khamenei. President Ebrahim Raisi is the top elected official and second in rank to the supreme leader. He is responsible for the day-to-day running of the government and has considerable influence over domestic policy and foreign affairs. However, his powers are limited, especially in security matters.

The population of Iran is around 86 million. The capital is Tehran. The currency, the Iranian rial, has been one of the weakest currencies in the world. Iran, officially known as the

Islamic Republic of Iran, is a country located in Western Asia. It borders Iraq, Turkey, Armenia, Azerbaijan, Turkmenistan, Afghanistan, and Pakistan. Iran has a rich history, dating back thousands of years, and has been home to various ancient civilisations. Its population is predominantly Persian but home to ethnic groups, such as Azerbaijanis, Kurds, Arabs, and Balochis. The official language is Persian (Farsi), but Iranians also speak regional languages or dialects. Economic sanctions, political unrest and high inflation have pressured Iran's currency. [179]

Iran is known for its rich oil reserves, making it one of the largest oil producers in the world.[180] The economy extends beyond oil and includes agriculture, manufacturing, tourism, and services.

I travelled to Iran between 2015 and 2017 when the sanctions were lifted. Iran opened itself to foreign business, showcasing the investment opportunities available to the world. Trade delegations visited Iran, eager to explore business opportunities. The reality on the ground differed from what the international press had reported. I used to read local English newspapers in my hotel and found the articles to be more balanced than in the West. The local newspaper may, of course, have been more biased.

When I participated in a conference on investing in Iran in Amsterdam, the Chairperson approached me and asked if I wanted to write an article. He said he would get it published.

The article I wrote on international investors' challenges when investing in Iran was published in the Tehran Times, the English-speaking newspaper in Iran[181]. In the article, I walked through all the perceived barriers of international investors. Surprisingly, no changes were made to the article besides adding a reference to an important person. A column was featured on the front page next to an Iranian Oscar winner, followed by a full page inside.

The day the article would be published, I was joining a trade delegation from Holland in shipping who were visiting the Iranian Government Maritime Organisation. I walked up to the second in command at the Dutch Embassy, who had organised the mission, and informed him my article would be published. I asked whether, in the future, I should pass it by the Embassy first. He reflected briefly and said, "No, Holland is a free country. You can write what you want."

Later, I got a heads-up and was warned because the article was written in Holland during the conference in Amsterdam, I would not be qualified as a local journalist. Being qualified as a journalist in Iran was not something I should aspire to as that potentially could endanger my life.

As I wrote in the article, when I first went to Iran in 2015, people asked me what it was like in Iran. Friends were eager to hear shocking stories. They expected me to say that the infrastructure was run down, with military and religious police on every corner and not much of a selection of quality consumer goods. I did not have much to report as it felt like going to Eastern Europe in the old days. There were more similarities than differences.[182] Surprisingly, there are excellent high-end restaurants like any other city. I also enjoyed a more traditional dinner in the hills outside of Tehran.

Iranians are exceptionally well educated, including the women, and charming. They had numerous titles on their business cards, indicating their extensive studies and expertise. Additionally, they possessed an entrepreneurial streak. During the business card exchange, I commonly received four of theirs in exchange for one of mine. They have a way of leaving a lasting impression and always made me feel like they had not seen a foreigner in years. They are superb relationship managers. Their hospitality extends to the airport, where they have a CIP section for Commercially Important People.

I never felt unsafe. Some people told me it was likely because I was being followed effectively and had bodyguards protecting me.

The European press had headlines of MOUs (Memoranda of Understanding) being signed. I soon discovered obstacles to doing business within Iran and internationally. As I wrote in the article, not all banks internationally were ready to do business with Iran after the sanctions were lifted.[183] Receiving funds originating from Iran, directly or indirectly, was difficult. Only banks with little or no US exposure seemed most open to doing business with Iran. In practice, you needed to be either an existing client of the bank or commercially interesting enough for a bank to be willing to take what they perceive as high risks of doing business with Iran.

At the same time, banks internationally were grappling with their business issues, which made them reluctant to take on more risk. Banks had been pulling out of emerging markets to focus on their home market.

Being paid a retainer for consultancy services out of Iran proved impossible. None of the European banks wanted to touch the transfer.

Companies maintained several sets of accounts, which did not comfort international investors. There was a significant information gap. Once the sanctions were lifted, huge strides were made in adopting international accounting standards.[184] I remember struggling to explain the importance of KYC (Know Your Client). Due diligence on counterparties was also challenging. Shareholder structures were opaque. It was hard to ensure you were not dealing with a sanctioned entity.

In navigating the intricacies of capital raising in Iran, I understood their perception of capital raising timelines. There was an inherent belief that securing a loan or equity was as straightforward as contacting a relative at a bank and obtaining funds the following day. A friend explained if a company in Iran wanted a loan, the management team would call their cousin or uncle, and the deal was done.

Similarly, there was not much business for recruitment agencies. If someone landed a prominent position at a company or in government, he would be expected to provide jobs for his struggling friends and family.

My role evolved into an educational one, shedding light on the complexities of fundraising processes abroad and dispelling misconceptions.

During a trade mission, I was asked to discuss project financing with the Secretary-General of the Government entity we were meeting. With prominent Dutch companies on the trade mission, I faced considerable pressure. In the Friday meeting with the Secretary-General and his team, they unveiled two projects, with an urgent request to secure funding by Monday. Having previously looked at the sector, I had a fairly good idea of what could be done. After briefly evaluating the two projects' feasibility, I conveyed that one project was achievable while the other posed significant challenges. Instantly, they withdrew the feasible project, focusing solely on the difficult one. To navigate this situation diplomatically, I explained that obtaining funding by Monday would be challenging, yet I committed to providing feedback by the stated deadline.

Another challenge related to the way projects were presented to companies internationally. The emphasis was put on showcasing the prized assets' immense potential and the vast returns investors could make by investing in Iran. Foreign investors were well-versed in assessing returns. Their focus was not on the potential – that was a given – but on understanding and mitigating risks, an aspect of fundraising overlooked by the Iranian side. The risks had to be incorporated into their presentations, explaining how they were mitigated to raise investors' comfort levels.

I was led to believe that people in Iran did not hold much cash, leading me to infer that lacking liquidity incorrectly signalled a sense of poverty. This was not entirely the case. In a country where the value of cash rapidly depreciated, it became a matter of urgency to spend or invest it as soon as possible. It took me time to grasp this concept and comprehend the profound impact of inflation on cash and investment behaviour. In an environment where the value of money was in constant flux, any available liquidity was promptly put to work.

The inflation led to a surge in real estate prices. The cost of real estate in Tehran reached levels comparable to those seen in cities like London, with the housing supply in Tehran being limited due to factors such as scarcity of available land, high construction costs, and government-imposed development constraints.

To effectively navigate the Iranian market, I assembled specialised teams, each focused on different industry sectors. These teams, comprised of former investment bankers who, like me, had transitioned into independent roles, allowed us to engage with Iran unburdened by the limitations of larger banks with substantial US interests preventing them from engaging with the country, even after sanctions were lifted.

A particularly intriguing revelation emerged from my interactions. I had believed the oil and gas sector was the most sensitive. However, the technology sector proved to be the most delicate sector within Iran. During discussions with a potential local partner we had selected for a technology fund we were looking to set up, he half-joking told me, "I hope your technology expert is not a spy." I relayed his comments to my

London business partner, who assured me I did not need to be concerned.

Together with the local partner, we successfully partnered with local funding to establish the tech fund. However, the tech investment banker based in London, who was meant to deliver a speech at a conference to further this initiative and close the deal, backed out at the last moment. The precise reasons for his change of heart remain unclear. Whether it was his ties to a prominent Iranian couple in the US or concerns about potential implications for his clients in Israel, questions lingered. He said his wife did not want him to go to Iran.

Iranians have honed their negotiation skills to a remarkable degree, drawing upon a rich cultural heritage of bargaining and haggling spanning generations, mixed with their high level of education and intellect. Their art of persuasion is evident as they skillfully navigate negotiations to achieve their desired outcomes. Unafraid to employ assertive tactics and push boundaries, they are adept at securing favourable deals. Engaging in negotiations with an Iranian counterpart is akin to attending a masterclass in negotiation strategies, and my two years in Iran significantly elevated my proficiency.

Negotiations in Iran are not mere transactions. They are intricate intellectual processes rooted in a desire to understand and connect. Failure to actively engage in the negotiation process is often considered an insult, underscoring Iranians' importance in forging meaningful connections through negotiation.

Stephanie told me she might have been under surveillance or subject to phone tapping. During a conversation with a client on her way to the airport, she repeatedly heard the same responses from her client played back to her. The same replies echoed despite her attempts to rephrase her statements, thinking he had not heard her correctly. Eventually, she had to hang up to break the loop. She would joke to friends she did not mind being followed around, as the government could then see her unwavering commitment to conducting business in Iran.

In another intriguing encounter, an individual in Tehran offered to share confidential information with her. He handed her a USB stick, urging her to download its contents onto her computer. He told her it had critical information he wanted to share with her but did not give any context. Stephanie felt uneasy about proceeding and declined. Subsequently, she never heard from him again. She never entirely understood what that had been about.

I could relate to her stories. During my time in Dubai, an Iranian contact once told me something intriguing: "I know exactly the dates and whom you met with during the years you were going up and down to Iran."

Puzzled, I asked him how he could know.

"It is quite simple," he explained. "I called the government. And taxi drivers are helpful too – they talk a lot among themselves."

This revelation shed light on the interconnectedness of information in Iran.

Reflecting on it, I recalled the subjective comments my taxi driver would make during my trips, such as labelling a company I was meeting with as "important" or questioning the significance of another. In hindsight, I could have leveraged my driver's insights to connect with the most influential families.

Alcohol is forbidden in Iran. This means no import, sale, production, or consumption. This comprehensive ban applies to citizens and foreign residents within the country. Even diplomatic missions, though typically afforded certain immunities and privileges, are bound by Iranian law regarding alcohol-related regulations.

Surprisingly, at a reception at the Dutch Embassy, alcohol was being served. Embassies operating within the confines of Iranian law have the prerogative to import alcohol for specific diplomatic functions, such as official receptions or formal dinners. This practice aligns with diplomatic conventions and allows foreign missions to adhere to their cultural norms while navigating the host country's regulations.

In meetings, everyone would ask me what sightseeing I had done. I instructed my driver to take me to all the sites one day. I remember being at the Persian carpet museum. It had not been set up for tourists. It was a bunker with carpets pinned on the wall. There was nothing to explain the history in English or show me how they were made. I was out after 30 minutes.

My driver said to me, "That was fast. When I take the Chinese here, they spend an entire day in the museum."

I replied, "They must be copying the carpets."

The country is also famous for its historical landmarks. Persepolis, an ancient ceremonial capital of the Achaemenid Empire, is a UNESCO World Heritage Site and one of the most visited attractions in Iran. Other notable sites include Naqsh-e Jahan Square in Isfahan and the ancient city of Yazd.

Stephanie, a veteran in the hotel sector, told me a story about engaging in business dealings with one of the prominent families associated with Rouhani to establish a fund focused on investing in hotels within Iran. They planned to set up this venture within the DIFC (Dubai International Financial Centre).

She found the interactions with the family highly engaging and enriching. The head of the family was solely fluent in Iranian, which necessitated the presence of a translator during all their conversations. He shared intriguing insights with her. He emphasised appearances can often be deceiving, and hidden dynamics were at play. Specifically, he disclosed the US and Iran had maintained a more favourable relationship than what was publicly perceived. The two nations had an agreement to support Rouhani's re-election. This revelation took aback the translator.

His statement came as good news to Stephanie. She recognised such an outcome would positively affect her business in Iran. Furthermore, she was informed the US had conveyed its acceptance of Iran's potential to become a dominant force in the region. Interestingly, contacts in Saudi relayed similar narratives, suggesting either the US gave the same message to both or there was miscommunication. The US possessed adeptness in tailoring their communication to align with the desires and expectations of their counterparts.

Stephanie said she thought part of the messages in the meeting got lost in translation.

Stephanie also told me that during her visit to the sovereign wealth fund in Iran, before the sanctions were lifted, she noticed in the signing-in book at the entrance that a major US private equity firm had checked in before her. Discussions during the preliminary stages were, of course, subject to the lifting of sanctions. Considering the prevailing sanctions, she said she was surprised to see a US private equity fund signing in. She likened this situation to the "sneak preview" of a Harrods sale, with items showcased before the sale begins.

I told her about firms at the time visiting Iran in anticipation of the sanctions being lifted, not just US companies. Iran will continue to struggle because of the US sanctions reintroduced in 2017. Hopes for the lifting of the sanctions are low. Stephanie had to discontinue business in Iran in 2017 but said she thoroughly enjoyed her time there and is eager to step back into the market if the sanctions are lifted.

An Iranian lawyer told me he remembers countless stories of his mother, who was not taken seriously as a businesswoman. She owns a meat slaughtering company in

Iran. Whenever she went to file documentation at the bank, she would be asked, "When is your husband arriving?"

While Saudi has quietly been reforming, in Europe, the newspapers have reported on protests across Iran for women's rights. Women can drive in Iran. When I was in Iran in 2017, everyone was wearing a hijab, including me. Women in Iran have since been rejecting the hijab, seen by some to symbolise repressive laws.

Parisa, who recently moved to Dubai, told me a lot has changed, and you may see around 30% of women without a hijab on the streets of Tehran. They will have their head scarf draped around their neck; when needed, they will put it back on, covering their hair.

In the past, not wearing a hijab or even wearing nail polish or sunglasses, anything associated with the West, could have resulted in being arrested by the moral police. The regime's enforcement of the hijab has undergone significant changes. Instead of directly enforcing it, the authorities insist that individuals who do not cover their hair face the risk of being fined.

Parisa was concerned anyone could report perceived misconduct, such as spotting a lady in a car not wearing the hijab, by sending an SMS with the vehicle's number plate to the authorities. This system is open to abuse. For instance, if someone sees a woman smiling at her husband, they could report her. Your car will be stopped and stored in a garage for 1-2 weeks. In the end, you may be fined. Moreover, not wearing a hijab may restrict your access to certain services. She gave examples of the lady at the counter in the duty-free shop at the airport not serving her because she was not wearing a hijab. At the airport, the lady at the check-in counter would not serve her either. Effectively, the population ensures compliance.

Parisa explained that the difference in policies towards women in Iran and Saudi could be attributed to their respective regimes. She told me, "In Iran, the country is governed by religious clerics. They will not relax the rules. The hijab is considered a religious obligation. This is what they believe."

I questioned whether my approach might be too assertive at a certain juncture. During this time, an Iranian colleague reassured me, "Not at all, you smile." This insight was enlightening at the time. Years later, I realised why women did not smile and that it may be inappropriate.

I had a fantastic time in Iran and loved every moment. When the sanctions are lifted again, I will visit again.

The Israelis: Value for Money

Israel's Prime Minister is Benjamin Netanyahu. The population of Israel is about nine million. The capital is Jerusalem. The currency is called the Israeli new shekel, in short, the Israeli shekel.[185]

Establishing diplomatic relations between the UAE and Israel in 2020, known as the Abraham Accords, marked a significant and transformative milestone in Middle Eastern politics. The agreement, which brought together former adversaries, ushered in a new era of collaboration between the two nations. This historic development led to flourishing bilateral relations, encompassing trade, tourism, technology, and cultural exchanges.

Before the Abraham Accords, there were notable challenges and restrictions surrounding interactions with Israel. Including Israel on roadshows was impossible: direct flights between the UAE and Israel were unavailable, and the country code of Israel was blocked within the UAE. Furthermore, having an Israeli stamp on one's passport posed difficulties for those intending to visit the UAE. Individuals, especially business travellers, resorted to using multiple passports or requesting separate pages for Israeli stamps to navigate these limitations. The Abraham Accords effectively removed these barriers, enhancing engagement and activity.

The newfound openness led to a surge of interactions akin to dealing with the US. I invested time, calling on investors in Israel and exploring business opportunities. Israel is known for its technological advancements and start-up ecosystem. It has become known as "The Start-Up Nation" due to its thriving high-tech industry and innovative spirit. The country excels in cybersecurity, biotechnology, agriculture, and renewable energy. Israel brought innovative technologies to the UAE, contributing to collaborations between the two countries.

However, one noteworthy challenge encountered was related to contract negotiations. Israeli counterparts insisted on conducting contracts under Israeli contract law, raising concerns regarding potential disputes and recourse. The unfamiliarity with the legal system and jurisdiction posed a dilemma, as pursuing legal action in a foreign country presented uncertainties.

Rachel raised a similar issue with a client.

"Don't worry," he remarked. "I am famous. Google me."

This was met with a thoughtful response. "All the more reason to exercise caution." This humorous exchange encapsulated the complexities of cross-border business dealings.

In conclusion, the Abraham Accords have fundamentally reshaped the dynamics of engagement between the UAE and Israel, opening new avenues for cooperation and growth. While the transformative nature of this development is undeniable, it has also brought to light certain challenges arising from divergent cultures. As both nations strengthen their ties, navigating such intricacies remains essential to conducting successful business.

Working for a multi-family office, Rachel was involved in a transaction between an Israeli family group and a government entity in the UAE, looking for funding for a retirement home development. She came across an Israeli family group interested in the retirement home market in the UAE. She connected them.

Traditionally, the elderly in the UAE were taken care of by their families. Although the local market was questionable, expats who had spent years in the UAE and considered it their home were seeking retirement options. The timing seemed right, given recent legislative changes allowing for retirement in the country. There were no retirement homes in the UAE.

It seemed a perfect match. However, despite the initial excitement of both parties, the transaction faced a significant challenge rooted in differing investment perspectives. The Emirate had plans for a lavish and grandiose retirement housing project, in line with the region's affinity for innovative and extravagant projects. The Israeli family group had a more pragmatic, cost-effective approach. Their idea of making money was to acquire and renovate an existing run-down 3-star hotel to cater to retirement living. This disconnect led to the deal falling through.

Sectors where the UAE and Israel have more in common include diamonds and gold. There is also a steady rise in financial services, technology, and telecoms.

Both countries have well-developed technology ecosystems and a strong focus on innovation. The UAE and Israel can foster partnerships in cybersecurity, artificial intelligence, and digital transformation by leveraging their strengths and expertise. The telecoms industry has witnessed significant growth. With the UAE's advanced infrastructure and

Israel's tech-savvy workforce, there is enormous potential for cooperation in areas like 5G networks, the internet of things (IoT), and smart city solutions.

The outbreak of COVID-19 impacted my plans to attend a 60th birthday party in Israel organised by a friend from Monaco. My excitement and anticipation to explore Israel were dashed when the hotels cancelled all bookings due to the pandemic, leading to the cancellation of her party. This turn of events was disappointing, especially considering my eagerness to visit Israel and deepen the contacts established and my interest in experiencing the country's culture and history. While circumstances prevented me from visiting Israel, I still would like to explore the country. I have added it to my list of future travel destinations. The disrupted plans remind me of the unpredictable nature of global events, but they have not dampened my enthusiasm to embark on these journeys eventually.

Recent tensions in Israel have caused flight disruptions from the UAE and other countries to Israel. The airlines have reported on their websites they are carefully monitoring the situation. Tourism will take a hit. Exporters will benefit should the currency weaken.

The Lebanese: The Charmers

The current prime minister is Najib Mikati. The population of Lebanon is about 5.5 million. It is estimated that 8 and 14 million Lebanese live abroad, making up about twice the total Lebanese population. The capital is Beirut. Their currency is the Lebanese pound.[186]

Beirut was once the glamourous financial hub of the Middle East, a role later assumed by Bahrain and then Dubai. During the 1920s and 1930s, the Lebanese banks became well-known for their secrecy. By the late 1960s, Lebanon earned the reputation of being "The Switzerland of the Middle East." Influenced by its strong French connection, it became an irresistible destination and drew celebrities from around the world. However, a civil war broke out in the 1970s, shattering its reputation.

The recent trajectory of events in Lebanon continues to paint a sad picture. It has experienced further setbacks recently, highlighting how unstable the country is. Lebanon has been in a dire economic situation, ranking among the most heavily indebted nations globally. The steep decline of its local currency, losing around 60% of its value, has sparked widespread protests as citizens voice their frustrations over deteriorating living conditions and government mismanagement. The devaluation of the Lebanese currency, coupled with soaring inflation, has dealt a severe blow to individuals' savings. The ramifications have been catastrophic, with the economy collapsing, unemployment surging, and businesses shutting down at an alarming rate.

Adding to the turmoil, people lack access to their money held at the banks. Capital controls imposed restricted the withdrawal of dollars. People could only withdraw local currency. As the value of the Lebanese pound plummeted, and the dollars were blocked, many individuals did not have sufficient funds to cover their expenses. And in unfortunate cases, they had nothing at all.

These distressing developments in Lebanon offer a sobering perspective on economic challenges, particularly as inflationary pressures take root in the West. The increased cost of living in cities like London prompts reconsidering lessons from places such as Lebanon and Iran. These nations can serve as valuable case studies, highlighting the dire consequences of unchecked economic policies and fiscal mismanagement. While discussions about impending crises in Europe have gained attention, there appears to be a notable absence of discourse on hyperinflation cases such as those in Lebanon.

The iconic Cedar of Lebanon tree on the national symbolises strength, longevity, prosperity, and hope. The cedar tree is an evergreen conifer that can grow tall and old. It is known for its strength and durability and can withstand harsh conditions. This makes it a symbol of strength and resilience, qualities the Lebanese people have often had to draw on throughout history. The cedar tree is also a symbol of longevity. It can live for hundreds of years. Its wood is known for its durability. This suggests Lebanon will continue to exist and thrive again in years to come.

On a positive note, Lebanon offers a refreshing departure from the landscape typically associated with the GCC region. Unlike the desert landscape of the Gulf, Lebanon has mountains, beaches, and even snow-covered peaks. Everything is close by. You could be swimming in the sea and, within an hour, skiing in the mountains. Beirut has gained international recognition for its nightlife and rooftop bars gracing its skyline. Alcohol is legal in Lebanon, contributing to a lively social scene.

The country's culinary offerings are equally celebrated, ranging from delectable kebabs and *shawarma* to the creamy delights of *hummus* and *tabbouleh*. The popularity of Lebanese cuisine extends far beyond its borders, evident in the abundance of Lebanese restaurants in places like Dubai and London.

The Lebanese excel at creating a welcoming atmosphere, making visitors feel like cherished friends. In the Middle East, the Lebanese are often found in sales roles, where their exceptional communication skills shine. A visit to Beirut provides a glimpse into a unique blend of influences.

I so enjoyed my trips to Beirut. The city's architecture, nestled against the mountain, reminded me of Monaco, while the vibrant beach culture and well-toned physiques evoke comparisons to Brazil's beach life in Rio de Janeiro. The Lebanese exude a certain Italian flair, characterised by a relaxed and easy-going disposition, all while exhibiting resilience from overcoming significant challenges in their history. Lebanon's allure lies not only in its stunning landscapes and culinary delights but also in the spirit of its people, who possess an unwavering ability to embrace life's joys and overcome adversities with grace.

During a pivotal moment, Tracy was in Lebanon on a roadshow when an unexpected announcement was made. The Saudi government ordered all Saudi nationals to leave Lebanon immediately. Tracy offered the management team the option to leave the country for safety. She would remain and stick to the scheduled meetings, but she completely understood if they wanted to leave. Tracy reasoned that any potential threat would take time to materialise, as all the Saudi nationals would need to have left the country first, which might take a few days. With their departure scheduled for the evening, she believed the immediate risk was limited. Her team concurred, proceeded with the meetings, and departed safely from Lebanon.

In the meetings, the investors shrugged their shoulders. They did not think anything of the announcement. These announcements happened all the time. They had become numb.

Again, this is an example of being prepared to review situations as they arise, and they inevitably always do. The Middle East is a region with high political instability and security risks. Before you travel, you must be aware of the risks and take steps to mitigate them.

Lebanese men possess a reputation for their charismatic and flirtatious nature. They are adept at sweeping females off their feet with grand romantic gestures and an air of masculinity, evoking a sense of being the most cherished person in the room. This propensity for amorous expressions is like the Italians. Brace yourself for "I love you!" declarations.

However, as a Lebanese friend in London recounts, such passionate words can sometimes be abundant, yet actions may not always align. As with any cultural stereotype, the reality may vary widely.

The Pakistanis: Safety and Security Not Guaranteed

The President is Arif Alvi. He has been in office since September 2018. The population of Pakistan is around 250 million. The Pakistani community in the Middle East is over 7 million people. Most of the population is Muslim. The capital is Islamabad.[187]

Perceptions of safety vary across the Middle East. While the UAE and broader GCC are considered safe, Pakistan is on the other side of the spectrum, perceived as less safe for expats and tourists. The crime rate is high, there is always a threat of terrorism, and the infrastructure needs an upgrade.

Pakistan's political situation is complicated and polarised. The country is embroiled in a power struggle over who should lead Pakistan. Its economy is on the verge of collapse, society is polarised, millions are still suffering from last year's disastrous floods, terror attacks are rising, and inflation is skyrocketing. Shehbaz Sharif was elected as Pakistan's new Prime Minister in April 2022, following the dismissal of former Prime Minister Imran Khan in a no-confidence vote that threatened to spark a constitutional crisis.[188]

Theresa shared a story of her first trip to Pakistan. She was aware Pakistan was considered dangerous, but as she was single without children, she was prepared to take the risk. She flew into Lahore, the second largest city, known as one of Pakistan's major industrial and economic hubs. "Flights from the GCC to Pakistan are like buses with wings," she said.

At the time, she was working for a Kuwaiti family, looking to invest with a co-investor from Singapore in a warehouse in a port in Pakistan. They all set off from Lahore to the port by car. The Singaporean investment team was provided with armoured vehicles for their security. At the same time, Theresa, who was sent out to complete due diligence for the Kuwaiti family, was offered a regular car with a male chaperone but without any armoured security.

During the journey to the port, two tires on the car went flat. They were stranded in the middle of nowhere, and Theresa, wearing a designer Shalwar Kameez[189], was also wearing a Cartier watch, which she had forgotten to take off before getting on the plane to Lahore. She stood out and felt unsafe. It was stupid. She had been warned, "Watches attract attention, and you can get your hand cut off by guys on motorcycles." She removed her watch and hid in the bushes while the driver fixed the car's tires.

Luckily, all ended well, but a week later, a massive bomb went off in the capital. According to the UK Government's travel advice, terrorist attacks have targeted public places and government or security forces.[190]

She felt she had a lucky escape. When she discussed the security matter with the Kuwaiti family, they explained that hiring security is tricky because they will sell you out without knowing it.

This story illustrates the importance of taking precautions when travelling to a place perceived as being less safe. Be aware of the risks and take steps to mitigate them, such as travelling with security, dressing inconspicuously, and avoiding dangerous areas off the beaten track.

Theresa shared another story with me. After the initial visit to the port, she was invited to several lavish dinner parties hosted by a government official, with no expenses spared. Hospitality is an essential part of Pakistani culture. Guests are treated with respect.

After one of the dinners, the government official asked her to pay him a bribe of one million dollars. The government official said this was "business as usual." He would have felt the wealthy Kuwaitis could easily afford this small token of gratitude. The Kuwaitis declined to pay the bribe, but the project continued. The government official was disgruntled, making Theresa feel highly uncomfortable with another two weeks to go until the project's completion.

These stories highlight the challenges of doing business in Pakistan. The high crime rate, the threat of terrorism, and the potential for corruption can make it a challenging environment.

She gave me another tip, "If you are looking to take photos, be careful about photos involving anything military-related. It will get you into trouble."

I have wonderful friends from Pakistan. One of my neighbours in Dubai was from Pakistan. I used to visit him and his wife, half Dutch and half Turkish, for tea and share the company pitches I was working on. He used to critique them, which was extremely helpful as it helped me improve the pitch and prepare for investor Q&A.

They told me not all of Pakistan is dangerous. Security concerns exist in the country's more isolated parts, but all of Pakistan's major cities, including Islamabad, Lahore, Karachi, and Peshawar, are safe to visit. Standard measures should still be taken, especially in Karachi, where thefts of phones and bags are a problem.

Having a trusted local accompany you is helpful. A local guide can give you significant insight into the country's culture and customs and help you navigate unsafe areas. Take appropriate steps and always remain watchful.

The Turks: the 100-year celebration in 2023

Turkey celebrates its 100th year as a Republic in 2023. Although Istanbul is the largest city, the capital of Turkey is Ankara. Its population is well over 80 million. The recently re-elected President is called Recep Tayyip Erdogan.[191]

Turkey has deep-rooted historical ties to the Middle East. As the successor to the mighty Ottoman Empire, which ruled over the region for an impressive 500-year period, Turkey has maintained a longstanding presence in this part of the world. Despite European powers eventually exerting their influence and diminishing Ottoman control, Turkey's historical legacy and impact in the Middle East cannot be ignored.

Turks are a proud people with a rich culture and heritage deeply rooted in the Middle East and Western influences. This unique blend positions Turkey as a bridge connecting the two regions. When I mentioned to a Turkish business associate that I felt I should include Turkey in the book, he commented, "But Turkish people never think of Turkey as a Middle Eastern country."

It is one of the leading powerhouses in the region. When it comes to exporting to the GCC, Turkey delivers food and beverages, textiles, machinery, and construction materials.

Turkey serves as a crucial hub for trade and travel between various regions. Its strategic location allows it to facilitate trade routes that may not be feasible in other countries like the UAE. Some say it was a route to enable business with Iran.

The Turkish lira has been losing its value for the last four years. The cost of living has been skyrocketing because of

Erdogan's monetary policies that have not managed to control inflation. Inflation has been running over 50%, partly because of his policy of cutting interest rates to stimulate growth. Recently, he changed his mind and set a new direction. He said, "With the help of tight monetary policy, we will bring inflation back down to single digits."[192] Inflation is slowing, and foreign investors are being drawn back into the market.

Turkey has always been a popular tourist destination. The weak lira pulled in more tourists, making the tourism industry one of the bright spots in the economy.

I had an unforgettable long weekend in Istanbul. Friends from London had planned a four-day trip, which included a glamorous ball and plenty of sightseeing opportunities. It was a large group of friends-of-friends. I have very fond memories of my time in Istanbul. I recall one of the girls in our group on the first night at a nightclub had her handbag stolen. Crowded places can be prime spots for thieves to strike. We were all alert after that incident.

While Turkey's foreign policy has been controversial in recent years, it remains a significant actor in the Middle East, and its role in the region will likely continue to grow. It shares borders with eight countries, including Iraq, Syria, and Iran. As a member of NATO, it plays a crucial role in maintaining regional security. Turkey's military has actively participated in various conflicts within the Middle East.

Armenia, Georgia, and Jordan: Weekends Away

A British friend started the "Long Range Dining Club," bringing together a group of adventurous individuals from Dubai who shared a passion for exploration and new experiences. He organised trips for us to Georgia and Armenia. We used to joke that he was on an intelligence mission, and we were his cover. I had a fun time, forming new friendships and fun memories. Both countries are perfect long weekend away destinations. You should also add Jordan to this list.

The capital of Armenia is Yerevan. Armenia declared independence from the Soviet Union in 1991. Russian remains the most spoken language. Armenia was the first nation to formally adopt Christianity in the early 4th century. Armenia is home to the oldest church in the world. There is a connection to the UK, as Churchill was fond of 'Ararat', an Armenian brandy he enjoyed drinking. Unfortunately, the Armenia-Azerbaijan conflict has escalated, and some expect more unrest in the corridor.

The capital of Georgia is Tbilisi. Georgia's hills and mountains are marvellous and offer many hiking trails. It is a lovely change of scenery, with lush greenery.

The capital of Jordan is Amman. Jordan is known for being a transit country, more flexible than others. For example, Pakistani passports are valid for all countries except Israel because. Pakistan does not recognise Israel. Some say Pakistanis who cannot board a plane to Israel find travelling through Jordan is possible.[193]

Spend time in Jordan. Go to Petra, a UNESCO World Heritage Site known for its ancient city carved from sandstone cliffs to the stunning landscapes of Wadi Rum, which provide a glimpse into the beauty of the desert. You can float on the salty waters of the Dead Sea, the lowest point on Earth, and venture to the crystal-clear waters of the Red Sea.

Chapter 32.

Who to contact in The Middle East?

Global financial institutions and bankers are shuttling back and forth to the Middle East. The word is out that the Middle East is booming and has a lot of illiquidity. Investment conferences have been inundated by those looking to raise money in the Middle East.

Identifying Institutional investors

In terms of the type of investors, you will find sovereign wealth funds, pension funds, government-owned enterprises, insurance companies, mutual funds, foundations, venture capital funds, private equity investors and family groups. Many rely on consultants. According to the Sovereign Wealth Fund Institute, the region's largest sovereign wealth funds manage nearly $4 trillion combined.[194]

You do not have many family offices like you do in Europe. Instead, there are what are called family groups or family businesses.

You can find the names in the public domain. According to Forbes Middle East, Saudi topped the list with 36 family businesses, with 21 UAE families ranked among the Arab world's 100 most powerful family businesses.[195] Forbes mentions many UAE businesses in their 'Top 100 Arab Family Businesses in The Middle East 2020'.[196]

Sourcing and Classifying Investors in the Middle East

Once you understand what type of investors are out in the Middle East, you need to determine who the right investor category will be, like elsewhere in the world. The landscape is diverse, with each investor having distinct criteria and preferences. Your pitch must be tailored to resonate with the specific investor with which you are engaging. What appeals to one investor may fall flat with another. Be prepared for the question: "Why are you raising money in the Middle East?" They may suspect something is wrong with the deal if the UK company cannot raise the funds in their home market.

When talking to Ultra High Net Worth Investors, find out if it is old or new money. Old money tends to be risk-averse, whilst new money may take more risk as they are still building their wealth. What do they invest in? Do they invest in startups or established profitable businesses? Which sectors and geographical regions interest them? How much capital do they deploy? What stake do they seek, and how does their decision-making process work? Such factors dictate the compatibility between an investor and your proposition.

Family groups will have made money in a particular industry, adding more business lines over time. They tend to be interested in the strategic angle for their existing business and like investing along the lines of their businesses. The Middle East offers fertile ground for fundraising for European companies with a proven product in one market. This is especially true if your product holds relevance in the region. A strategic approach might involve combined deals, linking equity raises with distribution rights within the GCC countries. Demonstrating prior success with local clients can bolster your pitch.

Are you talking to the principal about allocating his money, or has he hired a team? If it is a hired team, they will be concerned about losing their jobs and will unlikely take significant 'career risks.' If you are talking to the principal, he may take a punt if it is considered a small investment, under 1 million.

What I found interesting is that families were willing to invest a significant amount of money in a strategic deal much larger than any European family. The family in the Middle East believed they understood the risks because their business operations were in the same sector. Therefore, they thought they better understood the risks, making them perceive them as lower than an investor with little exposure to the industry.

I spoke to a CIO of a family group in Saudi, active in the mining industry. The owner had hired him to diversify the investment portfolio. He told me it was a struggle. The owner continued to prefer to invest in the mining sector. None of his recommendations for diversification were taken on board. It is an example of family groups preferring to invest along their existing business lines.

Do not have overly high hopes for the strategic value added by the investor after they put money into the business. It is essential to sell the investment based on its strategic benefits effectively. In practice, investors may make some introductions initially, but then their attention shifts as they move on to their next investment.

Government entities may be interested in the potential for localisation, which may involve technology transfer, on-the-ground operations, R&D partnerships with local universities, local hiring, and manufacturing or assembly facilities in their country, contributing to job creation and potentially repositioning a country's image in the field.

Having also travelled across Asia, I noted a difference between the investment appetite of government entities in China and the family groups and government entities in the Middle

East. Family groups are interested in companies with proven products that they can distribute in their home market and the GCC. The government entities are interested in products and technologies ready to market at the commercialisation stage. In contrast, government entities in China will ask, "What technologies are you working on that are not mentioned in the deck?"

Sovereign wealth funds are diversified across asset classes. They do not require the same degree of localisation or strategic angles as other entities. Sovereign Wealth Funds are the easiest to access and are often staffed with people from the West.

Private equity fund managers get paid to analyse investment opportunities and must allocate the money they have raised from third parties. They invest in themes and strategies, usually outlined on their website, including their criteria for investment. Many private equity funds in the Middle East allocate funds to the MENA region (Middle East and North Africa). Physical headquarters in the Middle East is not always mandatory to pitch for MENA allocations. Proving substantial on-the-ground operations and clientele within the region can substantiate your case for MENA funding.

You will come across asset managers looking to set up an SPV (Special Purpose 'Vehicle') for a specific deal. Some will have proprietary money to allocate to the transaction, and then they will raise more money from outside investors. Be careful and check how much principal money is available for the deal. I have several times been through the process with an investor, pooling external capital through an SPV, only to find out they did not have the money.

Pension Funds and Insurance companies look for yield to meet their long-term future liabilities. They do not tend to take significant risks. This is not a place to go for your start-up funding unless you have an insurtech company to present with a strategic angle for the business.

Besides understanding the differences between each investor, you will need to connect at the right level and tailor the pitch to the investor. Building connections is integral to the process. It is a blend of existing contacts, cold calls, and gaining introductions through well-connected intermediaries. First, you must build a bespoke list of potential investors, complete with contact details.

Reaching the right person within an organisation can prove a challenge. Turnover is high, so any database you consult will typically be outdated. If in doubt, start at the top. Be prepared – emails often go unanswered, necessitating direct calls. Yet, fixed lines also may go unanswered or be outdated, and switchboards are not always operative.

Do not give up if you do not hear back from an investor immediately. There are reasons why an investor may not have replied. The investor may not be interested in the company or its products or services and is too busy to respond to every person pitching to them. The investor could be on holiday or out of office. Or he may be interested but may have forgotten to respond or accidentally deleted your email.

Judith told me a story about how she was advising a company, raising capital for their profitable business. She thought it would be easy. Judith had researched and identified a potential investor in the Middle East, a perfect fit for the business. She sent an email to the investor, introducing herself and the company.

A few days later, she diligently followed up with the investor, but she again did not receive a response. She then tried calling the investor, but the phone number was not in service. She sent another email, but still no response. She was getting so frustrated. Her client kept asking her for feedback and did not understand why she still had not spoken to the investor. Ten days passed, and there had still been no contact. Judith said she was desperate.

Under pressure from her client, she took more extreme measures and turned up at the investor's office. She sat in the reception for three days in a row. Eventually, on the third day, the CEO agreed to see her. Persistence and determination are key traits you need to have in getting an audience with decision-makers. Turning up at someone's office or sitting at reception until a meeting is granted were tactics used to show genuine interest and commitment.

While such approaches might have been considered unconventional in many other parts of the world, they could be effective in the Middle East, where personal relationships and face-to-face interactions hold significant value. However, nowadays, there is a greater emphasis on arranging meetings through proper channels and respecting the preferences of potential business partners. While surprise visits might work in certain situations, it is recommended to establish contact through more formal means, like emails or direct messages, to ensure your intention to meet is clear and your request is respectful of the other party's time and schedule.

You can reach out to the investor on LinkedIn or Twitter. Or try the traditional way, a letter in the post. Alternatively, check for a mutual connection to the investor and ask them to open the door for you. There is no one way. If you cannot get in through the front door, try the back door, or you may even find one of the windows is open. The Middle East is the place to develop good relationships with the assistants to the CEOs and family members. Assistants are often powerful figures in the Middle East and can help set up meetings and get things done. If you can develop a good relationship with them, they can be invaluable assets to your business.

Acquiring the investor's mobile number is the best-case scenario. WhatsApp texting is seen as a perfectly acceptable means of business correspondence. It is your best course of action if you want an answer to anything.

Your job will be easier if you are raising capital for a big company or a well-known brand. I remember working on an M&A deal involving a large insurance company. Within 30 minutes, I had the relevant people at the sovereign wealth funds on the phone. They all already knew the company and were able, on the call, to express their interest.

The bigger the deal, the easier it is to get investors' attention. Getting their attention is difficult if you are raising below $50 million. Above $300 million, it becomes easier and easier. In the Middle East, the bigger the deal, the better. As there is little trust in foreigners, household names are preferred.

Scam Alert: Clones and Fraudsters

There are fraudsters in the marketplace cloning local investment groups' profiles. These individuals, driven by various motives, deceive others into believing they are part of a genuine family group.

The fraudster will often have what seems like a genuine LinkedIn profile, and their emails can also look real as they will have mimicked names and logos with links to pages from the actual website. It is straightforward to copy and paste real web pages onto a new fake address. So be careful out there and stay vigilant.

Always check the counterparty you are dealing with and be wary of incoming cold calls from those claiming to be an investor offering cheap loans. Occasionally, I am contacted by people in Europe asking me if I can check out such a counterparty for them in the Middle East. Usually, they have received a cold call and been offered a loan.

My initial step in verifying the authenticity of a potential counterparty is to examine the website's inception date. This crucial information is often found at the bottom of the webpage. If it says 2023, then you need to be alert. Additionally, I delve into the ownership details of the domain name by utilising the WHOIS domain lookup. This investigative process helps me discern the credibility of the entity.

The language employed and the titles used on the website also provide valuable insights. On one occasion, I encountered a website where an individual of importance was addressed as "Mr" instead of the appropriate "His Excellency," a clear and immediate indication of potential fraud.

You can also check the regulator's website. By cross-referencing with this official source, I use the contact details provided on the regulator's site, which ensures I am engaging with a legitimate entity. It is worth noting occasional name disparities may also arise, signalling the need for further investigation. A meticulous approach, including scrutinising website details, utilising domain ownership lookup, analysing language and titles, and cross-referencing with regulatory sources, is critical to authenticating potential counterparts in the Middle East.

Another giveaway is that genuine investors from the Middle East will not want to jump into a business deal with people they barely know. They prioritise building relationships before deciding if they wish to work with someone. So, if you received a cold call and feel like you are being rushed into a transaction by a lender, hold off. It is highly unlikely a lender in the Middle East would exchange emails and sign a business deal without further due diligence.

An example was given by Natasha, a real estate developer, who received a connection request from an American over LinkedIn. The American seemed credible. He subsequently introduced her to an investor in the Middle East. The investor offered a loan at 3% with no profit share, which was highly unusual and too good to be true. The investor was happy to proceed with no further due diligence. There was an upfront fee to proceed. Natasha felt the offer was odd and declined further meetings with the investor.

I received a message on LinkedIn from HH Sheikh Hamid Mohammed Bin Rashid Al Maktoum. He wrote, "Greetings Rebecca, how are you doing today? I would like to know more about your services. Hope you do not mind."

It was a fake profile, but surprisingly, he had almost 3 million followers on LinkedIn, more than the authentic profile of HH Sheikh Hamdan Bin Mohammed Bin Rashid Al Maktoum. When I checked the next day, the profile had disappeared.

What could be the motivation for cloning? By appearing to be part of a legitimate family group, individuals may believe they are less likely to attract suspicion or face investigation into their activities. This could potentially involve engaging in illegal activities.

Additionally, watch out for fake legal documentation. According to a lawyer, it is a significant issue that can have severe consequences for individuals and businesses. Producing and distributing counterfeit legal documents is not only unethical but also illegal. Always verify the legitimacy of documents through proper channels, such as trusted legal professionals or relevant government authorities, to protect against potential fraud.

I encountered fake documents in commodity trading, such as oil trading. Mandates would be faked. A party would pretend to have a government or corporate mandate. The counterfeit letters were often easily spotted by the different letter types, spelling mistakes or a clear copy and paste of government logos. Similarly, a party may pretend that they have supply and would fake a mandate letter of a factory. Certificates would be falsified. Certificates can be checked out online with the relevant authorities. Nothing can be assumed. Check everything.

While finding a legitimate investor in the Middle East is possible, do not be swayed by seemingly easy meetings without conducting comprehensive due diligence on the counterparty. Stay focused, and remember, thorough scrutiny is your best defence against potential pitfalls.

Perceptions Abroad of Middle East Investors

In addition to selling the transaction to investors in the Middle East, my job was to convince the European company management that the investor from the Middle East would be the right partner for them. Perceptions of the Middle East varied wildly. I ensure clients are thoroughly briefed on who they will meet and the investor's background.

Companies believe raising money in the Middle East is easy, and they approach me with unrealistic timelines. Some believe gold grows on palm trees. They may also think the wealth is what is referred to as dumb money, and all they must do is show up for a meeting, and funds will magically appear in their account. They read about large transactions in the newspaper and think it must be easy.

I must burst the bubble and manage the expectations. It will require patience to raise money in the Middle East. Yes, there is a lot of wealth, but investors have become incredibly savvy. It is not as easy as it used to be and has become increasingly competitive. You are not the only one pitching; you need to stand out and show relevance. The due diligence processes are like those in any other part of the world. They conduct their internal due diligence and often follow up with confirmatory due diligence done by third parties. It is not a short process. Investors are much more selective. And even post-due diligence deals can fall apart. There are political and ethical considerations.

Years ago, Marie had the Board over of one of her clients from Europe with well over €10 billion in assets under management. Their investors included European pension funds. Her first question was whether they had been in the Middle East before. For all the Board Members, it was their first time in Dubai. Marie then asked them about their first impressions, and the answer was, "It is like Las Vegas."

At that point, she knew she had to educate them. She explained there were no slot machines in Dubai. She proceeded to run them through the fundraising dynamics of each country in the GCC. At the time of the meeting, a journalist and critic of the Saudi government had disappeared in Istanbul. In the following months, conflicting narratives emerged over how he died, what happened to his remains, and who was responsible. Marie's client told her in the meeting that they considered it a reputational risk to do business with Saudi. They feared losing their super-conservative pension fund clients.

Marie told me about another incident where she faced a challenge when introducing an investor from Saudi to a US company. She had arranged a conference call between a Saudi multinational construction group and the CEO of a startup company in the US. The CEO agreed to the call, but he got an anxiety attack when he heard who the family was, a name associated with 9/11. Marie said she had to do a lot of convincing and handholding. Eventually, she had to conclude it was a bit of a stretch for him to imagine this Saudi family group as potential investors in his company. I said that even though the CEO may have been open-minded and accepted them as an investor, raising money in the US in the following rounds may have been challenging.

Chapter 33.

Regulatory Realities

Navigating legal frameworks and bureaucracy can be complex, especially for foreign companies unfamiliar with local laws and regulations. Middle Eastern countries have implemented various investor protection regulations to ensure transparency and fairness. Each country has capital market regulations governing fundraising activities such as initial public offerings (IPOs), debt issuances, and private placements. Complying with these regulations can be time-consuming and require extensive documentation.

Islamic finance principles are followed by some in the Middle East, which means businesses seeking capital may need to adhere to specific Sharia-compliant financing structures and guidelines. In some countries, you may need to employ local agents. Seeking legal counsel from Middle Eastern business law experts is vital to avoid pitfalls. There are strict rules when speaking to retail investors. Fewer restrictions apply to institutional investors. It is better to send an email from outside the country.

Marie took the initiative to obtain a legal opinion for one of her clients from a respected law firm in the UAE to figure out how they could market their product in the various GCC jurisdictions. She thought the legal advice the law firm produced was excellent. The lawyer did a great job outlining the rules in each country and explaining how companies navigate them in practice. *Perfect,* she thought. *We know how to execute.*

However, a small sentence was added at the end, stating, "Of course, we cannot recommend such practices."

When Marie spoke to Hanna, the head of legal, Hanna explained that she had a completely different view of the advice given. "No, Marie," said Hanna, "we cannot execute in line with how others execute. We must stick to the exact letter of the law as outlined."

Marie suggested arranging a call with the lawyer.

"Marie, we do not have calls with lawyers, as we can only rely on what is put in writing."

Hanna requested that Marie obtain an email from each investor explicitly asking Marie to provide them with more information about a fund they had heard about in the marketplace. Marie remembered attempting to work with what is called "reverse solicitation," but it proved to be impossible. Investors were wary of doing this. They felt it might be construed as a commitment while they had not even seen the pitch deck to establish interest. She did not blame the investor for not complying with the request. Even her most reliable contact would not send such an email. It was challenging to explain to Hanna that reverse solicitation would not happen.

After exchanging many emails on this matter, Marie and Hanna agreed to focus only on generating interest with institutional investors in the UAE, where the rules were clear. They debated family groups and eventually decided it was okay to approach investors, including family groups, in the UAE. So, even though her mandate initially covered the Middle East, it eventually narrowed down to the UAE. Marie explained to me that anything more was too challenging, not only from a legal perspective but also from being outside their comfort zone.

In my experience, some companies will work in the "grey zone," staying within the rules, whilst others stick to the letter of the law. If you stick to the letter of the law, execution will be expensive, as you will need to hire local agents in each market. This is only affordable for the big private equity firms.

Marie told me local agents sometimes only offer regulatory protection; you will need to reach out to investors yourself, giving the local broker a list of investors that have been contacted. Local agents can open doors, but sometimes, local family dynamics can be at work, hindering progress in the follow-up. They may be unwilling to make a second call as they will tiptoe around their relationships.

Chapter 34.

Pitching to get a Meeting

Pitches for Successful Business Presentations

A concise and strategic approach is paramount when pitching in the Middle East. I strongly advocate using a one-page executive summary of your investment opportunity, complemented by a brief email cover note. Your one-pager is more important than your pitch deck. Nobody will agree to take a call or a meeting without the one-pager being excellent. Back-of-an-envelope presentations are not suited to Middle Eastern investors. The email summary note is even more important, or nobody will be enticed to open your one-pager attachment. Tell the story concisely and outline the headline financials, desired investment amount and projected returns. Much more information than this in an introductory email tends to go unread. This approach respects the investor's limited time while facilitating their ability to brief higher-ups or other relevant departments. When speaking on the phone, especially with the family groups, tell them a compelling story to share within their organisation. Inspire investors.

Conversely, sovereign wealth funds often respond favourably to a more conventional Western-style pitch. When preparing for meetings, avoid arriving with a back-of-an-envelope pitch. Be thoroughly primed for your in-person presentation, armed with a well-structured introductory deck spanning 10-20 pages. Include supplementary materials such as financial statements or market research. Your goal is to deliver a compelling and distinctive narrative, capturing attention and making you stand out. Keep the story focused so as not to confuse. Clarity is critical to communicating your business purpose and value proposition.

Middle Eastern investors are often visual. Enhance your presentation with impactful visuals like charts, graphs, and images. Some visuals might be considered offensive, such as slightly suggestive images or depictions of alcohol consumption. Using video content can also be an effective tool for storytelling and engagement. Localise your content using appealing visuals.

Rather than divulging your information all at once, consider a strategic "drip-feed" approach. Begin with a one-page teaser during initial pitches, then expand your presentation during the meeting. After a meeting, offer more detailed information, including financials and supporting documentation, to sustain interest and foster a progressive rapport with potential investors. By tailoring your approach, you will effectively navigate the nuances of pitching in the Middle East, making a lasting impression.

Government Tenders: Business in the Public Sector

Government tenders are part of the business landscape in the Middle East. They are used to procure goods and services for government projects and can be worth billions of dollars. There have been allegations of corruption in government tenders in the Middle East, like elsewhere. These allegations have ranged from the rigging of bids to the awarding of contracts to unqualified companies. I have also heard about a company in Europe complaining it was impossible to compete with companies from Asian countries where exchanging gifts was acceptable and common practice.

In recent years, there has been a growing focus on transparency and accountability in government tenders in the

Middle East. Governments have implemented measures to combat corruption, such as requiring tenders to be open to all qualified bidders and publishing the results of tenders online.

However, there are still challenges to overcome. Sometimes, the tendering process is not transparent, making it difficult for businesses to know what is required to win a contract. The tendering process is sometimes conducted in the local language, which can create further hurdles for companies that do not speak the language to participate. Build relationships with government officials. This can help you to understand the tendering process. Before participating in a government tender, research and understand the tender's requirements and the country's culture. Be prepared to walk away if you believe the tendering process is unfair. There are other opportunities for business in the Middle East.

The government will evaluate the quality of the product or service being offered. They will look for companies with a good reputation for quality and reliability. Price will be a consideration as they want to get the best possible deal, but they also want to ensure they are not sacrificing quality for price. They will compare the prices of different companies and choose the one offering the best value.

Additionally, they prefer collaborating with companies with a proven track record of success. They will look for companies with a history of delivering high-quality products and services on time and within budget. Governments also prefer to work with financially stable companies with the resources to deliver on their commitments. As a loss-making startup, it will be hard to compete on this point. They will look for companies with a good credit rating and a history of paying their bills on time. Governments are increasingly looking for companies committed to social responsibility. They will look for companies with a good track record of environmental sustainability and ethical business practices.

In addition to these factors, governments in the Middle East may also look for other factors specific to their country or region. For example, governments may prefer companies owned or managed by nationals. They may also look for companies that understand the local market and culture and speak their language. If you find out they prefer local parties, a better route may be to partner with a local party and have them pitch. A local company cannot run away, giving the government more security and continuity.

Chapter 35.

Setting up Meetings

Roadshow Planning: Effective Outreach

The preference in the region is for face-to-face interactions in business dealings. While electronic communication and Zoom meetings have become more prevalent, Middle Eastern businesses still prioritise in-person meetings and negotiations.

E-mails will go unanswered. You will have to follow up with a phone call. E-mails are often perceived as less personal and may not carry the same weight as verbal communication. In countries like Saudi, they will only negotiate critical business matters in person. This preference for direct in-person contact can contribute to longer selling cycles.

Setting up meetings with investors in the Middle East can be daunting, especially if you are unfamiliar with the region's cultural norms and business practices.

Always check the work week, which may not always be Monday to Friday. In some countries, the work week is Sunday to Thursday. On Friday, a holy day, businesses close for congregational prayer. Do not be surprised if you are invited to a business meeting on a Sunday, the equivalent of a Monday if the work week is Sunday to Thursday. Also, make sure you check the local holidays. Historically, the work week in Dubai used to span from Sunday to Thursday. However, a recent shift has transitioned the official work week to Monday through Friday, aligning with Western countries. Despite this change, individuals are still open to Sunday scheduling meetings.

It is worth noting the public sector operates on a slightly different schedule. Public sector employees typically work from Monday to Thursday, with a shorter workday on Fridays, concluding at noon. This respects the Islamic holy day, allowing individuals to observe their religious practices and engage in community activities on Fridays. Sometimes, office hours may not be 9 am–5 pm. Especially during Ramadan, they may finish work at 3 p.m. If you suggest a meeting time coinciding with prayer time, a Muslim will decline politely. Prayer is important in the Islamic faith, and Muslims must pray five times daily. The prayer times are fixed, making them unchangeable. As it can be a bit of a minefield, you should ask them about their preferred meeting times or suggest several days and slots. Or ask the investor what the prayer times are in his country.

Even if you are familiar with the process, it can be stressful because meetings are often not arranged until the last minute. The management team may fly out with only a few meetings scheduled, which puts pressure on the placement agent and can lead to complaints about the partially filled roadshow schedule. I used to think being told, "Call me when you land, and we will arrange a time to meet," was a way of the investor saying they were not interested. They may not be able to predict their schedule. For example, they may receive a call to attend a presentation by someone higher up in the ranks, either the business owners they work for or someone in government. If this were to happen, the investor would have to cancel their meeting with you to make room for the more important person. For these reasons, he prefers to confirm on the day.

I received a WhatsApp from an expat working in Saudi. We were supposed to meet in London. He wrote, "Sorry Rebecca, I am not going to be able to meet up in London today.

Chairman asked me to do something urgent, so I cannot say later. Hope to see you soon." This is a typical scenario.

However, I have always had full roadshow schedules. I used to prepare a list of names and numbers before going on the roadshow. In the morning, I would wake up early and call down the list, setting up meetings for the day.

Just because meetings are not set up until after you land, it does not mean you can wait until one week before flying out to start arranging them. It would be best if you started at least a month in advance. Family groups often need buy-in from one of their business units regarding the technology's applicability to their business. It can take a couple of weeks for the Chief Investment Officer or CFO to hear back from their business units. They will not take a meeting unless they have the buy-in from one of the managers.

Suppose you did set up meetings in advance. In that case, it is advisable to reconfirm the appointments a day or two beforehand to avoid any last-minute changes or confusion regarding whether the meeting is confirmed. Keep in mind that priorities can shift unexpectedly, as explained above. Having a flexible mindset will be appreciated.

It is advisable to book internal flights within the Middle East at the last minute, as you may need to change the order of two countries in your itinerary. The most important is the last flight to Dubai before the weekend, as these flights tend to get booked quickly. Decide which country you will be in by the end of the week. Ideally, it would be best if you aimed to spend the last day of the week in the UAE to avoid this issue. Contrary to popular belief, investors rarely cancelled meetings with me.

However, a Royal once died as my client was about to fly out of London to the Middle East for a week-long roadshow. During the mourning period, all businesses would be closed. We were initially unsure how long the mourning period would last. So, we faced a dilemma: should we cancel the trip or go ahead with it? My client in London woke up to a string of voicemails before he was about to board his flight. As a precaution, I cancelled all hotels and decided to assess the situation further in the morning. However, I advised him to hold off on cancelling the flights for now. The hotels could be cancelled for free, so it was not a problem.

We decided to proceed with the roadshow despite not knowing the mourning period. We took a gamble based on rumours and were fortunate that the traditional two-week mourning period was shortened to a couple of days. As a result, all I had to do was rebook the hotels, and the schedule remained unchanged. Be prepared for such events and be flexible. Unexpected things will happen, and it is crucial to be able to adapt to them.

Chapter 36.

Ensuring Successful Dialogue

Punctuality in Business Meetings

In the Middle East, punctuality is not valued like elsewhere. I consider it respectful to be on time and expect the same in return. In the Middle East, being late is not regarded as disrespectful, and no apology is needed unless someone runs late by over an hour. Ensure you are always on time, even if you must wait for them. Often, you will find reading material in the waiting room, giving you more insight into the investor's interests.

Sarah told me a couple of stories about punctuality. She was sitting in Emirates Towers and overheard an argument.

A British 50-year-old was shouting to what looked like his junior, a 30-year-old. "Doesn't he understand I flew over specially to meet with him, and I go back to London on my private jet this afternoon?"

"Yes," the junior responded, "he knows we are having the meeting."

"Then why has he not responded to your messages for the last two hours? He needs to get his ass over here right now!"

Sarah, who had overheard the conversation, said, "It is likely he had a family incident, or someone in government called him in for a meeting. He will unlikely do any business with his attitude and bad language."

I, too, have witnessed such behaviour. It does not work well in the Middle East and is not a good look.

Looking at your watch in meetings is impolite. Make sure you leave sufficient time between meetings in case they start late or run over. Sarah usually assumes slots of 1½ hours, with an hour between meetings. She said she would be the timekeeper and agree on a discreet signal with her client. When she made the signal, he would know he had 15 minutes left to wrap up. It would be her discretion to let a meeting go over, knowing the route to the next meeting. She would have another signal for that. "The worst thing you can do," she said, "is to keep looking at your watch and then rushing out without taking the time to thank the investor for making time and agreeing on the next steps with some chit-chat."

Meetings have the potential to extend beyond their intended duration. In such cases, practising patience and maintaining courtesy is essential.

Sarah told me another story about being in Oman in a meeting with a company from Europe and a family group. It was time for them to round up the meeting. Sarah gave the pre-agreed signal to the CEO, her client.

Then, the head of the family group, thanking them for their presentation, asked them if they wanted to learn about their business. The Omani Group CEO gave them an hour-long presentation, including a 30-minute video. When he started the presentation, they had no idea how long it would take. They ended up being an hour late for the next meeting but felt it would have been incredibly impolite to leave without listening to their family history. But then it also was not great we were so late for the next meeting. Sarah managed to contact the CFO she was meeting next and inform him of the delay. He was very accommodating and told her not to rush.

Effective Business Dialogue

As I mentioned in a previous chapter, trust comes before competence. In Europe, people also prefer to do business with people they like and trust but expect them to be competent. Both are equally important. In the Middle East, competence is secondary. Your number one focus when doing business should continually be establishing a relationship and trust.

To make a good impression and signal you are serious about the region, learn key phrases in Arabic and have your business cards printed in Arabic on one side and English on the other.

Middle Eastern business settings tend to be more formal, so it is recommended to dress professionally and act respectfully during meetings. Addressing people by their titles and using appropriate greetings is also highly appreciated. Small gifts or tokens of appreciation are customary during business meetings or visits, emphasising *small*. A souvenir from your country will appreciated.

I once briefed a client to take a small gift along, and he completely overdid it and arrived with a huge hamper. Something small, no bigger than your hand, will be appropriate. I felt embarrassed. It looked like we were bribing them.

If you have a placement agent, I recommend sending her around to see all the investors you plan to meet first so she can screen their interest and start the trust building. So, when you arrive in town, you start from a base of trust. Your placement agent will be able to brief you well about their interest and potential for a partnership.

Make the meeting interactive. Start by asking the investor for an introduction about their business and ask relevant questions demonstrating that you are genuinely interested in them and are curious. It is always good to find common ground. It is worth researching what school they went to, the countries they lived in and their hobbies. Whilst chit-chatting, establish trust and rapport. Sports is a good topic. Many locals have been educated in the US and love talking about sports. Topics to avoid are religion, politics, and humour. I would avoid discussing the family in a first meeting unless they bring it up. You can ask about their children, but it will not go down well if you ask about their wife(s),

Remember, building trust takes time and patience. You can establish strong and enduring relationships in the Middle East by demonstrating respect, consistency, transparency, and a genuine commitment to long-term collaboration.

You can also ask them about their experience investing in your space. This will give you a good sense of their level of knowledge and interest. If an investor is familiar with the Middle East market, they will be able to assess the potential for your business to be successful in the region. They can also help you to identify the risks and challenges you may face.

Be engaging and enthusiastic about your business and tell stories with examples. Anecdotes will be remembered and repeated to their seniors or investment committee. If you look bored, they will be bored too. People will have forgotten most of a meeting two weeks on. Stories tend to get remembered.

Avoid any jargon and technical language in the meeting. Speak slowly and clearly, and repeat the essential points or rephrase your message, as English is not everyone's first language. I recommend you have a high-level pitch, which you can do at the beginning and the end so at least they will remember the headlines.

When presenting your business plan, be specific about your goals, target market, competitors, and financial projections – plus, of course, how much money you are looking for and the potential returns for the investor. Investors want to see you clearly understand your business and that you are realistic about your chances of success.

When presenting to a family group, focus on the mutual benefit of the relationship. The investor in the Middle East may ask you, "What is in it for me?" He is not referring to the return on investment but is asking if he can get distribution rights or if any other angles could benefit their family business.

Demonstrating your understanding of the local market, culture, and customs can go a long way in building trust with potential clients or partners. Highlight how your product or service caters specifically to the needs of the Middle Eastern market.

Do not expect much structure to the meeting. It can be frustrating not getting to tell your whole story, including your business plan, but it is best to go with the flow.

The first meeting is about building trust and should be about getting to know each other and starting the relationship. It is like dating. Few get married after one date.

It is crucial to be aware of your body language and social interactions, especially when you are in an unfamiliar cultural setting. Even seemingly innocent gestures may have unintended negative implications, depending on the specific location you are visiting. Being mindful of these nuances will help ensure your communication is respectful and well-received by the people you encounter during your travels.

Middle Eastern communication tends to be indirect, relying on implicit meanings rather than explicit statements. Be prepared for small talk, storytelling, and using metaphors or analogies. Listen actively, read between the lines, and be patient.

After your presentation, send a thank-you note to the investor and reiterate your interest in their investment and a partnership. In the meeting, you should encourage questions to send them additional information about your business or answer any questions they may have had after the meeting as a follow-up. Put anything specific agreed in writing to avoid misunderstandings due to the language barriers. This will help to prevent any disagreements down the road.

Coffee Culture: Embracing a Cultural Tradition

The coffee ritual in the Middle East is an experience beyond getting your caffeine fix. The coffee itself is called Arabic coffee or *qahwa*. It is made from lightly roasted beans and infused with cardamom for extra flavour. When you are in a business meeting, you may be served qahwa. The host will bring out a small cup (a *finjan*) filled with aromatic brew. If you do not drink coffee, at least take a sip out of politeness. Do not gulp coffee down like your morning espresso shot if you like coffee. Instead, you are supposed to take slow sips and savour the moment. Hold the cup while you are taking the sips in your right hand. Once you are finished, you hand back the cup. Do not forget to compliment your host on their excellent brewing skills.

Alongside your cup of qahwa, you will often find dates or other sweet treats to accompany your drink. It is impolite to reject any coffee or dates offered. The sweetness of the dates perfectly balances out the intense flavours of the coffee. You may see your business partner wiggling his cup of coffee. Wiggling a cup of coffee in the Middle East is a cultural ritual known as *"raqwa,"* believed to enhance the flavour and aroma of the coffee. It is like giving your brew a little shake to awaken its true potential.

They will keep topping up your cup unless you give a signal. I remember being wired because my cup was continuously being filled up, and it was unclear how I could signal him to stop. It is all about being respectful and mindful of local customs.

One way to go about it is by saying, "*Shukran* (thank you) for the delicious coffee, but I think I have had enough for now." This way, you show appreciation while clarifying that you have reached your limit. Remember, being polite is key here. Whether it is a friendly smile or a gentle wave of your hand as you decline another cup of coffee, make sure your message is delivered with genuine kindness. Another trick is to place your finger over the rim of your cup. It is code for "I have reached my coffee limit."

Reading Signals: Assessing Investor Engagement

Your job is to ensure you stand out and the party you pitch to is interested. After a roadshow, you will always return on a high because investors are incredibly courteous. You will hear phrases like: "Thank you for your time and coming to meet us." It is not necessarily reflective of their true thoughts. Converting positive meetings into investments is a whole different ballgame. If an investor is interested in your business, they want to learn as much as possible about it. They will make eye contact, nod, and ask critical questions about your product or service, market, team, and financials.

You should be concerned if they do not ask you any questions in the meeting. If they are interested in your business, they will want to meet with the rest of your team and will fly over to see the operations. Investors may not be interested in investing but are more interested in distributing your products. It is good to ascertain their intentions early on.

I have never ended a meeting where the investor said, "I think your presentation is rubbish." Getting a 'no' out of people is a challenge. You can end up being strung along for months.

The investor may hope you will get the hint and quietly go away so he does not need to confront you. You must continuously learn from feedback until the pitch is "bulletproof." The pitch is something you continue to improve until you reach perfection. That is usually the point at which you close a transaction.

It can be challenging to get constructive feedback in the Middle East. It is best to get an indication of interest when you are concluding a meeting. Do not ask them if they are ready to invest. This would be the completely wrong thing to say. You can say, "Would you be open to continuing our discussions and the potential for an investment in the business?"

Sometimes, investors from the Middle East will be indirect about their interests. They may not say they are interested in investing in your business, but they may comment, suggesting they are open to the idea. For example, they may say things like, "I think your business has a lot of potential" or "I am interested in learning more about your business."

If the man at the top is in the meeting, he may say "Execute" to the junior if he is interested. In Europe, this evasive behaviour is impolite, disrespectful and a waste of everyone's time. It would be so much more efficient if an investor could say no and give the reason for passing. In the US, an investor will provide you with a "not interested," including why they decided to pass, especially with the larger private equity firms.

In the Middle East, you never hear from an investor again. There can be many reasons for passing, and they will never tell you if they have no cash. Although you may think it is rude for the investor to vanish without an explanation, he is trying to spare your feelings and avoid any confrontation which may strain the relationship. Sometimes, they can disappear, go missing-in-action, for a month or so when suddenly, you will hear from them.

One way to get feedback is by alleviating the person from their responsibility, so it is not them personally giving negative feedback. "What do you think the obstacles may be for your Board to approve this proposal?"

Marie had an amusing conversation with an Indian investor at a private bank in Oman. She said he was not giving her a straight answer regarding their interest, and it was one of those days when her patience had run out. She told him, "I think I can mark you down for a 'no'."

He uhm-ed and ah-ed, trying to sound positive.

Marie then said, "Okay, that is a clear rejection."

He chuckled, but he would not give her any reason. It was difficult for him to admit somehow, he was not interested. What may appear as evasiveness is often an unwillingness to say "no."

Do not take direct or silent rejection personally. Investors are often busy and have numerous deals to consider. It is a competitive market. Because one investor does not get back to you, it does not mean your idea is not good. Keep improving your storyline and pitching your idea. The more people you talk to, the greater the chance of finding an interested investor. You can also ask for referrals. If it is not for them, do they know someone else who might be interested?

Chapter 37.

Long Selling Cycle

Long Road Ahead: Lengthy Sales Cycles

One determined salesperson told me it took him 10 years to close a deal involving military equipment. She told me all the competition had retired or moved to other jobs. She was the only one left standing and got the order.

Do not go to the Middle East expecting a deal to close overnight. Many factors contribute to the longer selling cycle in the Middle East. After the first meeting, Fiona told me she worked with naive CEOs who would tell her, "I will handle it from here," thinking the next step would be closing the deal. Then, inevitably, they would not get any replies from the investor. They completely underestimate how much time is invested in maintaining dialogue.

You will look at a minimum of six months if the process runs smoothly, which is not usually true. The Middle East has a significant amount of liquidity. Many companies in the region are privately owned. Families and family groups anywhere in the world are patient capital. Unlike private equity funds, they do not have to invest their money and can stay in cash. They have the flexibility to choose when to invest and can also choose to sit on the sidelines.

There is greater emphasis on personal relationships in the Middle East than in the West. Building relationships with potential customers and investors before selling to them would be best. Take the time to get to know them and their needs. They start with distrust. Foreigners have, historically, been seen as invaders or exploiters. They may be more hesitant to purchase and invest unless they are confident about making the right decision.

If you come with a brand name, your selling cycle will be much shorter. The trust factor comes with being a recognised brand with a reputation to uphold. Additionally, any "ready-made" transaction over a billion, especially profitable companies, will find an immediate audience, and decision-making can be speedy.

You will know when you have developed a relationship when you start getting calls on your mobile outside of office hours asking the name of the restaurant you had both visited together. Another good sign is when they refer to you as "Brother." They generally mean it. A client told me he worked in a firm reporting to an Emirati who was out of his depth as he had no private equity knowledge. He showed him how to do things and made him shine. The Emirati said to him, "You saved my life. You helped me when I did not ask you to do so." From then on, he was always there to help him and would send him invites to watch the World Cup at his house and invites for EID Celebrations at his father's house. He would be the only expat at these gatherings and felt honoured.

Not all companies possess the luxury of patience, often constrained by depleting financial resources. A client, new to the Middle East, expressed frustration whenever a Middle Eastern investor failed to meet his deadlines, suggesting, "The investor must not be interested if they hesitate to sign the term sheet."

The client's frustration is understandable. Raising capital can be time-sensitive; every day without an investment can risk a company's future. It is also understandable that the client would interpret the investor's hesitation as a lack of interest.

However, there are reasons leading to a longer decision-making process the client may not be aware of. In the Middle East, the decision-making process for buying a product or service or investing is often more complex than in the West.

Firms tend to be bureaucratic and hierarchical. There are often multiple decision-makers involved and many different committees. The emphasis is on consensus-building and respect for hierarchy.

Be patient, avoid pushing for quick decisions, and show respect for those in positions of authority. Although decisions are eventually taken at the top, there is a lot of initial decision-making at a lower level. They may have different needs and priorities.

Customisation is often necessary, meaning you may need to tailor your product or service to each customer's needs. Investors and companies will ask whether you have tested your product in the Middle East. Have you thought about this? It would be best if you had considered the unique circumstances in the Middle East. Will your product need to be modified to withstand the heat and dust?

Pippa, an Infrastructure Fund Board member, gave me a great example of customisation. She told me about the tires on cars in the Middle East differing from those in other regions. The extreme temperatures can accelerate the deterioration of rubber tires, necessitating specific adaptations for the Middle Eastern market. They need to be made with different materials and have different designs. For example, the tires may have more synthetic rubber, which is more heat-resistant than natural rubber. They have a thicker tread, which helps protect the tire from heat and objects commonly found on the roads, such as sand and rocks, which can all damage tires. Additionally, they feature a more robust sidewall that prevents the tire from bulging or cracking under hot temperatures. In addition to their ability to handle the harsh driving conditions in the Middle East, these tires also feature a special coating that helps reflect heat away from them. Not only will you need to customise your product. It will also have to be tested in the Middle East.

As a result of these factors, the selling cycle in the Middle East can be much longer than it is in the West and more costly, as you will have to fly over many times before a deal is closed. One friend claims it takes 12 meetings to complete a transaction. With Zoom, you may be able to bring this number down. I do not think it takes twelve visits, but more than one. I would say it takes 12 points of contact. If you want to be successful in the Middle East, be aware and adjust your sales strategy accordingly.

Putting deadlines in front of investors is counterproductive. *Inshallah, this* is the way to go. Whatever selling cycle you are used to in the West, you can double this in the Middle East. Having said that, when they are ready for the next steps, you need to be immediately on the ball. Sometimes, all the stars align, and there is a reason why they want to close a deal. You will know. After a year of nothing happening, suddenly, they may show a sense of urgency. For example, an investor may prioritise closing a transaction to showcase during COP28.

Marie told me about a recent experience of something simple taking forever. Her client in London was pitching to an investor in the UAE. The call went well. The client suggested they send an NDA to the investor to share more confidential information. The investor explained their legal team was busy and asked whether it would be okay if they sent their own NDA. The company in the UK agreed and immediately sent back a signed copy of the investor's NDA. The investor took over a month to countersign, even though it was their own NDA. This is an example of simple things taking time.

Raising capital can be challenging. Be persistent, and do not give up. If you are willing to work hard, go with the flow and put in the effort to build relationships, you can be successful in the Middle East.

Saskia, a friend's daughter, embarked on a new artificial intelligence venture, a tech company set up in the UK. With an unwavering passion for her idea, she was eager to bring it to life. However, she recognised the need for funding to kickstart her journey. She told me she decided to reach out to investors in the Middle East as she had heard a lot of money was looking for a place to invest. Saskia, however, was met with rejection after rejection. The investors were not convinced her idea was viable. She felt they did not think she had the right experience to make it a success. They mentioned they would first like to see the product on the market.

Saskia was discouraged, but she did not give up. Taking the feedback on board, she started to build a team of experienced professionals who could help her make her idea a reality and bring more credibility to the team. After a year of pitching, she finally got a break, leading to a $1 million investment in her company. The investor insisted on the headquarters being moved to the UAE, which she agreed to.

Her story is a reminder that it takes persistence to raise capital in the Middle East. Investors are often sceptical of new businesses, especially those started by young entrepreneurs. However, if you have a good idea, you can eventually find investors who are willing to support you, but it requires patience and persistence, finely balanced.

Sometimes, an investor you go in to see may tell you at the end of the meeting to come back and see them the following Tuesday. They are assessing whether you are committed to the region. Following up on such a request will be hard if you are flying in and out. Everyone these days has an office in the region. This is increasingly expected. It will be challenging if you are going to fundraise by going to the Middle East once every six months for the next 18 months. There are, of course, always exceptions. Sue, an event organiser, recalls the time guys turned up to try to raise money for a cannabis deal in the Middle East. She had told them there was not a market for cannabis transactions. They went to Abu Dhabi and found a Sheikh who, on the spot, put in a couple of million.

She said she was approached by a company looking to raise USD 6 million for a desperate company the other day. Their IPO had failed because there was no liquidity in the market, and now, they urgently needed money. Susie said she now ignores such emails. If you are looking to raise money with a deadline of three months or less, the Middle East is not the best market to focus on.

Onsite Visits by Middle Eastern Investors

When the investor visits you in your home country, understand he may not know his way around. Hospitality extends beyond the way a guest is received. It also includes making sure their trip is easy and comfortable. Suggest hotels and take control of the logistics. Entertain, such as lunches and dinners, and enquire if the investor has any dietary requirements. Remember – he may not drink alcohol, so you may want to refrain from drinking, too. He may be coming with his wife and staying the weekend. If so, suggest activities for them to do. And if you want to impress, you can suggest taking them to a special spot in your hometown on the weekend.

Check the office to ensure you have no offensive pictures on the wall. One year, I remember sitting at an Islamic finance conference in London and could not help but laugh when I noticed the statues of naked ladies behind the speakers.

Someone else may have also commented on this, as they replaced the naked ladies with statues of sculptured men covered in togas the following year.

Make sure you brief everyone at your company, from the lady at the reception to the rest of the team, on the investor's background so he feels special. Just like in a restaurant, it makes someone feel special if they are addressed by their name, including title, on arrival.

If they are coming by train, send them the train times. It would be good manners to pick them up at the airport or the train station. It is essential to think things through. I recall a situation where one of my clients suggested picking up the investors from the train station. I had to explain to the CFO that since the investors would be carrying suitcases, his car would be too small to accommodate the investors and their luggage.

After the meeting, it is good to have the CEO drive the investor back to the train station or airport to continue the conversation and discuss the next steps.

Chapter 38.

Decision-making Process

Cultural Cracks: Reasons for Deals Unravelling

Amidst the many successes, there were moments when cultural differences threatened to derail transactions. Alexandra told me about a deal she had been working on involving a company producing an EV (Electric Vehicle). She had arranged a meeting with an investor from Saudi who had made significant money taking a famous car brand into Saudi. He attended the meeting in person and had put in a lot of preparation beforehand. He walked into the meeting room with a pack of marketing documents. He had put colourful stickers on the relevant pages, highlighting relevant sections, and had a list of questions prepared. This potential investor was a billionaire. Surprisingly, he came to the meeting in person and did not send one of his analysts. He had researched the management team and was excited about the opportunity presented.

The CEO of the EV company used to be a CFO, which Alexandra said was not the best choice for a CEO. He did not have a good understanding of personal relationships. She would give a thorough briefing of the person the CEO would meet before the meeting. The idea was for him to say all the right things in the meeting so they would be impressed, and he would create a bond with the investor. Unfortunately, the CEO failed to tailor the pitch following the briefing beforehand.

On the other hand, the investor had conducted extensive research on the CEO and clearly understood that although accomplished in the venture capital industry, he had little exposure outside the UK.

He clearly understood that raising money in Saudi was a daunting venture for the CEO. So, he started the meeting by mentioning his background and specifically spent time discussing his investments, such as a famous department store in London and office buildings in New York. He also noted that he had studied in the UK and learned much from the British. These were all things the CEO could relate to.

Always fascinated and eager to learn, Alexandra asked him what he had learned from the British. He replied it was to be patient. He mentioned that in Saudi, people are not patient, which she found interesting. She always thought "inshallah" meant that they were patient. He explained to her that the British are good at playing the long game.

The following week, he boarded a plane to London to visit the company's offices. That meeting also went well, and he proceeded with due diligence. The process went smoothly, and then Christmas arrived. The investor called the CEO to wish him a Merry Christmas and inform him the investment vehicle had been set up and they were ready to invest.

One final meeting took place in London. Alexandra had briefed the CEO to treat him as if the Queen were coming for a cup of tea, ensure he had biscuits and offer him lunch. During the meeting, the investor asked the team if they were in contact with anyone else about a potential investment. Unfortunately, the CEO answered with a yes. He said, "We are talking to other people, and it is first come, first serve."

Well, this did not go down well. Alexandra told me, "The investor had behaved impeccably, delivering on all the promises made, yet here he was being treated disrespectfully."

Treating investors in the Middle East, and arguably any investor, as special is how to close a deal. They are potentially your future partner. Make sure they feel they are having an exclusive conversation. Of course, they understand you may be talking to other investors, but saying it is "first come, first served" is not a respectful remark and an excellent start to the relationship. The better answer would have been, "Yes, there has been other interest, but you are our preferred partner."

To make matters even worse, the company had made it up and was not engaged in other conversations. The company was bluffing and thought this remark would make him more eager to invest.

After the meeting, the investor decided to withdraw. The CEO blamed the investor, citing their Saudi origin for their alleged failure to deliver. However, it was clear to Alexandra that the CEO had mishandled the investor.

The CEO was later fired as the board decided Alexandra was not the only one he did not listen to. A new CEO came in. She called the billionaire investor back and reminded him about the deal they had been working on together. He said he did not remember who she was. Alexandra replied, "I remember you well, and I recall you mentioning in the meeting how you had learned from the British to be patient and play the long game. Anyway, you have shown great patience, and I believe the time has come to revisit this opportunity, as a new CEO has been appointed."

Without wasting time, the Saudi billionaire hopped back on his plane to meet the new CEO.

Top-Down: Decision-Making Hierarchy

The local business culture has a hierarchy. The business owners are at the top. Older, more experienced employees are given high-ranking positions and can be critical decision-makers. The influence of lower-level employees on the decision-making process is limited. They take instructions from above.

I start any engagement by initiating contact at the top of the hierarchy, knowing decisions will cascade down and ultimately return to the upper echelons for final approval. There is a difference between decision-makers and decision-takers. Decisions are taken at the top but do not dismiss the importance of the decision-making lower down.

Let me illustrate these dynamics with case studies, offering a glimpse into the potential scenarios. While some companies emphasise having robust processes for selection, the practical reality often diverges from these claims. Through my experiences, I have come to recognise that navigating this landscape successfully hinges on a fundamental principle: establishing a meaningful connection at the upper echelons of the hierarchy.

Tanya said she was recently close to finalising a transaction involving a UK-based manufacturing business. The investor, based in the GCC, was about to inject crucial principal capital into the venture, with plans to source additional funding externally. Exhaustive due diligence had been undertaken. The investment team was enthusiastic. A visit to the UK factory further solidified their confidence.

As all the pieces were falling into place, all that remained was the formal sign-off from the Board. This was supposed to be a formality. However, the outcome took an unexpected turn when a single Board member wielded his authority to veto the deal. His concerns were rooted in the implications of Brexit and the potential for supply disruptions, which may lead to empty supermarket shelves. The company made loo rolls, and during the pandemic, there were barely any loo rolls in the supermarkets, but not for the reasons envisaged by the investor. Loo rolls were sold out.

Tanya shared another situation where she was in the advanced stages of negotiations with an investor in a GCC country. Their journey through a structured selection process made them the preferred service provider. After months of meticulous evaluation, they had affirmed their suitability for the role. The counterpart called Tanya to say her team had been selected. The finish line seemed imminent, leading Tanya to anticipate the awarding of the contract.

A turn of events transpired following a dinner meeting attended by the CFO, wherein a rival provider secured the contract. Despite the formal evaluation process, it became evident that the personal relationship between the CFO and the chosen provider influenced the decision. The counterparty called Tanya to break the bad news. He also felt incredibly frustrated that his boss had made such an impromptu decision.

These stories underscore a fundamental reality within the business culture: while formal processes exist, personal connections at the upper echelons wield a powerful influence over outcomes. It is not about processes on paper but the interplay of relationships and hierarchies shaping the final verdict. Navigating this terrain effectively requires an acute awareness of these dynamics and a strategic focus on cultivating connections at the highest levels of the hierarchy. This approach, rooted in understanding the true pulse of the business culture, has proven to be an invaluable rule of engagement.

Chapter 39.

Negotiation Skills and Debt Collection

Business Diplomacy

Businesses and individuals in the Middle East may be reluctant to pay their bills, even with a signed contract. This can be a significant challenge for companies operating in the region, leading to cash flow problems, bankruptcy, and a bad taste of the region when they eventually leave.

Most of my business clients were located outside of the Middle East because clients in the region were reluctant to pay engagement fees. I preferred clients elsewhere who were comfortable engaging me fully. My motto has always been: 'If they can't find your bank account in the beginning, they will never find it.' I also firmly believe that people listen to advice when paid for. Giving it out for free is not a good idea.

There is an expectation among some business owners in the Middle East that businesses will be flexible with their payment terms and prepared to negotiate. Sometimes, you feel you are in a souk. It is not uncommon for companies to pay their bills late or even not at all.

In Northern Europe, we believe what is put in writing is exactly what is agreed at the time of the signing of the agreement and should be honoured. These negotiations around payment terms after the signing of contracts can cause friction between parties.

A Western party will consider the haggling a waste of time and money.

The legal system in some countries in the region is not as robust as in other parts of the world. This means it can be difficult and expensive to enforce contracts, which makes it less likely that businesses will be paid what they are owed. It will be tough for small businesses to enforce getting paid as it will take so long to research the local laws, which would distract from the core business. When freelancers, like designers and IT consultants, struggle to get paid, they cannot cover their costs, forcing them to close shop.

Knowing there may be negotiations around payment terms in the Middle East, there are things you can do. Firstly, personal relationships are essential. Building solid relationships with your business partners will make you more likely to get paid on time. Also, you should carefully review contracts before signing them.

I would not sign a contract in Arabic, only like I would not sign a contract in Chinese. I would not sign contracts under Shariah Law simply because I am unfamiliar with it, just as I would not sign anything under Thai Law. Lawyers may advise you to sign the contracts outside of the country of your counterparty to avoid falling under Shariah Law.

Some parties take a practical view and will gross up the payment terms when signing, expecting they will not receive the last payment.

Verbal contracts with a handshake hold significant value in Arab culture and carry more weight than written agreements. A written contract is often considered a necessary formality but does not have the same level of trust and commitment as a verbal agreement. To cover all fronts, include a handshake when you sign an agreement.

Do not start work without a contract. When negotiating a contract, be clear and transparent about your payment terms. Do not let anyone sign without reading the agreement. This will help to avoid any misunderstandings later.

One Saudi introducer, Abdullah, signed an agreement without reading it. He said to me, "I trust you 100%." Although flattering, I told him this did not work for me. I sat him down, read the contract, and explained each clause. He found it amusing. I told him I did not want him to sign anything he had not read to avoid any issues down the line.

When there is a disagreement around fees due, it is advisable to take an indirect approach initially. If the other party feels that they are losing face, they may take it personally, leading to a breakdown in negotiations and preventing any possible positive outcome.

If friendly negotiations fail and a business or individual does not receive payment for their goods or services, they should take immediate action. This may involve filing a lawsuit or seeking help from a debt collection agency. However, most people are not familiar with the legal systems in the Middle East. There is also the perception that because of the many laws, you can be jailed for unrelated matters to pressure you to drop your case.

Payment Issues: Case Studies

Marillyn, an interior designer, thought she had landed a huge client. She got to supply candles to one of the palaces of a Royal. She could not believe her luck. Unfortunately, she was not paid. She never could have imagined this happening as they were a wealthy client with no cash constraints. When she asked about the outstanding invoices, they said, "We assumed you had gifted these to us." She decided not to pursue the matter out of fear of repercussions. She said the Royal may not have known what happened to her. It may have been that the purchasing manager siphoned off the money by getting one of his friends to invoice for the goods she delivered. She could not imagine the Royal would have endorsed such behaviour.

Anna, a capital raising professional, also shared her experience of not getting fully paid. Her client was a company in the agricultural sector, majority owned by a Middle Eastern government entity. The investor from the Middle East unilaterally decided to stop paying further instalments of the pre-agreed fees.

Anna told me she had brought in the government entity. They had put in a large ticket with the promise of follow-on investments. It was fantastic news for the company as they never needed to go fundraising again, and this should have been great for Anna, too. She was immensely proud, especially considering the company had been weeks away from bankruptcy. The government entity remained supportive and continued to invest in the business.

Anna then discovered that her client, a German company, did not tell her of the follow-on investment. She initially gave the company the benefit of the doubt as there had been a lot of firing and hiring with a new CEO and a new Chairman. Notifying her of the additional investment may have fallen between the cracks. Anna told me she had flown over to the Middle East to meet with the investors in person to see if she could help them with their investment in the company.

In the meeting, the investor confirmed they had made follow-on investments and were a majority shareholder. To her surprise, the investment manager said, "We instructed the company not to pay you."

Anna was shocked. That was the last thing she expected to hear.

When she asked why, he suggested, "Haven't you received enough money? We are now the majority shareholder and have decided not to pay you."

Anna replied, "We would not have this conversation if my company were a large investment bank."

"We treat every introducer in the same manner," he claimed. "It is our policy not to pay trailers. It is not personal."

Anna explained to the investor it would have been acceptable if they had wanted to buy her out of her claim, and they could have discussed it and come to a mutual understanding. However, unilaterally deciding not to notify her and refusing to pay her was unacceptable. She did not know what was more shocking, the unilateral decision not to pay her or the admission that they did this to everyone.

In a follow-up meeting with the company, the Chairman of the German company threatened her for pursuing the success fees. The Chairman said, "Don't provoke the big bear. It will not end well for you." She was told to remain quiet and accept the situation.

She explained that the management team had changed, and the new guys did not know all the work she had done for the company. The Chairman said this was not his problem as it was before his time.

Anna told me she felt angry, bullied, treated disrespectfully, and tossed aside. She was incredibly disappointed in the investor with whom she thought she had developed a good relationship. It left her with a bad taste of the region, leading her to conclude respect was a one-way street in the Middle East.

She did not feel safe after she took legal action and told me she was busy closing down her business and bank accounts in the Middle East. She would not be returning any time soon.

In the example above, although her contract was with a German company, with an entity from the Middle East becoming a majority shareholder, it effectively had become a

Middle Eastern company. The investor controlled the decision-making.

I told Anna I was not surprised they told her, "Haven't you received enough money." Some locals think women do not need the money and are taken care of by their husbands, resulting in a reluctance to honour contracts with female counterparts, even more so if you are unmarried with no children. The road to equal pay is a long one.

These stories are not unique. I had a similar experience. Many consultants and suppliers can feel frustrated by a perceived lack of clear rules of engagement in the Middle East. Signed contracts are sometimes seen as mere guidelines to be renegotiated at any time. My one-liner to clients who pay late: "I have prioritised you and expect you equally to prioritise me."

The issue of getting paid remains one of the most significant challenges for consulting firms new to the region. You think you finally landed a nice client in the Middle East after years of hard work and building relationships. Getting paid for services or products delivered can pose a significant challenge for those unfamiliar with the region's negotiation tactics. There can be months and months of delay in payments, or you will not get paid at all.

Ideas also can get copied, according to several entrepreneurs I spoke to, so tread carefully. Non-disclosure agreements (NDAs) are hard to enforce. These issues are not specific to the Middle East and can happen anywhere.

I have also heard about employees being underpaid or forced to wait months for their wages. When this happens, some hesitate to file a case because they worry that doing so could lead to immediate termination. Additionally, they fear termination may result in losing their visa, which could negatively impact their entire family. That is why, although it may seem natural in Europe to file a court case, people are unwilling to do so and see it as a last resort. When dealing with the government, many do not think they stand a chance – or worse, they are afraid their lives will be made complex.

Priya, a young software developer, moved from India to the UAE to pursue a better life. She had heard about the UAE's reputation as a thriving hub for tech workers, offering lucrative salaries and abundant career prospects. She found a job as a developer at a small startup company. The work was challenging and rewarding, and she was thrilled to live in Dubai.

However, after a few months, she started experiencing issues with her salary. Her boss frequently delayed payments, and then she was not paid at all. She tried to talk to him about the problem, but he always had an excuse. He said the company was experiencing financial difficulties and started questioning the quality of her work. She was beginning to feel desperate because she could not afford to live in Dubai without being paid and did not know what to do. She was left with no other choice than to return to India. She was disappointed and angry but knew she had made the right decision.

Other tech workers, like Priya, have been victims of wage theft. It is an excellent workplace for most expats, but some workers are exploited.

There are things tech workers can do to protect themselves. First, they should always ensure their salary agreement is in writing. This will help to avoid any disputes later. Secondly, individuals must keep track of their hours worked and ensure they are compensated for all their time. Thirdly, they should not hesitate to voice their concerns if they are not being paid accurately.

There are things Priya could have done. She could have filed a complaint with the Ministry of Labour. She could have also contacted a lawyer or a labour rights organisation.

Wage theft is a significant issue that can be addressed and overcome. By being aware of your rights and speaking up, you can protect yourself and fellow workers from exploitation.

We are taught that confronting anyone in power can risk retaliation at home, school, university, or the workplace. Some may take advantage of this power imbalance. Speak up because others may not know what you know on topics that could change and lead to a better future.

In Europe, the perception is that getting what is rightfully yours is impossible if you find yourself opposite the ruling powers. There are success stories of people getting paid through the courts, but many do not even try to collect their money because they are concerned about retaliation and deportation.

Acquaintances from the GCC, including citizens, told me stories in which people were threatened with jail if they did not simply accept not being paid.

I also hear complaints from locals who didn't have an agreement in place and expected to get paid for a favour that they did. I explained to them it is crucial to have terms in writing with their Western parties, and they can't assume they will be taken care of if they did not ask to be paid in advance of the introduction. They should communicate their expectations and put them in writing.

Debt Collection Solutions

Interestingly, I was told by Anna that the Middle East has a long tradition of debt collection by Sheikhs. This is often seen as a more effective way to collect debts than through the legal system, which can be slow and expensive. Sheikhs who offer debt collection services typically have a network of contacts in the business community. They can use these contacts to pressure debtors to pay their debts. In some cases, they may even threaten to use their political influence to get the debts paid.

Sheikhs collect debts by inviting the debtor to lunch at their home. This is seen as a sign of respect and can put the debtor in a more cooperative mood. During lunch, the Sheikh may explain the importance of paying the debt, and they may even offer to help the debtor find a way to do so. Of course, not all Sheikhs who provide debt collection services are legitimate.

However, if someone in the Middle East owes you money, Anna suggested it may be worth contacting a trusted Sheikh to see if they can help you collect your debt. The success rate of debt collection by Sheikhs is high, as most people do not want to get on the wrong side of them. You should also be aware the process may take time, as Sheikhs often have a lot of other commitments. They may charge a percentage of the debt recovered as a commission.

Concluding, debt collection by Sheikhs appears to be a unique and thriving mediation practice rooted in the culture of the Middle East. While it may not be for everyone, Anna said she considered this an effective way to collect debts in a region where some deem the legal system unreliable. Unlike a court case that becomes public, it helps save face for the parties involved. It comes with an apology letter.

In recent years, according to the government's website, the UAE "has introduced new debt laws to strengthen the legal framework for debt collection and insolvency proceedings, providing a more modern and comprehensive approach to debt collection."[197]

There are also positive stories. For instance, Erika, the head of business development and M&A at a large family group in Saudi, decided to resign and join another company in Saudi due to an offer she could not refuse. The company she was leaving handled her decision with maturity and treated her well. They even exceeded her expectations by surprising her with a generous discretionary bonus as a token of gratitude for her outstanding work throughout the years. Erika gave it her best until the last day of her employment. It was a wonderful story, and I told Erika that this is how reputations are built.

An investment banker in the UK recently told me, "Rebecca, the world has become cutthroat everywhere. Even in the UK, known for saying 'Your word is your bond,' and where business is done with a handshake, an investment banker often must step to the lawyers to enforce payment." I agree, but accessing a lawyer in the Middle East is much more complicated than in the UK.

Chapter 40.

Do your Due Diligence

Due Diligence on Local Partners and Investors

I am frequently asked about potential partnerships with the ruling families. Western groups like having a Ruler or Royal involved because they want to delegate and believe these prominent individuals can make things happen for their business and protect them if an issue arises.

One client from India looking to set up a hospital in the UAE specifically asked me to find a local party she could JV (joint venture) with. It had to be an entity owned by one of the Royals.

Whether you do business with a Royal, a Ruler or another prominent family, always do due diligence on them. Check out what their reputation is like in business. Also, as much as they value building a personal relationship, you should. It lets you learn more about them and evaluate your value sets' alignment.

Diana, a successful entrepreneur, recalls the early days she went on a roadshow, meeting investors in the Middle East for her startup business. One of them, a wealthy businessman, Abdullah, was excited and wanted to invest in her company and set up a company locally. Abdullah and Diana's team negotiated the terms of an investment and signed a binding term sheet. The term sheet outlined the key terms of the investment, including the amount of money to be invested. It also stated the agreement was binding, and Abdullah was obligated to send the funds before the stipulated date.

Abdullah never sent the funds. Diana tried to contact him, but he never returned her calls or emails. Diana was left without the funding she needed to start her company. She was furious. She did not understand why Abdullah would sign a binding term sheet and not send the funds. She felt like she had been defrauded. She consulted with a lawyer, who told her she had a good case against Abdullah. However, she decided not to pursue legal action because it would be expensive and time-consuming. Diana learned a valuable lesson from this experience – she needed to be more careful when dealing with investors.

She was determined to start her company. She continued reaching out to other investors, eventually raising her needed funds. She launched her company, which turned out to be a unicorn. She recently sold the business for a lot of money to a strategic acquirer.

Diana's story is a reminder there are risks involved in raising money from investors. It is essential to do your due diligence and check the investor has money in their account. Even if you encounter setbacks along the way, you can succeed. In this case, the term sheet was legally binding. Abdullah could have been sued for breach of contract. However, Diana must prove she suffered damages because of Abdullah's breach. The legal process can be expensive and time-consuming, so Diana had to weigh the costs and benefits of suing Abdullah before deciding.

A client who used to work on the buy side at an international asset manager told me that their investors from the Middle East did not pay in the funds, even though they had signed agreements for their commitments. Of course, she said, they could not insist on the payments because of who the investor was.

A friend of Diana's, the CEO of a small French company, was eager to expand its operations into the Middle East. The team had learned about the region's promising business environment, characterised by a thriving economy and a well-educated, youthful workforce. After careful consideration, they initiated their expansion by establishing a joint venture with a local company based in the Middle East.

The negotiations initially went smoothly. Both sides seemed happy. They reached an agreement on the terms of the deal, and the French company promptly dispatched a team of executives to the Middle East to kickstart the business.

However, the situation turned for the worse, and tensions escalated rapidly. The local partner began making demands not included in the original agreement. They requested additional funds, a bigger portion of the profits, and sought control over the business's day-to-day operations. The management team attempted to negotiate, but the local partner showed no interest. In response, they threatened to withdraw from the deal unless their demands were met.

This put the company in a challenging position. The French company had already invested over a couple of million into the joint venture and was concerned about losing it. However, they were also wary of being taken advantage of.

They decided to walk away from the deal. Despite losing a significant amount of money, they learned a valuable lesson about doing business in the Middle East. In hindsight, they realised they had not researched their local partner sufficiently. The local party had a reputation for renegotiating terms. The CEO now looks back and sees they went in with a complete lack of understanding of the culture and business practices prevalent in the region. Make sure you agree to terms so there can be no misunderstanding.

A university friend in Holland, a serial entrepreneur, had a similar experience with a local partner in Saudi. He told me the local partner tried to renegotiate the terms – and took his passport away from him. The local told him, "You will only get your passport back if you sign on the dotted line. Try getting out of Saudi without your passport."

He managed to escape and had to get the embassy involved. This occurred a long time ago, and things have improved since, but always keep in mind the risks in business, and hold on to your passport and all other original documents.

A local partner should be a positive, bringing value add and connections, but can sometimes work against you. With dreams of starting her own business and making a mark in the UAE, Lilian set out to establish a pet food business that would thrive in this land of opportunities. Little did she know that her journey would be far from smooth sailing.

Lilian partnered with a local Sheikh in her pursuit, hoping to benefit from his knowledge of the region and his network of influential connections. He was arrogant, making it challenging for Lilian to navigate the bureaucracy to set up their company.

As Lilian began engaging with service providers and government agencies, she could not help but notice the disdain they held for her partner. Her encounters were met with cold shoulder and passive-aggressive behaviour, making it clear that her journey would be far from straightforward. The service providers seemed to go out of their way to make things difficult for her. The local partner was not able to expedite the process. She had to start giving out "wasta fees."

These are exceptional cases, and there are bad actors everywhere. It highlights that dealing with any Ruler, Royal, or other prominent family has risks attached. Make sure you do your homework on their reputation in business. Get references and check them out.

A Lebanese businessman explained it is culturally accepted in Lebanon to bribe a bank employee to send the bank statements of a potential client. This was the way they performed due diligence on counterparties. He said, "The worst case is a local Partner, a Royal with no money. Just because someone is called a Sheikh does not mean he has any money. " The lesson I learned from him is the importance of making sure you are dealing with a wealthy local partner who has a good reputation.

In the past, I heard people hacked other people's emails. "Trust but verify" is what they would say to me. In conversation, they would tell their future business partner, "I trust you," and then hire a hacker to check out the other party.

Chapter 41.

Exploring Investment Interest

Investors in the Middle East have a diverse range of interests in investing. They often allocate their capital across various asset classes, including real estate, fixed income, commodities, infrastructure, real assets, venture capital, private equity, and listed equity, either directly or through funds. Funds and alternative investment vehicles attract Middle Eastern investors looking for diversified portfolios. Some Middle Eastern investors adhere to Islamic financial principles, which prohibit certain types of investments, like those involving interest. Islamic finance provides a unique set of investment opportunities compliant with these principles.

While Middle Eastern investors have investment preferences, individual preferences and strategies vary significantly. As with any region, investment decisions are influenced by risk tolerance, financial goals, market conditions, and regulatory considerations. Many family groups will invest along the lines of their businesses. They will be interested in private equity investments, investing in privately held companies or projects, especially if synergies exist with their businesses.

Investors tend to be hands-on. In the past, they would prefer direct investments into companies to funds. They like having a sense of control. Although risk-averse, with the rise of new technologies, venture capital investments are gaining popularity among investors in the Middle East.

It struck me that investors often preferred investing in emerging markets through direct investments, while they may allocate to the US through a fund structure. The logic behind their decision was that they had a good understanding of emerging markets, being in an emerging market themselves, and believed they could make a difference there through direct investments. They perceived the potential returns lower in developed markets, so they allocated funds to these markets.

Foreigners see investments by investors in the Middle East going into what they describe as "crazy real estate developments" and, therefore, often think investors are happy taking a lot of risk. At a conference, one person asked me, "Why would they build such high buildings in the UAE, the Burj Khalifa, when they have so much land?" The story around risk appetite is more complex and nuanced. Perception of risk is subjective.

Investing for Safety and Diversification

Middle Eastern investors have a strong affinity for real estate investments, both domestically and internationally. They often seek opportunities in commercial properties, residential developments, and hospitality projects.

They like markets like UK real estate for diversification and relative safety. The investment value may decrease, but they are unlikely to lose everything, which is always a perceived possibility in their own country. So, they invest in UK residential and commercial real estate for safety and diversification from their home country.

When one client in Germany offered much higher yields than the UK, it was still hard to attract attention from Middle Eastern investors. The language in Germany was perceived as a barrier, so even though yields were higher, the investors preferred investing in the UK. Instead of London, they started investigating opportunities in secondary cities, with Manchester being one of the favoured destinations.

They also have more of an affinity for the country. Many have studied or worked in the UK and may have family or friends living there. This can make them feel more comfortable investing in property in the UK.

The sterling-USD exchange rate is crucial. Whenever Sterling is weak, it leads to more interest from the Middle East. Investors and businesspeople from the Middle East visiting London traditionally stay in high-end hotels like The Dorchester or The Ritz. But then they end up purchasing their own homes in high-end locations. Many Bahraini, Kuwaiti and Saudi individuals send their children to study in the UK to places like Oxford University and Cambridge University and buy homes for their children to live in.

I heard one amusing story from Irina, a real estate broker in Abu Dhabi, about an investor buying commercial real estate in the UK. In the Middle East, investors often go through Arab brokers to keep their identity anonymous. The investor ended up outbidding himself. He paid GBP 25 million for a building in the West End of London, estimated to be worth less than GBP 15 million. He will not sell to avoid losing face.

Kira, a Dutch real estate asset manager, told me the story of a Sheikh. The Sheikh flew to London in his private jet and checked into one of the best hotels in Mayfair. The next day, he called her and said, "I am in London and would like to visit the property you bought for me last month." She replied, "The property is in Scotland." He replied, "Where is Scotland?"

Where is my Dividend?

Some Middle Eastern investors have shown a preference for investments offering high returns in the form of yield to provide them with a regular income. One fund manager mentioned that one of his investors in Saudi called him, asking, "Where is my dividend yield?" He had to explain that he was invested in a growth equity fund, which is all about capital gains.

Dividends are a way for companies to share their profits with their shareholders and a popular way for investors to generate income.

There are several reasons why investors in the Middle East like receiving dividends. Dividends provide a regular stream of income, which can be helpful for investors looking for a steady source of income. This can be especially important for retired investors or those living on a fixed income.

Investments in infrastructure projects, such as transportation, utilities, and energy, are also common, as these investments can provide stable income streams over the long term. Middle East investors are often interested in infrastructure projects such as airports, seaports, roads, and railways, especially if they contribute to the region's development.

Fixed-income investments, including bonds and government securities, also appeal, as they provide a steady income stream, which can be attractive to investors looking for a more conservative investment.

Returns not High Enough

Mary told me about a meeting with a client, an investment fund, visiting a Sovereign Wealth Fund. The meeting was going incredibly well. The investor could not contain his excitement about the space and shared that he had already invested in similar niche funds. He was more than happy to allocate more, he said. The presentation was going smoothly. The conversation was engaging and interactive.

Then, right at the end, the investor dropped a bombshell: "I like everything you said, and I like this space, but I will not be able to invest in your fund."

Naturally, Mary was curious and asked, "Why not?"

"Because your returns are too low," he said, pointing to the 12-14% IRR numbers. "We need a minimum of 15%."

Unfortunately, her fund manager had been much more conservative with his projections than the competition and did not want to promise a higher number. All the competitors had a targeted return of 15% in their deck. The sovereign wealth fund had been a great lead, but they left empty-handed.

Mary told me about another meeting with a real estate platform in the UK. They were promising a 6% yield on UK residential real estate. She had scheduled a Zoom call with an investor from Qatar she had met in person. He gave a reality check: "We get a 6% interest rate on our bank deposits in Qatar!"

And just like that, the discussion came to a screeching halt.

Mary did not give up.

Next, she visited a Sovereign Wealth Fund, introducing a Brazilian infrastructure project. They promised a 17% return, much higher than other infrastructure funds. She was told they got similar returns by investing in government bonds. She learned that Sovereign Wealth Funds take a portfolio approach, so make sure you not only compare your returns to the sector locally and globally but also against the returns the investor can get by investing in lower-risk instruments in the same country.

Can you Guarantee my Returns?

Many investors in the Middle East look for "guaranteed returns." Middle Eastern investors are more risk-averse than investors in other parts of the world because of religious beliefs, cultural values, and the region's political instability.

Not all guaranteed returns are created equally. Very high guaranteed returns may come with hidden risks.

Bianca, a Swiss family office's CEO, told me she had a wonderful time in Saudi. She was picked up in Saudi by a Sheikh, her client, in a luxurious car. She stayed at a delightful hotel in Riyadh. They reviewed his investments, and the Sheikh asked whether she could guarantee a 13% annual return. She replied that she could not make such a commitment. She did not hear from him again.

Through the grapevine, she heard he had invested money with a company that told him they could deliver 13%, guaranteed. They paid him his 'guaranteed return' in year 1, then ran off with the rest of the money.

She was told the Sheikh lodged a complaint with the Swiss authorities and urged them to track down these gangsters. In response, the government provided him with a lovely apartment at one of the best ski resorts. However, they also made it clear that this issue was his responsibility to handle. If something looks too good to be true, it often is.

Investing for Status: Investing in Trophy Assets

The Middle East is known for investing in trophy assets. Trophy assets are typically high-profile and expensive assets purchased for prestige rather than their financial returns. Trophy assets include luxury real estate, sports teams, and iconic landmarks. Middle Eastern investors have a long history of investing in trophy assets, particularly in Europe and North America.

Investors are attracted to trophy assets for several reasons. First, they offer a way to diversify investment portfolios and reduce risk. Trophy assets are typically located in major cities and are often considered recession-proof. Second, trophy assets can provide a steady income stream and capital appreciation over time. Third, trophy assets can be used to enhance the prestige and reputation of an investor.

Companies in Europe may not have heard of certain prominent family groups. When a principal of a family group shared an investment made in a trophy asset in Europe, this was an immediate tick in the box.

Not all Middle East investors go for trophy assets. Mary explained the difference in investment preferences between the GCC countries. Qataris are the teenagers on the block regarding their investment style, and they like trophy assets. Kuwaitis have been through many investment cycles and are more mature and likely to invest in high-grade property than trophy assets.

Investing in Sports

The Middle East has been buying up football clubs. In 2021, Saudi made headlines when it purchased Newcastle United for over GBP300 million. Others include Manchester United, bought by Sheikh Mansour bin Zayed (UAE), Paris-Saint Germain, bought by Qatar's Nasser Al-Khelaifi, and Sheffield United, owned by Saudi's Abdullah bin Mosaad bin Abdulaziz al-Saud.[198]

There are several reasons why the GCC countries are investing in football clubs. Sport evokes emotions, leading to extensive media coverage. They invest in sports to diversify their economies. Tourism is a significant driver of economic growth in the GCC, and owning football clubs can help attract tourists worldwide. Sports can be used to improve the image of GCC countries internationally. The GCC countries can show they are modern and progressive by investing in successful football clubs. Sports can be used to enhance commercial ties with the West. For example, Emirates Airlines, Etihad Airways, and Qatar Airways signed major sponsorship deals with European football clubs. Saudi has stated it wants to promote sports activities and achieve excellence in sports regionally and internationally.

Saudi wants to get the population moving, 20% of whom are classified as obese. In the money directed towards football, there is a link to public health. There has been an explosion in football academies and coaching programmes. Some say it may be a strategy to brush up its image internationally.[199]

Any rules on spending do not bind Saudi clubs, so they can offer high salaries to lure away top players to the Middle East. Some of the biggest football names are expected in Saudi next season. Portugal's Cristiano Ronaldo (Saudi Pro League Club Al Nassr) will receive around $200 million annually.[200] Brazil's Neymar Junior (Saudi Pro League Club Al Hilal) is moving for $100 million per season. Neymar will have a private plane and a mansion with all the staff he could want. He will reportedly make a $87,000 bonus for every Al-Hilal win and $545,000 for every post or story he creates on social media that promotes Saudi.[201] In the big scheme of things, it is a small marketing budget.

Saudi's sovereign wealth fund PIF is taking over four big domestic football clubs.[202] They want to invest more and grow the sector, turning them into proper businesses with good corporate governance, eventually attracting private funding.

Saudi has also made a bid to host the FIFA World Cup 2030. The Middle East is becoming a significant player and investor in the global sports industry, not only football, and it will likely continue to invest in sports in future years.

Basketball icon and NBA legend LeBron James, the LA Lakers star, four-time NBA champion and all-time leading point scorer in the history of the world's most famous basketball league, went on a three-day visit to the Kingdom. His visit received a lot of press. During his visit, he immersed himself in training sessions with aspiring athletes to help them sharpen their skills on the court. Media reports have suggested that the iconic basketball star could potentially be offered a two-year contract worth $1 billion to play professionally in the Kingdom.[203]

The Middle East has recently become a major hub for Formula One racing. The region hosts several Grand Prix races, including the Abu Dhabi Grand Prix, the Bahrain Grand Prix, and the Qatar Grand Prix.

The region hosts several ATP and WTA tournaments, including the Dubai Tennis Championships, the Qatar Open, and the Saudi Arabian Tennis Open.

It also hosts major golf tournaments, including the Abu Dhabi HSBC Championship, the Dubai Desert Classic, and the Saudi International.

Horse racing is also popular in the Middle East. Major horse racing events in the Middle East include the Dubai World Cup, the Saudi Cup, and the Qatar Prix de l'Arc de Triomphe.

Golden Pursuits: Commodity investments

The Middle East is a region with political and economic instability. Investors in the region often look to gold and commodities to protect their wealth from these risks. Given the Middle East's position as a major oil producer, energy investments remain popular among Middle East investors. They may consider investing in oil and gas, renewable energy projects, or even technology advancements within the energy sector. The mining sector also attracts attention.

Gold has been used as a store of value for centuries. Gold has a long history in the Middle East and is often used in jewellery and other decorative items. It is a popular investment for people in the Middle East. It is commonly used as a hedge against inflation and political instability. It can be easily bought and sold and is widely accepted as a form of payment in many countries. This characteristic makes it a relatively liquid asset.

People often buy gold bars or coins, which they keep in safes at home. They like to have something to trade should they suddenly need to flee the country. I remember when I first arrived in Dubai, one of the topics of discussion was the exit plan. Many expats would have a backpack next to their bed just in case something was to happen, and they needed to leave the country immediately.

In the past, vending machines selling gold were prevalent in locations like Dubai Mall. These machines offered a convenient way for people to purchase gold in various forms, from small 2.5-gram coins to one-ounce bars of pure 24-karat gold. The machines were equipped with advanced technology, updating the prices regularly, ensuring customers received real-time market rates. Such convenience and adaptability made these vending machines appealing to those looking to invest in gold.

In recent years, there has been a renewed interest in gold in the Middle East, as countries in the region have been diversifying their economies and looking for ways to protect their wealth from inflation and political instability. One of the Saudi government-owned mining companies is now investing in producing assets abroad.

At a Canadian Mining Conference in London, one of the gold companies told me an amusing story of a potential investor from the GCC passing on an investment because their private plane was too big to land at the local airport. I thought it was a joke, but he was serious.

He also noted that many investors in the Middle East can relate to production but struggle to understand greenfield projects as they are used to oil just coming out of the ground. Investors believe you similarly open a tap, and gold will come out. He said, "Mines are made, not found." Concluding, raising money for producing assets is easier than greenfield projects.

Ma'aden is Saudi's largest mining company, leading the charge in developing the mining sector. Several other companies are also investing in the sector. Several other companies in Saudi and elsewhere are also investing in the sector. The Saudi government, in parallel, is investing in the development of new mining technologies, such as artificial intelligence and robotics. These technologies will help improve the mining sector's efficiency and productivity. The Future Minerals Summit in Riyadh is a must-attend event for mining professionals.[204]

The gold reserves in the Middle symbolise the region's wealth and power. According to the World Gold Council, the Middle East has about 1,174 tonnes of gold reserves, equivalent to about 3.8%. The top five countries in the Middle East with the most gold reserves are Saudi, Lebanon, Iraq, UAE, and Qatar. This number is a rough estimate, and the amount of gold stored in the Middle East may be higher or lower. The gold reserves of countries in the Middle East are often kept secret, so it isn't easy to get accurate information.[205]

Samantha, a commodity trader, told me an amusing story. An investor held gold reserves in London and decided they wanted them back in their home country. The gold was flown in and put on a truck. A man was sent to guide the truck to their building. He turned up in a Ferrari at the airport. As he led the way in his fast car to the investor's premises, the truck struggled to keep up with his speed and got lost. The truck eventually showed up with all the gold intact, and the gold was stored in the basement of the building. In any other country, the gold, without any security, would have vanished before it arrived at the premises.

Investing Abroad - Sectors of Interest

Although deal activity globally has slowed, the Middle East remains a hub for both inbound and outbound investment. Sovereign wealth funds hold most capital in the Middle East. As the region seeks to diversify its holdings and move away from oil dependence, new private equity opportunities are available, with investments focused on food, healthcare, industrials, education, technology, and consumer goods and services.

Due to limited arable land and water resources, food security is a priority for Middle Eastern countries. Therefore, investments in agriculture and agribusiness are of interest to investors seeking opportunities in food production, technology-driven farming methods, and agricultural infrastructure.

Industrial markets are growing – especially in civil aerospace, defence, and automobiles. Saudi's decision to lift the ban on women drivers immediately impacted the demand for passenger vehicles. Suddenly, a new segment of female consumers sought to purchase their cars.

The healthcare industry is another area attracting the attention of Middle Eastern investors. I did not find the Middle East a good market for raising money for biotech ventures. Investors prefer products on the market instead of investing in development. It may also be the result of a lack of local winners. Looking at the largest companies in a country gives a good guide to what sectors investors are comfortable investing in.

Education is highly valued in the Middle East, which makes it an attractive investment sector. Investors focus on private schools, universities, vocational training centres, and educational technology platforms.

The tech sector has been gaining traction in recent years among Middle Eastern investors. They are keen on investing in innovative startups, digital platforms, e-commerce ventures, and technology-driven solutions across various industries. Recently, a significant amount of money has been going into financials, such as investment banks, locally and internationally. The prominence of cryptocurrencies and central bank digital coins is on the rise.

Pots of money, including grants, exist for companies willing to move their headquarters to the Middle East.

Domestic Focus

Localisation is the buzzword. Important sectors for national security in the Middle East include energy, defence, food and water security, cybersecurity, and public health.

Many countries in the region invest heavily in their defence. The Middle East increasingly faces cyber threats. Countries are investing in cybersecurity capabilities.

The Middle East is a water-scarce region, and food and water security are major concerns for many countries, as much of the food is imported. Countries are developing new water desalination technologies to increase their water supply and reduce their reliance on imported food. The Saudi government is investing heavily in its agricultural sector, to increase domestic food production by 50% by 2030. This includes investments in new irrigation systems, greenhouses, and other agricultural technologies. The UAE also invests in food production, focusing on sustainable and innovative farming methods. For example, the UAE invests in vertical farming, which uses less water and land than traditional farming methods.

Many countries in the region are investing in their public health sectors to improve access to quality healthcare for their citizens. Investments in hospitals, medical centres, pharmaceuticals, and healthcare services are popular, providing financial returns and contributing to societal well-being.

In addition to these sectors, education, infrastructure, and social development are important for national security. These sectors are essential for building a stable and prosperous society, which is key to reducing the risk of conflict and instability.

Remember that although there is more liquidity because of the higher oil price, much of the fresh liquidity is invested locally. During the Saudi Aramco IPO, I heard family groups in Saudi received a call strongly encouraging them to invest. We also see PIF, Saudi's Sovereign Wealth Fund, pour billions into domestic landmark projects, such as NEOM. This, of course, leaves less liquidity for investments abroad. There is more interest in localisation of the activities of companies abroad.

Chapter 42.

ESG and Islamic Finance

Ethical Business: ESG Practices in the Middle East

The world is uniting under the framework of ESG (Environmental, Social, and Governance). ESG is a comprehensive framework that assesses an organisation's business practices and performance regarding sustainability and ethical issues. Companies face increasing pressure from stakeholders to comply with ESG. ESG investing can help investors avoid holding companies engaged in risky or unethical practices.

Most people, especially the younger generation, agree that sustainable investing is crucial to transitioning to a greener and more sustainable future. The next generation is not solely focused on the bottom-line results of companies. They also consider whether the company, as well as countries, are adhering to ESG principles.

When I spoke to Angela, an economics and business teacher in her 30s, she mentioned that she would need to consider whether Dubai adheres to ESG before contemplating a move. Following her remarks, I decided to include an ESG chapter in the book. Her husband said he would check if the company he interviewed with behaved ethically before signing any employment contract.

Having participated in Ernst & Young's 2019 workshop in Dubai: Integrated Thinking and Integrated Reporting (ESG) for Integrated Investor Questioning, and after attending The World Economic Forum in Davos in Switzerland in January 2020[206] before the COVID-19 pandemic, it became clear to me that ESG and climate change is a trend hard to ignore. When I first moved to the Middle East, I heard no talk about ESG. In the last couple of years, governments in the Middle East have been acknowledging the significance of integrating ESG principles into their economic development strategies. Governments have recently been announcing ESG policies. For example, Abu Dhabi's SWF Mubadala announced the creation of a standalone ESG Unit and has been concentrating on assessing ESG-related risks and the potential for current and future investments.[207]

COP28[208], the 28th Conference of the Parties to the United Nations Framework Convention on Climate Change (UNFCCC), will be hosted by Dubai from November 30 until December 12, 2023. I plan to attend. This promises to be a big event. The main objective of COP28 is to accelerate action towards the goals of the Paris Agreement. COP28 is a critical opportunity for governments, businesses, and society to unite and act on climate change. The decisions made at COP28 will have a significant impact on the future. World leaders, activists, and others will be coming together in Dubai to find solutions for pressing environmental issues.

Countries will produce ambitious plans to reduce their greenhouse gas emissions. This will require a major shift to clean energy sources and reduced fossil fuel consumption. Developing countries need financial support to help them mitigate and adapt to climate change. This support can come from grants, loans, and investments. The transition to a net zero emissions economy must be fair and equitable so no one is left behind. Climate change is already having a devastating impact on people and ecosystems around the world. Countries must build resilience to these impacts by investing in early warning systems and reducing disaster risk.

As a result of COP28, the Middle East will be in the spotlight. Middle Eastern countries are known for their heavy reliance on hydrocarbon resources. There will be more focus and attention on the corporate agendas to achieve sustainability ambitions and net zero commitments.

The 'E' in ESG stands for Environment. Environmental criteria consider how a company safeguards the environment, including corporate policies addressing climate change, for example, energy use, waste, pollution, and natural resource conservation. The Middle East's reliance on oil and gas challenges reaching net zero by 2050. Air conditioning, water-guzzling sprinklers, and pollution add to the challenge. The UAE is still heavily reliant on fossil fuels for its energy needs, making it a significant emitter of greenhouse gases.

The UAE continues to invest in renewable energy to reduce its reliance on fossil fuels and become ESG-compliant. It has invested heavily in renewable energy in recent years. It could develop energy efficiency standards for businesses and homes.

The Middle East is in the heart of the global sunbelt. The GCC countries have the highest sunlight exposure in the world. The UAE has some of the world's largest solar and wind farms. They have implemented ambitious solar projects like the Mohammed bin Rashid Al Maktoum Solar Park[209]. These efforts showcase a commitment to sustainable development and serve as inspiring models for others to copy.

The Emirates Nuclear Energy Corporation (ENEC) is developing the Barakah Nuclear Energy Plant as the first peaceful nuclear plant in the UAE and the Arab World. It comprises four nuclear units, each producing up to 1,400 megawatts of electricity. Once all four Units are fully operational, the Barakah plant will generate up to 25% of the country's electricity with zero emissions, preventing the release of 21 million tons of carbon dioxide into the atmosphere.[210] Similarly, Saudi has launched ambitious plans to develop a sustainable energy sector through initiatives like the Vision 2030 program.

The UAE is facing a water scarcity crisis. It needs to take steps to conserve water and develop new water sources to become ESG-compliant. The country could invest in water conservation projects and develop new water sources, including more desalination plants. The UAE generates significant waste and needs to develop more sustainable waste management practices, such as recycling and composting. It could also invest in waste-to-energy projects.

The 'S' in ESG stands for social criteria. It examines how a company or country manages relationships with employees, suppliers, customers, and the communities where it operates. Positive change is happening on the 'S,' arguably from a low base.

The UAE has been criticised for its human rights record and is taking steps to become ESG-compliant. The UAE could improve its human rights record by upholding the rule of law, protecting freedom of speech, and ensuring fair trials. The country could also work to strengthen the rights of women and minorities.

Middle Eastern governments are increasingly promoting gender equality and empowering women in the workforce. Initiatives include Saudi's decision to allow women to drive so they can get to work. Recognising the untapped potential of their female population, governments are implementing policies and initiatives to support women's participation in various industries. By providing equal opportunities and access to education and promoting inclusive work environments, countries are creating a more balanced and diverse workforce, contributing to national development and global progress. The UAE has also been criticised for its labour practices. It could improve its labour practices even more by enforcing labour laws, protecting migrant workers, and providing fair wages and working conditions. With COP28 around the corner, new initiatives have been announced.

The 'G' stands for governance. Governance involves a company's leadership, executive pay, audit, internal controls, and shareholder rights. It requires analysis, verifying whether a company embraces diversity on its board of directors and whether the company practice corporate transparency. Although there has been a lot of talk about governance, there is still more to do to strengthen trust and confidence within the countries and abroad.

Nathalie told me it was around the time of the Saudi Aramco planned IPO that she suddenly saw a change. Conferences around corporate governance were organised, with the first one in Saudi. She attended the Pearl Initiative conference in Saudi[211]. At this conference, many family groups' principals were gathered in Riyadh to discuss governance. At the time, she thought this was an attempted quick fix to demonstrate Saudi's commitment to corporate governance as they were looking for investors for the Saudi Aramco IPO. It was a good initiative, but governance cannot be fixed overnight.

ESG risks have emerged as one of the biggest threats to businesses, potentially impacting their long-term performance and profitability. These risks can also affect their ability to secure new capital. Moreover, as regulations emerge and fines are increasingly issued, organisations must comply with them at a basic level. There is an increasing emphasis on investments having a positive social or environmental role.

Corinne, an investment banker, said she did not see ESG truly prioritised by investors when making investment decisions. It is at the government level that changes are visible.

They understand that aligning themselves with ESG principles can attract socially conscious international investors who prioritise environmental sustainability, social responsibility, and good governance. Corinne feels investors can further enhance the focus on ESG in their annual reporting.

A lot still needs to be done in the private and government sectors. Corinne explained, "There is awareness at the top, but as you get to mid-level management, there appears little interest in ESG." She explains the significance of international investors expecting co-investors in transactions to adhere to the same ESG principles. Improving the perception of them as an investor would also make fundraising for companies they are invested in easier internationally.

The UAE has promoted ESG awareness. As outlined on the government's website, initiatives include the UAE Net Zero by 2050 strategic initiative, a nationwide initiative to achieve net-zero emissions by 2050.[212] Other initiatives worth mentioning are the UAE Vision 2021[213], the Dubai 2040 Urban Master Plan[214], the UAE Green Agenda 2015-2030[215], the Paris Agreement, and the UN Sustainable Development Goals.

The UAE Green Agenda is a national plan to promote sustainable development. The program includes goals such as increasing the use of renewable energy, reducing water consumption, and protecting the environment. The Dubai Clean Energy Strategy plans to make the country a global hub for clean energy. It includes goals such as increasing the share of renewable energy in Dubai's energy mix to 75% by 2050.

The Abu Dhabi Sustainability Week is an annual event that brings together businesses and governments to discuss sustainability issues. It includes workshops, conferences, and exhibitions. According to Morgan Lewis, a law firm in Dubai, Abu Dhabi Global Market (ADGM) recently announced the implementation of one of the first sustainable finance frameworks in the region, coming into effect immediately. The framework includes rules for sustainability-oriented investment funds, discretionary-managed portfolios, bonds, and *sukuks* (sharia-compliant bond-like instruments used in Islamic finance). It also sets requirements for ESG disclosures by companies domiciled in ADGM.[216]

Some say climate change is the new world religion. It is interesting to note religious leaders are attending COP28.[217] They believe that their moral authority can be used to influence and provide guidance on how to live sustainably.

Shariah Law and Islamic Finance

Islamic finance and environmental, social, and governance (ESG) investing are two approaches to responsible investing that have gained attention in recent years. Both approaches emphasise ethical investment practices and can complement one another in promoting responsible and ethical financial practices.

Islamic finance is a financial system operating under the principles of the Shariah, Islamic law. At its core, Islamic finance prohibits the payment or receipt of interest and instead promotes risk-sharing and profit-sharing between parties involved in financial transactions. This means investments must be made in tangible assets or ventures generating genuine economic activity.[218] Many investors in the Middle East and beyond have taken steps to integrate their Islamic beliefs via Shariah-compliant strategies. The most developed markets in Islamic finance are Saudi, UAE, and Bahrain.

Islamic finance currently offers various products and services to cater to different needs. Examples include *Murabaha* (cost-plus financing), *Ijarah* (leasing), *Musharakah* (partnership), *Sukuk* (Islamic bonds), *Takaful* (Islamic insurance), and many more. [219]

ESG investing is an investment approach that seeks to identify companies that are good stewards of the environment, socially responsible, and have good governance practices. ESG investors believe that companies focusing on these factors are more likely to be successful in the long term.

There are overlaps between Islamic finance and ESG investing. Both approaches emphasise ethical investment practices and focus on investing in companies looking after the environment and society. The complementary nature of Islamic finance and ESG investing can be seen in several ways. For example, Islamic finance prohibits investments in companies involved in activities harmful to the environment or society, such as gambling, alcohol, tobacco, the adult entertainment industry, pork and non-Halal food, weapons, conventional derivatives, conventional banks, and insurance companies.[220] This list overlaps with the ESG investing approach, which also seeks to avoid investing in companies involved in some of these activities.

In addition, Islamic finance emphasises risk-sharing and profit-sharing between parties involved in financial transactions. This can lead to more sustainable and equitable outcomes, as it aligns the interests of investors with the interests of the companies in which they invest. This key ESG investing principle is promoting sustainable and equitable business practices. Islamic finance and ESG investing are two complementary approaches to responsible investing, with the potential to promote sustainable and equitable outcomes. By working together, these two approaches can help to create a responsible and ethical financial system.

In practice, Islamic finance is rule-based and open to interpretation. This can sometimes lead to challenges, as there may be different interpretations of what constitutes a permissible investment under Islamic law.

A hospitality sector specialist, Stephanie, told me she was involved in a European hotel transaction. It had a restaurant that served alcohol. According to Shariah principles, investments in businesses involving alcohol are prohibited. However, some argue that if the primary revenue of the hotel is not derived from alcohol sales, it might be permissible to invest in the hotel. Others may say that the percentage of alcohol sales constituting the hotel's revenue is the determining factor. Still, others may say that the hotel could be structured in a way that makes it permissible to invest in it, such as by separating alcohol-related activities from the rest of the business.

The permissibility of an investment under Shariah law is a matter of interpretation by scholars. However, the fact there are different interpretations of Shariah law can create challenges for investors who are seeking to comply with Islamic finance principles.

The structuring of a transaction takes place under Shariah law, while the remaining aspects are governed by conventional law. Combining Shariah and conventional law in structuring transactions allows for a comprehensive approach that addresses religious and legal considerations. By incorporating conventional law, businesses can ensure compliance with legal frameworks and regulations that govern commercial transactions within a specific jurisdiction. This ensures the transaction is legally binding and establishes a solid foundation for resolving disputes, if necessary.

It is worth attending IFN's conferences to learn more about Islamic Finance. I continue to participate in the conference in London in September, discussing the critical topics shaping Islamic Finance in the future.[221] The UK's Islamic finance leadership in Europe is undisputed. It has more

Islamic banks than its European peers and was the first to issue a sovereign Sukuk facility in 2014. London Stock Exchange lists around 70 Sukuk. IFN also organises conferences in the Middle East.[222]

The future of Islamic finance and ESG is bright. As these two approaches to responsible investing both gain attention, there is more collaboration between the two communities. This collaboration could lead to new products and services, combining the best of both worlds. It could also lead to a more sustainable and equitable financial system.

Chapter 43.

Reverse Culture Shock

I hope this book offered you a glimpse into the chaotic world of business in the Middle East. I have had a peek behind the shadows, like in Plato's *"Allegory of the Cave."* Wikipedia summarises it nicely as a philosophical concept that explores how our perception of reality is shaped. The allegory describes a group of people who have lived chained in a cave, facing a blank wall. The people observe shadows being cast on the wall by objects passing in front of a fire behind them. These shadows serve as the prisoners' reality but do not accurately represent the real world. One day, a prisoner is freed from his chains and realises that the shadows on the wall do not represent reality. He can perceive the true form of reality, unlike the other prisoners who can only see the mere shadows. Initially, he is blinded by the light of the fire outside the cave, but eventually, he gains the ability to perceive the true nature of reality.

This allegory serves as a metaphor for the soul's journey. The cave represents the material world, while the shadows symbolise our perceptions of reality. The fire, however, represents the sun, a symbol of truth and knowledge. The prisoner, freed from his chains, symbolises the philosopher who has gained a profound understanding of the true nature of reality.[223]

The allegory of the cave has been interpreted in many ways over the centuries. Some people believe that it is a metaphor for the journey from ignorance to enlightenment, while others believe it is a critique of the limitations of our senses. Whatever its interpretation, the allegory of the cave remains one of the most powerful and influential philosophical concepts ever written. The journey to true knowledge is difficult and requires us to relinquish our preconceived notions. The cave allegory is a powerful reminder that our perception of reality is limited. It encourages us to question our assumptions and to seek out the truth.

I am happy back in London, but time will tell whether this is a station to refuel or my destination. The main reason for moving back was Brexit. My application for the pre-EU Settlement Scheme has been approved. I am looking to embark on a new chapter.

Reflecting on my ten years in the Middle East, I am grateful for the lessons learned and the friendships forged. Friendships get solidified after you leave a country. Many connections got much better after I left. The region has increased my resilience, adaptability, and appreciation for diverse cultures. It has given me great memories and hours and hours of dinner party stories, some of which I have shared with you here and some which I can only tell behind closed doors.

Returning to the UK after 15 years abroad was a journey through reverse culture shock, encompassing a series of distinct phases. I felt like a fish out of the water. I was not only relocating physically but also mentally. Some refer to this phenomenon as emotional jet lag.

At the outset, I was excited by the novelty factor. This initial phase is often referred to as the "honeymoon phase." While I did not anticipate a grand reception, the timing aligned well with the post-COVID-19 pandemic reopening of London. Everyone was in the mood to go out and socialise. Invitations to various parties poured in, offering a seamless reintegration. Revisiting cherished haunts and clubs like Annabel's and 5

Hertford Street stirred a sense of familiarity, as did indulging in traditional English clubs, restaurants, tennis clubs, and countryside escapes. My perspective had shifted, and I observed the city and its inhabitants through fresh eyes, comparing my past self to the one I had become.

However, alongside the initial excitement, I had to acclimate to certain aspects of London I had forgotten about during my time abroad. The visible litter everywhere and garbage bags on the streets are realities requiring readjustment. Winter brought an intense cold, starkly contrasting the Middle Eastern climate. Yet it provided an opportunity to retrieve cherished cashmere jumpers and winter coats stowed away.

As I reacquainted with London, I found myself experiencing moments of profound nostalgia. Familiar streets triggered flashbacks to the past, evoking memories going back 20 years. This introspective phase left me feeling 10 years of my life had vanished. Upon reuniting with friends from the past, our connections effortlessly rekindled, but I grappled with the sensation I was no longer entirely the same person. This internal shift led to moments of disconnection as if I were a stranger amidst familiar surroundings. Discussions with fellow expats who had similarly returned shed light on this common sentiment of losing part of their timeline during their years abroad.

While integrating back into society in London posed no significant hurdles, reconciling the gap between my time in Monaco, the Middle East and London posed a challenge. Documenting these seemingly "lost" years in the form of this book provides a space for these experiences in my timeline, granting them the recognition they deserve. This exercise allows me to weave these disparate threads into a cohesive narrative.

I thoroughly enjoy visiting the recently renovated Jumeirah Carlton Tower, a splendid establishment owned by Dubai Holding. Dubai Holding, a government-backed investment company, boasts ownership of an array of enterprises in the UAE, including the prominent Jumeirah Group managing this upscale hotel. This elegant venue often hosts a diverse gathering of people in business from the Middle East, contributing to its vibrant atmosphere. In addition to the Jumeirah Carlton Tower, I have discovered a few coffee shops nestled in the heart of Knightsbridge and Mayfair, earning the reputation of "Middle East locals hot spots." The ambience of these establishments resonated with individuals from the region, fostering a sense of connection and shared comfort. Notably, Edgware Road is a favoured hub for the Middle Eastern community. Hanging out in these areas enables me to harmoniously bridge my experiences in the Middle East and the UK, aiding my transition back to the latter.

I have found my sense of belonging is most pronounced when interacting with fellow expats in the UK who share a similar background from emerging markets or who have lived on multiple continents. These connections and other close friendships provide a strong anchor, helping me navigate the intersection of my Middle Eastern and UK lives. There are plenty of people from the Middle East in London to socialise with. London is home to a significant Middle Eastern community, with an estimated population of 1.2 million. This group constitutes approximately 8% of the city's total population. Among the various nationalities forming the Middle Eastern community in London, the largest contingent comes from Iran. Following closely are individuals from Iraq, Turkey, and Egypt contributing to the city's rich cultural tapestry.

My 10 years in the Middle East remind me of the character's journey in the book, *"Candide"* by Voltaire[224]. The main character, Candide, travelled all over the world to eventually be content simply tending to the plants in his backyard. Candide believed in the philosophy of optimism. But he gets a reality check as he travels the world. From being kicked out of his castle to witnessing natural disasters and encountering crazy characters, poor Candide cannot catch a break. Voltaire uses this hilarious adventure to poke fun at society and question the idea that everything works out for the best.

A Saudi friend says: "If you fail to prepare, you prepare to fail." I would expand on his quote for anyone moving to the Middle East: "Always be prepared. Everything will go wrong, and occasionally, it may go according to plan."

People often inquire about my plans and sometimes playfully suggest destinations, even proposing the idea of a venture to a potential conflict zone in the Middle East. However, my true fascination lies in the prospect of conversing with extraterrestrial beings, should they visit our planet. A group of beings from another galaxy landing on Earth is enthralling to me. I envision an opportunity to engage in meaningful dialogue, gaining insights into their unique ways of life. While the moon has been suggested as a destination, the physical location does not captivate me. Instead, it is the people, their experiences, and perspectives. Naturally, the environment plays a role in shaping these experiences, a factor integral to understanding people. Diverse human experiences, thoughts and ideas captivate my curiosity, especially when they differ from mine. I love analysing a new theory of anything.

The owners of the apartment where I have been cat-sitting have arrived back from their holiday. My five weeks in the south of France are over, and the first draft of the book has been written. The darling cat looks confused. I prepared a nice *couscous* for my friends, who had a long journey from Mauritius to Dubai, and then Dubai to Nice. They told me their flight was packed with people from the Middle East. I explained that August is the month people from the Middle East come to Europe.

On the day I was leaving, they got an offer from a Middle East family for their apartment. The head of the family office had done a viewing during my stay. The purpose was to house their staff, as they had bought into an expensive development in Monaco. They told them they would revert in a couple of days.

'Inshallah.'

In the Fire of Capital

EPILOGUE

In the Fire of Capital

In the Fire of Capital

Why I Chose the Title "In the Fire of Capital"?

The book's title, "In the Fire of Capital," may evoke different associations with fire depending on people's backgrounds and religious beliefs.

Choosing a title was quite tricky. I did not start with a tile. One evening, I had an idea: "In the Fire of Capital". I immediately fell in love with this title.

I created an image that captures the essence and emotion of writing the book. I selected the photo of a campfire in the desert because it perfectly represented the concept of storytelling.

However, I faced significant pushback on my title. At a conference in London, several people from the Middle East expressed concern, stating that the title had associations with hell. This feedback stressed me, and I tried finding an alternative title.

Not everyone liked my front cover. Opinions were very divided. Either they loved it or really did not like it. One person from the Middle East suggested I change the front cover to a photo of a kid building a sandcastle with one of the iconic buildings, such as the Burj Khalifa, shining in the background. It was a creative idea. I initially thought he may be stereotyping and thinking of me as a mother with kids. He may have thought the book would be about schooling and family life. On the other hand, the kid with the sandcastle may have been symbolic of a startup or a newcomer to the Middle East. The visual required an explanation by the creator.

Eventually, I came up with an incredibly dull but non-offensive title, "More than oil and fast cars." I held that title for about two weeks. It had a green cover, resembling the colour commonly found in flags across the Middle East. However, the more I contemplated it, the more the title and the green colour were too dull and uninteresting.

I started yearning for my old title, which I absolutely loved and felt passionate about. It is fascinating that the title and front cover evoke such diverging emotions.

For me, fire symbolises strength, energy, passion, warmth, comfort, light, wisdom, and truth. Additionally, fire represents the sun and the hot climate of the Middle East.

Fire is central to numerous cultural celebrations and festivals worldwide, symbolising joy, happiness, and the spirit of togetherness. The book begins with fire as my journey starts in Dubai with a memorising fireworks display, marking a new chapter in my life.

Fire provides light in darkness, both literally and metaphorically. It is often associated with knowledge, wisdom, enlightenment, and clarity of thought. It symbolises the journey I have been through, from ignorance to a glimpse of the shadows.

Fire has the power to transform, purify, and regenerate. It is associated with change, growth, and overcoming challenges or obstacles. It symbolises the incredible transformation that the Middle East is going through.

Fire has long been associated with energy and power. In the context of capital, fire can symbolise the energy and power needed to fuel economic growth and inspire innovation. It represents the dynamic force that propels businesses forward, ignites ideas, and creates opportunities for prosperity.

Fire symbolises passion and ambition. In the realm of capital, it embodies the entrepreneurial spirit that propels individuals to embrace risks and chase their aspirations. Capital provides the means to transform ideas into reality, fuelling innovation and creating opportunities for success. It reflects the passion and ambition of the emerging venture capital community in the Middle East to be a catalyst for change.

Fire is a transformative element that has the power to turn raw materials into valuable resources. Similarly, in the realm of capital, fire symbolises the potential for transformation and growth. Capital represents the ability to invest wisely, nurture businesses, and generate wealth. It can function as a catalyst for change, driving progress and creating new possibilities.

Fire has historically played a crucial role in the development of civilisations. In the context of capital, fire represents economic development and prosperity. It symbolises the creation of jobs, the growth of industries, and the overall improvement of living standards. Capital is a vital resource that can be channelled towards fostering economic progress.

Fire has traditionally served as a community gathering point, offering warmth, light, and security. In the realm of capital, it symbolises the potential to sustain communities by supporting social initiatives, investing in infrastructure, and promoting social responsibility. Capital can be harnessed to create a positive impact, ESG, improve lives, and contribute to the well-being of society.

Fire is also unpredictable and can spread rapidly. Similarly, the world of capital is filled with risks and uncertainties. Investors frequently encounter the possibility of losing their investments or experiencing financial instability because of market fluctuations or unforeseen events. The fire of capital symbolises the inherent volatility and unpredictability of financial markets. Raising money in the Middle East is not an easy job. A friend jokingly told me it suggested the word of my book spreading rapidly.

Why I Wrote the Book?

I had long wanted to write the book and had already created an outline, including the stories I would share at dinner parties.

The trigger for sitting down and writing the book was emotional, sparked by the non-payment of success fees by someone in the Middle East for whom I had done a lot of work over the years. I found it difficult to focus on other business. I decided to channel my emotions and fire within me productively and write my story. Writing gave me back my voice after being pressured to remain silent and accept non-payment. I felt like the main character in Forest Gump, an American comedy-drama movie. He could not stop running. I could not stop writing.

Additionally, documenting these seemingly "lost" years in the form of this book creates a space for these experiences in my timeline. This exercise allows me to weave these separate threads into a coherent narrative.

People are rushing to the Middle East to raise capital. I receive numerous incoming calls from individuals seeking guidance on what to expect. It takes me hours to share my lessons with these newcomers. I now refer people to my book. I have written it as advice to those new to the Middle East like I was.

I will only collaborate with potential clients who have read the book and understand the time-consuming nature of the process and the additional expenses involved. I would not advise anyone to only work on a success fee basis. Even small retainers do not compensate you for the risks you run of not being paid. It is time to start my next chapter, possibly another book. My interest now is in advisory and non-executive roles.

Standing at this juncture, I find joy in sharing and giving back, passing on the wisdom I have gathered. People say wise men stay silent and listen. I am afraid I must disagree. Wise men and wise women should be talking and sharing their experiences with the next generation. After I had written my book, I met several people who had been in jail in the Middle East, a very unpleasant experience. By pointing out the rules, I hope to create awareness and prevent expats from inadvertently doing the wrong thing and getting into trouble.

Why are the Stories Fictional?

Initially, the idea of attributing the stories to women was sparked by a friend from Pakistan who expressed deep concern for my safety, "People have been knocked off for a lot less than you are doing." Other friends shared the same concerns and attempted to discourage me from writing the book. Some suggested I should write the book under a pseudonym. Many were happy to share their stories but did not want to be quoted.

On the other hand, some told me there was nothing to worry about. They explained the government monitors social media posts, not books, as books are considered slow burns - a social media post risks going viral. Some friends agreed the Middle East is more tolerant than some may think.

I had a fun time in the Middle East and believe my opinions are balanced. I have written a book with all the advice I wish I had been given before moving to the Middle East.

Taking on board the concerns, I decided to fictionalise the stories, loosely based on reality, so as not to embarrass anyone. It has become a collection of stories, some my own and some shared by friends, acquaintances, or people I met through business.

Contrary to the picture I may portray in this book, there are not many women in finance in the Middle East, like in

Europe. However, there are phenomenally successful and influential women. Doing business as a woman in the Middle East is not impossible.

Author Biography

I was born in the Netherlands and studied International and European Law at Leiden University. In addition to my academic pursuits, I engaged in numerous extracurricular activities and completed several internships abroad. Back then, I was an idealist, fuelled by a strong desire to make the world a better place and passionate about driving change, and I still am.

I was selected for the ABN AMRO Traineeship Program, where I got a first taste of finance within Private Banking in Gibraltar. Geneva was next with a traineeship at the United Nations International Labour Organization and Human Rights Commission. And then I had a great time in Brussels, the buzzing epicentre of the European Union. I spent six months as a *stagiaire* in DG I, diving into the dynamics of the relationship between the US and the EU. I had a front-row seat during all the anti-dumping trade negotiations in the steel industry. These experiences were transformative chapters, each carrying lots of stories.

Following the internships, I worked for several American banks like JP Morgan, Salomon Brothers, Citigroup, Robertson Stephens, and Bear Stearns. Although people often lump them together, they each have a distinct culture.

Salomon Brothers captured my heart. This chapter still brings a twinkle to my eye. The mid-90s marked an era of excitement on the trading floor, and Salomon Brothers was centre stage. I barely knew the difference between an equity and a bond but was quickly brought up to speed. I spent time in New York on the famous Salomon Brothers Training Program, featured in "Liar's Poker" by Michael Lewis[225], before working on the trading floor in London, learning on the job advising institutional investors on which equities to buy and sell. IPOs were doubling on the opening. The rush was unlike anything else. It was a time to be in the thick of it.

By the age of thirty, I had made a considerable sum of money from my time working in the city. Then, in 2002, I decided to take a break, a year off the grid, and set off on a global adventure. It was time to check off every item on my wish list, things I had always wanted to experience and explore, but working in the city had kept me from pursuing it.

I improved my French and learned Spanish. I travelled around the world, landing in South America, Australia, Asia, and China. I took a fascinating course at Sotheby's, which taught me how to distinguish the genuine from the counterfeit and tell the difference between bone and ivory. I delved into Feng Shui in Singapore, walked the Great Wall of China, and explored the Coral Reef in Australia. It was an amazing time, full of unforgettable memories. In Argentina, I played polo at several farms. It was a thrilling experience. The speed, the smell of horses, and their nostrils trembling as we galloped together on the field was exhilarating. I also enrolled in a culinary arts course at Prue Leith's, a renowned cooking school in London. I cannot say I transformed into a Michelin chef, but I found myself much more appreciative and in awe of the culinary creations crafted by others. Returning to the city in London and resuming work at another bank proved challenging after all the incredible experiences and freedom I had enjoyed. I was keen to embark on more adventures.

After a year of fun and inspiration in 2003, a new chapter started. I decided to set up an investment advisory company in London. My focus initially was on the emerging world of hedge funds, raising capital for these financial newcomers. It was an exciting time. Hedge funds were the place to be. I then expanded into private equity funds and private companies.

Setting up my business, AlphaBet Capital Advisors, an award-winning investment advisory business, was about creating a life combining my love for globetrotting with my professional aspirations. I chose to move to the South of France. It was my way of seizing the reins and embracing life on my terms. In Monaco, I had a marvellous time in my 30s, meeting many new people from different backgrounds. And then, in my 40s, I traded one sunny place for an even sunnier one, the UAE. My driving force is the excitement of new experiences. If there is a chance to learn something new, something unexplored, consider my attention fully captured.

I recall an interview where someone said, "Your comfort zone is being a stranger in your environment." It was a revelation, and I realised he was spot on. I felt in my element in a room full of people from diverse cultures. That sense of familiarity amidst the unfamiliar is where I feel at home—having said that, I am pleased to be back in London again.

In Dubai, I met many people like me, with dual nationalities. Dubai is a home for people without a home. You will find people from diverse backgrounds in every country. You may get along better with a person with a similar personality or experience in another country than someone in your own country speaking the same language.

In the Fire of Capital

Endnotes

1 Emmanuel Tchividjian "The ethics of silence and speaking up", Public Relations Society of America, PR Say [online] Available on:
"https://prsay.prsa.org/2018/02/27/the-ethics-of-silence-and-of-speaking-up/ (Accessed online 13 September 2023)

2 Wikipedia, Expo 2020 [online] Available on:
https://en.wikipedia.org/wiki/Expo_2020 (Accessed online 25 August 2023)

3 Guinness World Records [online] Available on:
https://www.guinnessworldrecords.com/news/2014/1/watch-live-stream-here-dubai-attempts-new-year%E2%80%99s-eve-fireworks-world-record-54187/ (Accessed online 14 August 2023)

4 Jason Hanna, Ashley Fantz and Catherine E. Shoichet ,"Dubai Address Hotel fire", CNN, 31 December 2015 [online] Available on:
https://edition.cnn.com/2015/12/31/middleeast/dubai-address-hotel-fire/index.html (Accessed online 14 August 2023)

5 Official Portal of the UAE Government, Political System and Government [online] Available on: https://u.ae/en/about-the-uae/the-uae-government/political-system-and-government (Accessed online 14 August 2023)

6 Wikipedia, Mohamed bin Zayed Al Nayan [online] Available on: Mohamed bin Zayed Al Nahyan - Wikipedia (Accessed online 25 August 2023)

7 Official Portal of the UAE Government, About the UAE, Fact Sheet [online] Available on: https://u.ae/en/about-the-uae/fact-sheet (Accessed online 14 August 2023)

8 Official Portal of the UAE Government, About the UAE, Fact Sheet [online] Available on: https://u.ae/en/about-the-uae/fact-sheet (Accessed online 14 August 2023)

9 Worldometers, World Population, United Arab Emirates Population [online] Available on: https://www.worldometers.info/world-population/united-arab-Emirates-population/(Accessed online 14 August 2023)

10 CIA World Factbook, "UAE" [online] Available on: https://www.cia.gov/the-world-factbook/countries/united-arab-Emirates/ (Accessed online 30 July 2023)

11 Official Portal of the UAE Government, About the UAE, Fact Sheet [online] Available on: https://u.ae/en/about-the-uae/fact-sheet (Accessed online 14 August 2023)

12 The National News, "A historical perspective of the Abu Dhabi border" [online] Available on: https://www.thenationalnews.com/opinion/feedback/a-historical-perspective-of-the-abu-dhabi-dubai-border-1.1044490 (Accessed online 8 September 2023)

13 Wikipedia, Mohammed bin Rashid Al Maktoum [online] Available on:
https://en.wikipedia.org/wiki/Mohammed_bin_Rashid_Al_Maktoum (Accessed online 15 August 2023)

14 Wikipedia, Mohammed bin Rashid Al Maktoum [online] Available on:
https://en.wikipedia.org/wiki/Mohammed_bin_Rashid_Al_Maktoum (Accessed online 15 August 2023)

15 His Highness Sheikh Mohammed bin Rashid Al Maktoum – Ruling Family [online] Available on: https://sheikhmohammed.ae/en-us/RulingFamilyDubai (Accessed online 15 August 2023)

16 Lauren Holtmeier, "Build it and they will come: Dubai as a creative hub", Arabian Business, 8 December 2021 [online] Available on:
https://www.arabianbusiness.com/politics-economics/build-it-and-they-will-come-dubai-as-a-creative-hub#:~:text=The%20adage%20%E2%80%98build%20it%20and%20they%20will%20c

ome%E2%80%99,ambition%20to%20transform%20itself%20into%20a%20creative%2
0hub. (Accessed online 14 August 2023)

17 Bloomberg, "Dubai's the Very Model of a Modern Mideast Economy" [online] Available on: https://www.bloomberg.com/view/articles/2018-01-14/dubai-s-the-very-model-of-a-modern-mideast-economy (Accessed online 14 August 2023)

18 The Economist "The world's most valuable resource is no longer oil, but data", 6 May 2017 [online] Available on: https://www.economist.com/leaders/2017/05/06/the-worlds-most-valuable-resource-is-no-longer-oil-but-data (Accessed online 14 August 2023)

19 UAE Minister of State of Artificial Intelligence, Digital Economy & Remote Work Application Office. AI Adoption Guidelines in Government Services, in collaboration with Accenture, May 2023 [online] Available on: https://ai.gov.ae/wp-content/uploads/2023/05/AI-Report-EN-v4.pdf (Accessed online 14 August 2023)

20 BBC, Episode 351 The Rest is History [online] Available on: https://podcasts.apple.com/gb/podcast/the-rest-is-history/id1537788786?i=1000621311029 and Episode 352 The Rest is History, https://open.spotify.com/episode/5SRsIfXVRRL4DJsi9t2Rj9 Historians Tom Holland and Dominic Sandbrook are interrogating the past, and attempting to de-tangle the present. (Accessed online 15 August 2023)

21 Government of Dubai, Dubai 2040 Urban Master Plan [online] Available on: http://www.dubai20240.ae/en (Accessed online 30 July 2023)

22 Tawfiq Nasrallah, "Sheikh Mohammed: UAE will send the first Arab mission to the moon by 2024", Gulf News, 6 September 2020 [online] Available on: https://gulfnews.com/uae/science/sheikh-mohammed-uae-will-send-the-first-arab-mission-to-the-moon-by-2024-1.1601117725190 (Accessed online 16 August 2023)

23 His Highness Sheikh Mohammed bin Rashid Al Maktoum - Quotes [online] Available on: https://sheikhmohammed.ae/en-us/Quotes (Accessed online 14 August 2023)

24 Ministry of Possibilities [online] Available on: https://mop.gov.ae/ (Accessed online 5 September 2023)

25 His Highness Sheikh Mohammed bin Rashid Al Maktoum - Quotes [online] Available on: https://sheikhmohammed.ae/en-us/Quotes (Accessed online 14 August 2023)

26 AZ Quotes, Quotes by Louisa May Alcott [online] Available on: https://www.azquotes.com/author/200-Louisa_May_Alcott (Accessed online 16 August 2023)

27 Quotefancy, Yasmin Mogahed [online] Available on: https://quotefancy.com/quote/941202/Yasmin-Mogahed-Resilience-is-very-different-than-being-numb-Resilience-means-you (Accessed online 16 August 2023)

28 Costas Mourselas in London and Ortenca Aliaj in New York, "Lure of Sovereign Wealth Funds fuels hedge funds rush to Dubai", Financial Times, 9 August 2023 [online] Available on: https://www.ft.com/content/80d1538c-3ac9-48c7-bf2c-b54635d32c5c (Accessed online 16 August 2023)

29 Andy Sambridge, "$33bn hedge fund hails 'unprecedented opportunity' in GCC", 20 July 2023 [online] Available on: https://www.agbi.com/articles/brevan-howard-hedge-fund-gcc/ (Accessed online 1 October 2023)

30 BBC News, "Wealthy Russians flee to Dubai to avoid sanctions" 5 May 2022 [online] Available on: https://www.bbc.co.uk/news/business-61257448 (Accessed online 14 August 2023)

31 Natasha Turak, "Rich Russians fleeing sanctions are pumping up Dubai's property sector", CNBC, 7 July 2022 [online] Available on:

https://www.cnbc.com/2022/07/07/rich-russians-fleeing-sanctions-are-pumping-up-dubais-property-sector.html (Accessed online 16 August 2023)

32 Simeon Kerr, "Wealthy Russians flock to Dubai as West rightens Sanctions", Financial Times, 10 March 2022 [online] Available on: https://www.ft.com/content/d6d3b45a-35cc-4e32-b864-b9c0b1649a79 (Accessed online 16 August 2023)

33 Quotefancy, Top50 Alan Watts quotes [online] Available on: https://quotefancy.com/alan-watts-quotes (Accessed online 14 August 2023)

34 The Arabic Language Centre [online] Available on: https://www.arabiclanguagecentre.com/about-us/why-alc/ (Accessed online 16 August 2023)

35 Burj Khalifa [online] Available on: https://www.burjkhalifa.ae/en/index.aspx (Accessed online 30 July 2023)

36 Wikipedia, Burj Khalifa [online] Available on: https://en.wikipedia.org/wiki/Burj_Khalifa (Accessed online 16 August 2023)

37 Wikipedia, Palm Islands, Dubai [online] Available on: https://en.wikipedia.org/wiki/Palm_Islands (Accessed online 30 July 2023)

38 Wikipedia, The World [online] Available on: https://en.wikipedia.org/wiki/The_World_(archipelago) (Accessed online 16 August 2023)

39 Britannica, "Rene Descartes | Biography, Ideas, Philosophy, 'I Think, Therefore I Am,' & Facts" [online] Available on: Rene Descartes | Biography, Ideas, Philosophy, 'I Think, Therefore I Am,' & Facts | Britannica (Accessed online 5 September 2023)

40 Victoria Seveno, Video, "How did Dutch create Netherlands", Iamexpert.nl [online] Available on: https://www.iamexpat.nl/lifestyle/lifestyle-news/video-how-did-dutch-create-netherlands (Accessed online 5 September 2023)

41 His Highness Sheikh Mohammed bin Rashid Al Maktoum – Quotes [online] Available on: https://sheikhmohammed.ae/en-us/Quotes (Accessed online 14 August 2023)

42 Khaleej Times, "UAE holds highest number of Guiness World Records across MENA" [online] Available on: https://www.khaleejtimes.com/uae/uae-holds-highest-number-of-guinness-world-records-across-mena (Accessed online 30 July 2023)

43 Dubaitravelplanner, Guiness World Records Dubai [online] Available on: https://www.dubaitravelplanner.com/guinness-world-records-dubai/ (Accessed online 30 July 2023)

44 Wikipedia, Princess Tower, Dubai [online] Available on: https://en.wikipedia.org/wiki/Princess_Tower (Accessed online,30 July 2023)

45 The Capital Club [online] Available on: https://capitalclubdubai.com/ (Accessed online 16 August 2023)

46 IMDbm "Lawrence of Arabia" [online] Available on: Lawrence of Arabia (1962) - IMDb (Accessed online 14 August 2023)

47 Hamed Ghelichkhani, RERA Certified Agents, Training Dubai Real Estate Agents Part 2, YouTube [online] Available on: https://www.youtube.com/watch?v=jcmTrUjo7mQ (Accessed online 14 August 2023)

48 Wikipedia, Dubai Housing Crash in 2009 [online] Available on: https://en.wikipedia.org/wiki/Dubai_housing_crash_in_2009 (Accessed online 14 August 2023)

49 Hamed Ghelichkhani, RERA Certified Agents, Training Dubai Real Estate Agents Part 2, YouTube [online] Available on: https://www.youtube.com/watch?v=jcmTrUjo7mQ (Accessed online 14 August 2023)

50 Hamed Ghelichkhani, RERA Certified Agents, Training Dubai Real Estate Agents

Part 7, YouTube [online] Available on:
https://www.youtube.com/watch?v=GdmohAJk3wU (Accessed online 14 August 2023)
51 Official Portal of the UAE Government, "Leasing a property in the UAE" [online]
Available on: https://u.ae/en/information-and-services/moving-to-the-uae/leasing-a-property-in-the-uae (Accessed online 30 July 2023)
52 Hamed Ghelichkhani, RERA Certified Agents, Training Dubai Real Estate Agents
Part 6, YouTube [online] Available on:
https://www.youtube.com/watch?v=GdmohAJk3wU (Accessed online 14 August 2023)
53 MyBayut, "Everything you need to know about Dubai Tenancy Laws" [online]
Available on: https://www.bayut.com/mybayut/rera-tenancy-laws-dubai/ (Accessed
online 14 August 2023)
54 Jumeirah, Burj Al Arab [online] Available on:
https://www.jumeirah.com/fr/stay/dubai/burj-al-arab-jumeirah (Accessed online 30 July
2023)
55 ATP Tour, ATP 50: "Agassi, Federer, & The Heliport Court", 5 October 2022
[online] Available on: ATP 50: Andre Agassi, Roger Federer, & The Dubai Heliport
Court | ATP Tour | Tennis (Accessed online 16 August 2023)
56 Wikipedia, Ciel Tower [online] Available on:
https://en.wikipedia.org/wiki/Ciel_Tower (Accessed online 17 August 2023)
57 UK Government Foreign Travel Advice [online] Available on:
https://www.gov.uk/foreign-travel-advice/united-arab-emirates/local-laws-and-customs
(Accessed online 14 October 2023)
58 Chambers and Partners, "Corporate Immigration" [online] Available on:
https://practiceguides.chambers.com/practice-guides/corporate-immigration-2023/uae
(Accessed online 8 August 2023)
59 Chambers and Partners, "Corporate Immigration" [online] Available on:
https://practiceguides.chambers.com/practice-guides/corporate-immigration-2023/uae
(Accessed online 8 August 2023)
60 Official Portal of the UAE Government, Residence Visas [online] Available on:
https://u.ae/en/information-and-services/visa-and-Emirates-id/residence-visas (Accessed
online 30 July 2023)
61 Official Portal of the UAE Government, Golden Visa [online] Available on:
https://u.ae/en/information-and-services/visa-and-Emirates-id/residence-visas/golden-visa (Accessed online 30 July 2023)
62 Wikipedia, Agarwood [online] Available on:
https://en.wikipedia.org/wiki/Agarwood (Accessed online 16 August 2023)
63 Argawood, "Why is Oud SO Expensive? Top 10 Reasons that Might Surprise You
[online] Available on: https://www.agarwoodgroup.com/oud-so-expensive/ (Accessed
online 16 August 2023)
64 Alphaaromatics, "What is Oud Fragrance and why is it so expensive?" [online]
Available on: https://www.alphaaromatics.com/blog/what-is-oud-fragrance/ (Accessed
online 16 August 2023)
65 Elyakim Kislev, "The "Marriage Problem" in the Arab World", Psychology Today, 8
April 2022 [online] Available on: https://www.psychologytoday.com/us/blog/happy-singlehood/202204/the-marriage-problem-in-the-arab-world (Accessed online 22
August 2023)
66 Khaleej Times, " Dubai Police warns of Cybercriminals and scammers" [online]
Available on: https://www.khaleejtimes.com/uae/dubai-police-warns-of-cybercriminals-and-scammers (Accessed online 30 July 2023)
67 Khaleej Times, " Dubai Police warns of Cybercriminals and scammers" [online]
Available on: https://www.khaleejtimes.com/uae/dubai-police-warns-of-cybercriminals-

and-scammers (Accessed online 30 July 2023)

68 UK Government Foreign Travel Advice [online] Available on: https://www.gov.uk/foreign-travel-advice/united-arab-emirates/local-laws-and-customs (Accessed online 14 October 2023)

69 Omar Ul-Ubaydli, "Cousin Marriage and Gender Inequality ", Discourse, 4 May 2021 [online] Available on: Cousin Marriage and Gender Inequality - Discourse (discoursemagazine.com) (Accessed online 26 August 2023)

70 Marcia C. Inhorn, Daphna Birenbaum-Carmeli, Soraya Tremayne and Zeynep Gurtin, Reproductive BioMedicine and Society Online (2007) 4 41-51 "Assisted reproduction and Middle East kinship: a regional and religious comparison", Elsevier [online] Available on: https://discovery.ucl.ac.uk/id/eprint/10055504/1/C%20Inhorn_Assisted%20reproductio n%20.pdf (Accessed online 26 August 2023)

71 Food Tech Valley [online] Available on: https://www.foodtechvalley.ae/ (Accessed online 30 July 2023)

72 ArabianBusiness, "Dubai scraps alcohol tax: Cheaper drink, higher hotel profits and everything you need to know", 3 January 2023 [online] Available on: Dubai scraps alcohol tax: Cheaper drinks, higher hotel profits and everything you need to know - Arabian Business (Accessed online 14 August 2023)

73 UK Government Foreign Travel Advice [online] Available on: https://www.gov.uk/foreign-travel-advice/united-arab-emirates/local-laws-and-customs (Accessed online 14 October 2023)

74 UK Government Foreign Travel Advice [online] Available on: https://www.gov.uk/foreign-travel-advice/united-arab-emirates/local-laws-and-customs (Accessed online 14 October 2023)

75 UK Government Foreign Travel Advice [online] Available on: https://www.gov.uk/foreign-travel-advice/united-arab-emirates/local-laws-and-customs (Accessed online 14 October 2023)

76 The National News, "A historical perspective of the Abu Dhabi border" [online] Available on: https://www.thenationalnews.com/opinion/feedback/a-historical-perspective-of-the-abu-dhabi-dubai-border-1.1044490 (Accessed online 8 September 2023)

77 The Official Portal of the UAE Government, Civic facilities, [online] Available on: https://u.ae/en/information-and-services/infrastructure/civic-facilities (Accessed online 23 August 2023)

78 His Highness Sheikh Mohammed bin Rashid Al Maktoum - Quotes [online] Available on: https://sheikhmohammed.ae/en-us/Quotes (Accessed online 14 August 2023)

79 The Official Portal of the UAE Government, Civic facilities, [online] Available on: https://u.ae/en/information-and-services/infrastructure/civic-facilities (Accessed online 23 August 2023)

80 Wikipedia, Port of Jebil Ali, [online] Available on: https://en.wikipedia.org/wiki/Port_of_Jebel_Ali#:~:text=With%2067%20berths%20and %20a,port%20in%20the%20Middle%2DEast. (Accessed online 23 August 2023)

81 Dubai Opera House [online] Available on: https://www.dubaiopera.com/en-US/home (Accessed online 30 July 2023)

82 Wikipedia, Alserkal Avenue [online] Available on: https://en.wikipedia.org/wiki/Alserkal_Avenue (Accessed online 30 July 2023)

83 Mall of the Emirates [online] Available on: https://www.malloftheEmirates.com/en (Accessed online 30 July 2023)

84 Dubai Mall [online] Available on: https://thedubaimall.com/en/about-us/about-the-dubai-mall (Accessed online 30 July 2023)

85 Sharmila Dhal, "No place like Dubai to buy, wear – and make a statement with - your gold jewellery", Gulf News, 7 February 2022 [online] Available on: https://gulfnews.com/uae/no-place-like-dubai-to-buy-wear---and-make-a-statement-with---your-gold-jewellery-1.85478353 (Accessed online 17 August 2023)

86 ArabianBusiness, UAE phishing scam: Dubai Police issues 'urgent alert' warning against clicking on emailed links to pay fines, 25 July 2023 [online] Available on: https://www.arabianbusiness.com/culture-society/uae-phishing-scam-dubai-police-issues-urgent-alert-warning-against-clicking-on-emailed-links-to-pay-fines#:~:text=Dubai%20Police%20has%20warned%20the%20public%20of%20a,the%20public%2C%E2%80%9D%20warning%20them%20against%20phishing%20email%20scams. (Accessed online 30 July 2023)

87 Wam, "Dubai Police warns of cybercriminals and scammers", Khalaaj Times, 3 July 2020 [online] Available on: Dubai Police warns of cybercriminals and scammers - News | Khaleej Times (Accessed online 25 August 2023)

88 Economist, "Why women are fatter than men in the Arab world " [online] Available on: https://www.economist.com/middle-east-and-africa/2022/07/28/why-women-are-fatter-than-men-in-the-arab-world (Accessed online 8 September 2023)

89 Jomana Karadshed, "Dubai unveils golden reason to lose weight", CNN, 19 July 2013 [online] Available on: https://edition.cnn.com/2013/07/19/health/dubai-gold-diet/index.html (Accessed online 7 September 2023)

90 His Highness Sheikh Mohammed bin Rashid Al Maktoum - Quotes [online] Available on: https://sheikhmohammed.ae/en-us/Quotes (Accessed online 14 August 2023)

91 Official Portal of the UAE Government [online] Available on: https://u.ae/en/about-the-uae/the-uae-government/government-of-future/happiness/national-programme-for-happiness-and-wellbeing (Accessed online 8 August 2023)

92 Saeed Saeed, "From Beyonce to Stormzy: 45 artists who played at the Abu Dhabi F1 After-Race Concerts", The National News, 13 December 2021 [online] Available on: https://www.thenationalnews.com/arts-culture/music/2021/12/13/from-beyonce-to-stormzy-45-artists-who-played-at-the-abu-dhabi-f1-after-race-concerts/ (Accessed online 21 August 2023)

93 Dutchnews, "The Netherlands most wanted man is arrested in Dubai", 16 December 2019 [online] Available on: https://www.dutchnews.nl/2019/12/the-netherlands-most-wanted-man-is-arrested-in-dubai/ (Accessed online 15 August 2023)

94 Logan Fish, Video Editor and Ali Al Shouk, Senior Reporter, 1 "Dubai Police arrest one of the world's most wanted criminals", Gulf News, 8 December 2019 [online] Available on: https://gulfnews.com/videos/news/dubai-police-arrest-one-of-the-worlds-most-wanted-criminals-1.1576681985813 (Accessed online 15 August 2023)

95 Logan Fish, Video Editor and Ali Al Shouk, Senior Reporter, 1 "Dubai Police arrest one of the world's most wanted criminals", Gulf News, 8 December 2019 [online] Available on: https://gulfnews.com/videos/news/dubai-police-arrest-one-of-the-worlds-most-wanted-criminals-1.1576681985813 (Accessed online 15 August 2023)

96 Afkar Ali Ahmed, "Dubai Police arrest 597 most wanted criminals, repatriate 85 fugitives over two years", Khajeel Times, 7 March 2023 [online] Available on: https://www.khaleejtimes.com/uae/crime/dubai-police-arrested-597-most-wanted-criminals-repatriated-85-fugitives-over-past-two-years (Accessed online 15 August 2023)

97 David Dunn, "Climbing Kilimanjaro with Camels", CNN, 12 October 2015 [online] Available on: https://edition.cnn.com/travel/article/climbing-kilimanjaro-with-camels-

uae-tanzania/index.html (Accessed online 15 August 2023)

98 WorldAtlas, Top Horse and Equine Animal Exporter, [online] Available on: https://www.worldatlas.com/articles/top-horse-and-equine-animal-exporters.html (Accessed online 15 August 2023)

99 Goldolphin [online] Available on: https://www.godolphin.com/about-us/our-founder/ (Accessed online 15 August 2023)

100 Darley Stud [online] Available on: https://www.darleyeurope.com/ (Accessed online 15 August 2023)

101 Royal Ascot [online] Available on: https://www.ascot.com/enclosures/Royal-ascot/enclosures/Royal-enclosure (Accessed online 15 August 2023)

102 Wikipedia, Dubai World Cup [online] Available on: https://en.wikipedia.org/wiki/Dubai_World_Cup (Accessed online 25 August 2023)

103 CNBC, "Casino Giant Wynn to open a 1000 room resort in UAE Emirate introducing legal gambling [online] Available on: https://www.cnbc.com/2022/01/25/casino-giant-wynn-to-open-a-1000-room-resort-in-uae-Emirate-introducing-legal-gaming.html (Accessed online 30 July 2023)

104 Qasr al Hosn Festival, 2014 [online] Available on: archive.qasralhosnfestival.ae/the-show/the-show/ (Accessed online 8 August 2023)

105 Wikipedia, Adolfo Cambiaso [online] Available on: https://en.wikipedia.org/wiki/Adolfo_Cambiaso (Accessed online 23 August 2023)

106 PEW Research Center, "Mapping the Global Muslim Population", 7 October 2009 [online] Available on: https://www.pewresearch.org/religion/2009/10/07/mapping-the-global-muslim-population/#:~:text=An%20overwhelming%20majority%20of%20Muslims%20are%20Sunnis%2C%20while,200%20million%20Shia%20Muslims%20in%20the%20world%20today. (Accessed online 17 August 2023)

107 BBC Bitesize, "What is Islam and what do Muslims believe in?", [online] Available on: https://www.bbc.co.uk/bitesize/topics/zpdtsbk/articles/zrxxgwx (Accessed online 30 July 2023)

108 BBC, "Religions – Islam: Sunni and Shi'a", 19 August 2009, [online] Available on: https://www.bbc.co.uk/religion/religions/islam/subdivisions/sunnishia_1.shtml (Accessed online 30 July 2023)

109 PEW Research Center, "Mapping the Global Muslim Population", 7 October 2009 [online] Available on: https://www.pewresearch.org/religion/2009/10/07/mapping-the-global-muslim-population/#:~:text=An%20overwhelming%20majority%20of%20Muslims%20are%20Sunnis%2C%20while,200%20million%20Shia%20Muslims%20in%20the%20world%20today. (Accessed online 17 August 2023)

110 BBC Bitesize, "What is Islam and what do Muslims believe in?", [online] Available on: https://www.bbc.co.uk/bitesize/topics/zpdtsbk/articles/zrxxgwx (Accessed online 30 July 2023)

111 Wikipedia, Islamic New Year [online] Available on: https://en.wikipedia.org/wiki/Islamic_New_Year (Accessed online 30 July 2023)

112 BBC, Religions "Islam: Hajj: Pilgrimage to Mecca" [online] Available on: https://www.bbc.co.uk/religion/religions/islam/practices/hajj_1.shtml (Accessed online 17 August 2023)

113 VOANews, Middle East, Mecca Women Take Part Hajj Guardian Rule dropped 20 July 2021 [online] Available on: https://www.voanews.com/a/middle-east_mecca-women-take-part-hajj-guardian-rule-dropped/6208472.html (Accessed online 17 August 2023)

114 BBC Newsround, "What is the Hajj pilgrimage", 26 June 2023 [online] Available

on: https://www.bbc.co.uk/newsround/24566691 (Accessed online 17 August 2023)

115 Islamic Landmarks, "Can Non-Muslims Enter Mecca or Madinah? | Can Tourists Enter?" [online] Available on: https://www.islamiclandmarks.com/makkah-other/can-non-muslims-go-to-mecca (Accessed online 17 August 2023)

116 Freddy Hayward ,"The lonely atheist – why denouncing your religion is Saudi Arabia can be deadly", The New Statesman, 29 August 2019 [online] Available on: https://www.newstatesman.com/world/2019/08/the-lonely-atheist-why-renouncing-your-religion-in-saudi-arabia-can-be-deadly (Accessed online 17 August 2023)

117 UK Government Foreign Travel Advice [online] Available on: https://www.gov.uk/foreign-travel-advice/united-arab-emirates/local-laws-and-customs (Accessed online 14 October 2023)

118 Daily Mail, "£7m Christmas tree: Abu Dhabi Emirates Palace hotel unveils fir draped in diamonds", 17 December 2010 [online] Available on: https://www.dailymail.co.uk/news/article-1339068/7m-Christmas-tree-Abu-Dhabi-Emirates-Palace-hotel-unveils-fir-draped-diamonds.html (Accessed online 17 August 2023)

119 Lucy Fisher, "UK asked to obtain assurances from UAE over right to protest at COP28", Financial Times, 11 August 2023 [online] Available on: https://www.ft.com/content/9e736585-f20d-482a-9cb3-3575741b4c6e (Accessed online 17 August 2023)

120 Middle East Jokes [online] Available on: https://upjoke.com/middle-east-jokes (Accessed online 8 August 2023)

121 Lauren Smith-Spark, "The ban on Saudi women driving is ending: Here's what you need to know", CNN, 22 June 2018 [online] Available on: https://edition.cnn.com/2018/06/22/middleeast/saudi-women-driving-ban-end-intl/index.html (Accessed online 31 July 2023)

122 Forbes Middle East, Top 100 most powerful businesswomen [online] Available on: https://www.forbesmiddleeast.com/lists/top-100-most-powerful-businesswomen-2023/ (Accessed online 30 July 2023)

123 Noor Alsalhi, "How women in MENA are taking on the status quo – and winning", World Economic Forum [online] Available on: https://www.weforum.org/agenda/2019/04/how-menas-young-women-are-fighting-to-change-the-status-quo/ (Accessed online 30 July 2023)

124 Jemima Shelley, "Women's Rights—Why the West Shouldn't Abandon the Middle East", Washington Institute [online] Available on: Women's Rights—Why the West Shouldn't Abandon the Middle East | The Washington Institute (Accessed online 30 July 2023)

125 Farah Elbahrawy, Filipe Pacheco and Abeer Abu Omar, ,"UAE to require listed firms to have at least one woman on board", Bloomberg, 14 March 2021 [online] Available on: https://www.bloomberg.com/news/articles/2021-03-14/uae-to-require-listed-firms-to-have-at-least-one-woman-on-board (Accessed online 30 July 2023)

126 AlJazeera, "UAE struggles with new rule to get women on company boards" ,18 May 2018 [online] Available on: https://www.aljazeera.com/economy/2021/5/18/bbuae-struggles-with-new-rule-to-get-women-on-company-boards (Accessed online 31 July 2023)

127 UNODC, Global Study on Homicide, 2018 [online] Available on: https://www.unodc.org/documents/data-and-analysis/GSH2018/GSH18_Gender-related_killing_of_women_and_girls.pdf (Accessed online 15 August 2023)

128 Official Portal of the UAE Government, Health and Safety at Workplace [online] Available on: https://u.ae/en/information-and-services/jobs/health-and-safety-at-workplace (Accessed online 31 July 2023)

129 Museum of the Future [online] Available on: https://museumofthefuture.ae/en (Accessed online 30 July 2023)

130 Official Portal of the UAE Government [online] Available on: https://u.ae/en/information-and-services/justice-safety-and-the-law/entities-responsible-for-security-and-safety-in-the-uae (Accessed online 31 July 2023)

131 The New York Time "Emirates secretly sends Columbian Mercenaries to fight in Yemen", 26 November 2015 [online] Available on: https://www.nytimes.com/2015/11/26/world/middleeast/Emirates-secretly-sends-colombian-mercenaries-to-fight-in-yemen.html (Accessed online 31 July 2023)

132 Melissa Dalton and Hijab Shah, "Evolving UAE Military and Foreign Security Cooperation: Path Toward Military Professionalism", Carnegie Middle East, 12 January 2021 [online] Available on: https://carnegie-mec.org/2021/01/12/evolving-uae-military-and-foreign-security-cooperation-path-toward-military-professionalism-pub-83549 (Accessed online 31 July 2023)

133 Saudi Arabia Vision 2030 [online] Available on: https://www.vision2030.gov.sa/thekingdom/explore/economy/ (Accessed online 30 July 2023)

134 PWC, "KSA Regional headquarters program" [online] Available on: https://www.pwc.com/m1/en/services/tax/me-tax-legal-news/2023/ksa-regional-headquarters-program.html (Accessed online 30 July 2023)

135 The National, "Saudi Arabia to allow some companies to operate without local headquarters" [online] Available on: https://www.thenationalnews.com/business/2023/01/08/saudi-arabia-to-allow-some-companies-to-operate-without-local-headquarters/ (Accessed online 17 August 2023)

136 Hudhaifa Ebrahim, "Saudi Arabia and UAE's Rivalry Intensifies in Race for Foreign Investments", The Media Line, 6 February 2023 [online] Available on: https://themedialine.org/top-stories/saudi-arabia-and-uaes-rivalry-intensifies-in-race-for-foreign-investments/#:~:text=A%20source%20told%20The%20Media%20Line%20that%20at,to%20be%20able%20to%20conduct%20direct%20government%20contracts. (Accessed online 17 August 2023)

137 Official Portal of the UAE Government [online] Available on: https://u.ae/en/information-and-services/finance-and-investment/taxation/corporate-tax (Accessed online 30 July 2023

138 His Highness Sheikh Mohammed bin Rashid Al Maktoum - Quotes [online] Available on: https://sheikhmohammed.ae/en-us/Quotes (Accessed online 14 August 2023)

139 Gulf News, "UAE passes draft law to combat fake degrees" [online] Available on: https://gulfnews.com/uae/government/uae-passes-draft-law-to-combat-fake-degrees-1.1613492199106 (Accessed online 30 July 2023)

140 Official Portal of the UAE Government, Starting a business in a free zone [online] Available on: https://u.ae/en/information-and-services/business/starting-a-business-in-a-free-zone (Accessed online 30 July 2023)

141 Official Portal of the UAE Government, Starting a business in a free zone [online] Available on: https://u.ae/en/information-and-services/business/starting-a-business-in-a-free-zone (Accessed online 30 July 2023)

142 PWC, "UAE - Important Regulatory Updates and Compliance Requirements" [online] Available on: UAE - Important Regulatory Updates and Compliance Requirements (pwc.com) (Accessed online 30 July 2023)

143 The National, Private companies with 20-49 employees now included in Emiratization drive [online] Available on:

https://www.thenationalnews.com/uae/government/2023/07/11/private-companies-with-20-to-49-employees-now-included-in-emiratisation-drive/ (Accessed online 30 July 2023)

144 Ted Kemp and Natasha Turak, "UAE is placed on money laundering watchdog's 'gray list'", CNBC, 5 March 2023 [online] Available on: https://www.cnbc.com/2022/03/05/uae-is-placed-on-money-laundering-watchdogs-gray-list-.html (Accessed online 25 August 2023)

145 KPMG UAE "Grey Listing of the UAE" [online] Available on: Grey Listing of the UAE - KPMG United Arab Emirates (Accessed online 16 August 2023)

146 Tala Michel Issa, Inside the UAE's crackdown on money laundering, Arabian Business, 8 September 2023 [online] Available on: https://www.arabianbusiness.com/abnews/uae-cracks-down-on-money-laundering (Accessed online 8 September 2023)

147 Maysaa Ajjan, "The psychology of fraud in the Middle East", Middle East Economy, 29 December 2022 [online] Available on: https://economymiddleeast.com/news/fraud/ (Accessed online 13 September 2023)

148 Investopedia, "Corruption: Its Meaning, Type, and Real-World Examples", By James Chen, 13 May 2023 [online] Available on: https://www.investopedia.com/terms/c/corruption.asp (Accessed online 30 July 2023)

149 Rebecca Meijlink, "Iran means business", Tehran Times [online] Available on: https://www.tehrantimes.com/news/411526/Iran-means-business (Accessed online 30 July 2023)

150 AZ Quotes, Quotes by Louisa May Alcott [online] Available on: https://www.azquotes.com/author/200-Louisa_May_Alcott (Accessed online 16 August 2023)

151 Euromoney Conferences [online] Available on: https://www.euromoneyconferences.com/ (Accessed online 30 July 2023)

152 Dubai World Trade Centre [online] Available on: https://www.dwtc.com/en/about/ (Accessed online 30 July 2023)

153 Britanica, "Gulf Cooperation Council (GCC) | History, Member Countries, Purpose, & Summits", Updated 24 August 2023 [online] Available on: https://www.britannica.com/topic/Gulf-Cooperation-Council (Accessed online 25 August 2023)

154 CIA World Factbook, "Bahrain" [online] Available on: https://www.cia.gov/the-world-factbook/countries/bahrain/ (Accessed online 30 July 2023)

155 Jane Millard, "30 Historic sites in Bahrain", Time out Bahrain, 20 July 2018 [online] Available on: https://www.timeoutbahrain.com/travel/11781-30-historic-sites-in-bahrain (Accessed online 25 August 2023)

156 Jane Millard, "30 Historic sites in Bahrain", Time out Bahrain, 20 July 2018 [online] Available on: https://www.timeoutbahrain.com/travel/11781-30-historic-sites-in-bahrain (Accessed online 25 August 2023)

157 CIA World Factbook, "Kuwait" [online] Available on: https://www.cia.gov/the-world-factbook/countries/kuwait/ (Accessed online 30 July 2023)

158 ExpatWoman.com, "Alcohol in Kuwait - Kuwait Drinking Laws to Know", 4 July 2017 [online] Available on: https://www.expatwoman.com/kuwait/money-finance/alcohol-laws-in-kuwait-complete-guide (Accessed online 25 August 2023)

159 CIA World Factbook, "Oman" [online] Available on: https://www.cia.gov/the-world-factbook/countries/oman/ (Accessed online 30 July 2023)

160 Paul Legg, "Obituary Sultan Qaboos bin Said", The Guardian, 12 January 2020 [online] Available on: https://www.theguardian.com/world/2020/jan/12/obituary-sultan-qaboos-bin-said (Accessed online 29 August 2023)

161 Wikipedia, Ibadi Islam [online] Available on: Ibadi Islam - Wikipedia (Accessed online 29 August 2023)

162 Ministry of Energy and Minerals [online] Available on: https://mem.gov.om/en-us/About-Us/Oman-Vision-2040 (Accessed online 29 August 2023)

163 David Belcher, "In Oman, a Dagger Symbolizes National Pride", NY Times, 4 December 2020 [online] Available on: https://www.nytimes.com/2022/12/04/fashion/craftsmanship-oman-khanjar-dagger.html (Accessed online 29 August 2023)

164 CIA World Factbook, "Qatar" [online] Available on: https://www.cia.gov/the-world-factbook/countries/qatar/ (Accessed online 30 July 2023)

165 Statista, Global LNG exporting companies by capacity 2022 | Statista [online] Available on: https://www.statista.com/statistics/859126/largest-lng-exporting-companies-by-capacity/ (Accessed online 25 August 2023)

166 Wikipedia, Al Jazeera [online] Available on: https://en.wikipedia.org/wiki/Al_Jazeera (Accessed online 25 August 2023)

167 BBC, "Saudi Crown Prince Mohammed bin Salman, power behind the throne", 6 October 2020 [online] Available on: BBC https://www.bbc.co.uk/news/world-middle-east-40354415 (Accessed online 30 August 2023)

168 CIA World Factbook, "Saudi Arabia" [online] Available on: https://www.cia.gov/the-world-factbook/countries/saudi-arabia/ (Accessed online 30 July 2023)

169 Vivian Nereim, "Dubai Suspends Alcohol Tax as Regional Competition Heats Up", The New York Times, 2 January 2023 [online] Available on: Dubai Suspends Alcohol Tax as Regional Competition Heats Up - The New York Times (nytimes.com) (Accessed online 16 August 2023)

170 Wikipedia, Al Waleed bin Talal Al Saud [online] Available on: https://en.wikipedia.org/wiki/Al_Waleed_bin_Talal_Al_Saud (Accessed online 16 August 2023)

171 Wikipedia, Kingdom Holding Company [online] Available on: https://en.wikipedia.org/wiki/Kingdom_Holding_Company (Accessed online 16 August 2023)

172 DiscoveryWalks Blog, "Top 10 Amazing Facts about Al-Waleed bin Talal [online] Available on: Top 10 Amazing Facts about Al-Waleed bin Talal - Discover Walks Blog (Accessed online 16 August 2023)

173 CIA World Factbook, "Egypt" [online] Available on: https://www.cia.gov/the-world-factbook/countries/egypt/ (Accessed online 30 July 2023)

174 Wikipedia, Ancient Egypt [online] Available on: https://en.wikipedia.org/wiki/Ancient_Egypt (Accessed online 25 August 2023)

175 BBC, Religions, Christianity, Coptic Orthodox Church, Updated 25 June 2019 [online] Available on: BBC - Religions - Christianity: Coptic Orthodox Church (Accessed online 18 August 2023)

176 Wikipedia, 2011 Egyptian revolution [online] Available on: https://en.wikipedia.org/wiki/2011_Egyptian_revolution (Accessed online 18 August 2023)

177 CIA World Factbook, "India" [online] Available on: https://www.cia.gov/the-world-factbook/countries/india/ (Accessed online 30 July 2023)

178 Wikipedia, Indians in the United Arab Emirates [online] Available on: https://en.wikipedia.org/wiki/Indians_in_the_United_Arab_Emirates (Accessed online 30 July 2023)

179 CIA World Factbook, "Iran" [online] Available on: https://www.cia.gov/the-world-factbook/countries/iran/ (Accessed online 30 July 2023)

180 Wikipedia, List of countries by oil production [online] Available on:

https://en.wikipedia.org/wiki/List_of_countries_by_oil_production (Accessed online 30 July 2023)

181 Rebecca Meijlink, "Iran means business", Theran Times [online] Available on: https://www.tehrantimes.com/news/411526/Iran-means-business (Accessed online 30 July 2023)

182 Rebecca Meijlink, "Iran means business", Theran Times [online] Available on: https://www.tehrantimes.com/news/411526/Iran-means-business (Accessed online 30 July 2023)

183 Rebecca Meijlink, "Iran means business", Theran Times [online] Available on: https://www.tehrantimes.com/news/411526/Iran-means-business (Accessed online 30 July 2023)

184 Rebecca Meijlink, "Iran means business", Theran Times [online] Available on: https://www.tehrantimes.com/news/411526/Iran-means-business (Accessed online 30 July 2023)

185 CIA World Factbook, "Israel" [online] Available on: https://www.cia.gov/the-world-factbook/countries/israel/ (Accessed online 30 July 2023)

186 CIA World Factbook, "Lebanon" [online] Available on: https://www.cia.gov/the-world-factbook/countries/lebanon/ (Accessed online 30 July 2023)

187 CIA World Factbook, "Pakistan" [online] Available on: https://www.cia.gov/the-world-factbook/countries/pakistan/ (Accessed online 30 July 2023)

188 Madiha Afzal, "Pakistan: Five major issues to watch in 2023", Brookings, 13 January 2023 [online] Available on: https://www.brookings.edu/articles/pakistan-five-major-issues-to-watch-in-2023/ (Accessed online 30 July 2023)

189 Fabricoz Seattle USA, "Shalwar Kameez: A Guide To The Ultimate Pakistani Dress" [online] Available on: https://www.fabricoz.com/blogs/pakistani-fashion/shalwar-kameez-a-guide-to-the-ultimate-pakistani-dress (Accessed online 30 July 2023)

190 UK Government Safety and Security – Pakistan travel advice [online] Available on: https://www.gov.uk/foreign-travel-advice/pakistan/safety-and-security (Accessed online 17 August 2023)

191 CIA World Factbook, "Turkey" [online] Available on: https://www.cia.gov/the-world-factbook/countries/turkey-turkiye/ (Accessed online 30 July 2023)

192 Adam Samson, "Recep Tayyip Erdoğan abandons cheap money to counter Turkey's soaring inflation", Financial Times, 6 September 2023 [online] Available on: https://www.ft.com/content/63a9de8b-de5c-4044-a250-40d691c4ceed (Accessed online 17 September 2023)

193 "Traveling to Israel from Pakistan in 2023: Passport, Visa Requirements" [online] Available on: https://www.hinterlandtravel.com/pakistan/destinations/israel (Accessed online 20 September 2023)

194 SWF Institute [online] Available on: https://www.swfinstitute.org/ (Accessed online 30 July 2023)

195 Forbes Middle East, "Top 11 arab family businesses in the Middle East 2020 [online] Available on: https://www.forbesmiddleeast.com/list/top-100-arab-family-businesses-in-the-middle-east-2020-1 (Accessed online 30 July 2023)

196 Forbes Middle East, "Top 11 arab family businesses in the Middle East 2020 [online] Available on: https://www.forbesmiddleeast.com/list/top-100-arab-family-businesses-in-the-middle-east-2020-1 (Accessed online 30 July 2023)

197 Khairallah Advocates & Legal Consultants, "New UAE debt collection laws", 6 April 2023 [online] Available on: https://www.khairallahlegal.com/uae-law/new-uae-debt-collection-laws/ (Accessed online 15 August 2023)

198 Investguiding "Which football clubs are owned by Saudi Arabia" 2023 [online]

Available on: https://investguiding-com.ngontinh24.com/articles/which-football-clubs-are-owned-by-saudi-arabia#toc-0 (Accessed online 25 August 2023)

199 Paul MacInnes, 'It's not a fad': the truth behind Saudi Arabia's dizzying investment in sport | Saudi Pro League", The Guardian, 12 August 2023 [online] Available on: https://www.theguardian.com/football/2023/aug/12/its-not-a-fad-the-truth-behind-saudi-arabias-dizzying-investment-in-sport (Accessed online 19 August 2023)

200 Fabrizio Romano, "Cristiano Ronaldo completes deal to join Saudi Arabian club Al Nassr", The Guardian [online] Available on: https://www.theguardian.com/football/2022/dec/30/cristiano-ronaldo-al-nassr-saudi-arabia (Accessed online 5 September 2023)

201 Moneycontrol, "The many perks of Neymar's Al Hilal deal: private plane, 25-bedroom mansion and..." [online] Available on: The many perks of Neymar's Al Hilal deal: private plane, 25-bedroom mansion and... (moneycontrol.com) (Accessed online 5 September 2023)

202 BBC Sport, "Saudi Arabia's PIF takes over Al-Ittihad, Al-Nassr, Al-Hilal and Al-Ahli", 5 June 2023 [online] Available on: https://www.bbc.co.uk/sport/football/65813662 (Accessed online 19 August 2023)

203 "LeBron James visits Saudi Arabia amid rumours of $1bn contract offer –", Arabian Business, 9 September 2023 [online] Available on: LeBron James visits Saudi Arabia amid rumours of $1bn contract offer - Arabian Business (Accessed online 9 September 2023)

204 Future Minerals Forum 2024 [online] Available on: https://www.futuremineralsforum.com/ (Accessed online 14 October 2023)

205 Forbes Middle East, "Saudi owns biggest gold reserves in the arab region followed by economically battered Lebanon" [online] Available on: https://www.forbesmiddleeast.com/industry/economy/saudi-owns-biggest-gold-reserves-in-the-arab-region-followed-by-economically-battered-lebanon (Accessed online 10 August 2023)

206 World Economic Forum [online] Available on: https://www.weforum.org/events/world-economic-forum-annual-meeting-2020 (Accessed online 30 July 2023)

207 Mubadala, ESG Journey - Mubadala Annual Review 2020 [online] Available on: https://annual2020.mubadala.com/esg-journey/#:~:text=The%20Responsible%20Investing%20Unit%20will%20act%20as%20the,our%20business%20development%2C%20asset%20management%20and%20corporate%20functions. (Accessed online 25 August 2023)

208 COP28 [online] Available on: https://www.cop28.com/en/ (Accessed online 30 July 2023)

209 Wikipedia, Mohammed bin Rashid Al Maktoum Solar Park [online] Available on: Mohammed bin Rashid Al Maktoum Solar Park - Wikipedia(Accessed online 30 July 2023)

210 Emirates Nuclear Energy Corporation [online] Available on: https://www.enec.gov.ae/doc/factsheet-commercial-operations-eng-606bfa39803d4.pdf (Accessed online 30 July 2023)

211 Pearl Initiative [online] Available on: https://www.pearlinitiative.org/corporate-fundamentals/ (Accessed online 30 July 2023)

212 Official Portal of the UAE Government, UAE Net Zero 2050 [online] Available on: https://u.ae/en/information-and-services/environment-and-energy/climate-change/theuaesresponsetoclimatechange/uae-net-zero-2050 (Accessed online 25 August 2023)

213 Vision21 [online] Available on: https://www.vision2021.ae/en (Accessed online 25

August 2023)

214 Official Portal of the UAE Government, Dubai Urban Master Plan 2040 [online] Available on: https://u.ae/en/about-the-uae/strategies-initiatives-and-awards/strategies-plans-and-visions/transport-and-infrastructure/dubai-2040-urban-master-plan (Accessed online 25 August 2023)

215 Official Portal of the UAE Government, The UAE Green Agenda - 2030 [online] Available on: https://u.ae/en/about-the-uae/strategies-initiatives-and-awards/strategies-plans-and-visions/environment-and-energy/the-uaes-green-agenda-2030 (Accessed online 25 August 2023)

216 Morgan Lewis, "Sustainable Finance a strategic priority for the UAE, 26 July 2023" [online] Available on: https://www.morganlewis.com/pubs/2023/07/sustainable-finance-a-strategic-priority-for-the-uae (Accessed online 30 July 2023) or [online] Available on: https://www.adgm.com/initiatives/sustainable-finance (Accessed online 30 July 2023)

217 UNEP, Faith based engagement [online] Available on: https://www.unep.org/events/conference/faith-based-engagement-cop28 (Accessed online 28 August July 2023)

218 Mufti Ismail Desai,, "Your Guide to Islamic Finance", GIFS, 2015 [online] Available on: https://www.gifsrv.com/wp-content/uploads/2018/11/Your-Guide-to-Islamic-Finance.pdf (Accessed online 19 August 2023)

219 Mufti Ismail Desai,, "Your Guide to Islamic Finance", GIFS, 2015 [online] Available on: https://www.gifsrv.com/wp-content/uploads/2018/11/Your-Guide-to-Islamic-Finance.pdf (Accessed online 19 August 2023)

220 GIFS, "What is Shariah Compliant Investment", [online] Available on: https://gifsrv.com/faq/what-is-a-shariah-compliant-investment/ (Accessed online 19 August 2023)

221 IFN, Press release, "IFN UK Forum: Europe's premier Islamic finance conference returned to London on the 4th of September 2023". 6 September 2023 [online] Available on: https://www.islamicfinancenews.com/ifn-uk-forum-europes-premier-islamic-finance-conference-returned-to-london-on-the-4th-of-september-2023.html (Accessed online 6 September 2023)

222 IFN UK Report 2023, 12 October 2023 [online] Available on: https://www.islamicfinancenews.com/supplements/ifn-uk-report-2023?utm_medium=email&_hsmi=277870729&_hsenc=p2ANqtz-8E12pyy3jAzPyC2tBj9oQT9BSJkMASyFIGpY4tYD-8C4G-Ie9lZNEX0L1lyKUua3_MZbEK9wCyl3gt1nxC3mSKbIef7DSaJpxkFFpqtfH0RIHuXXI&utm_content=277870729&utm_source=hs_email (Accessed online 12 October 2023)

223 Wikipedia, Allegory of the cave [online] Available on: http://en.wikipedia.org/wiki/Allegory_of_the_cave (Accessed online 29 August 2023)

224 Wikipedia, Candide [online] Available on: https://en.wikipedia.org/wiki/Candide (Accessed online 19 August 2023)

225 Wikipedia, Michael Lewis [online] Available on: https://en.wikipedia.org/wiki/Michael_Lewis (Accessed online 14 August 2023)